ART
and
PERSPECTIVE

Unravelling the secrets of the masters

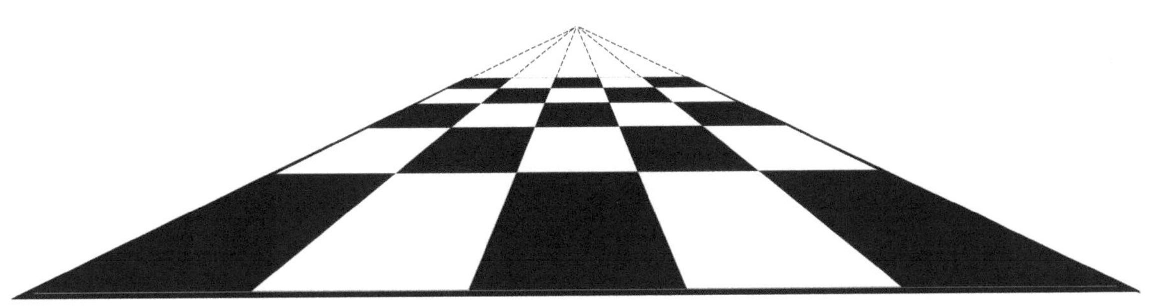

Trevor A White
BEng MSc MBA

ART and PERSPECTIVE

Unravelling the secrets of the masters

EAN (ISBN-13): 978-0-9990933-6-8

ISBN-10: 0-9990933-6-3

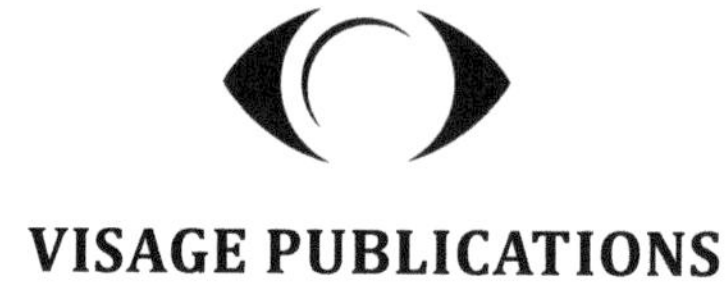

VISAGE PUBLICATIONS

Cover art: *The Arnolfini Portrait,* Jan van Eyck, 1434

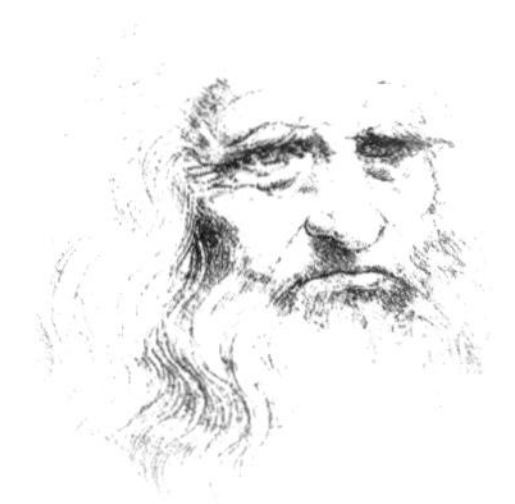

Perspective is the guide and the gateway; and without this nothing can be done well in the matter of drawing

Leonardo da Vinci

Acknowledgements

My warm thanks to Emma Kemp, professor at Otis College of Art & Design, Los Angeles, California for reading the draft and suggesting some structural improvements.

My warm thanks also to Ruth Le Lion, artist/designer, for offering commentary on the first draft and suggesting some additional material to reinforce the story.

Finally, my appreciation, as ever, to my wife, Valerie White, who has read the text multiple times and is a constant source of support and inspiration.

Contents

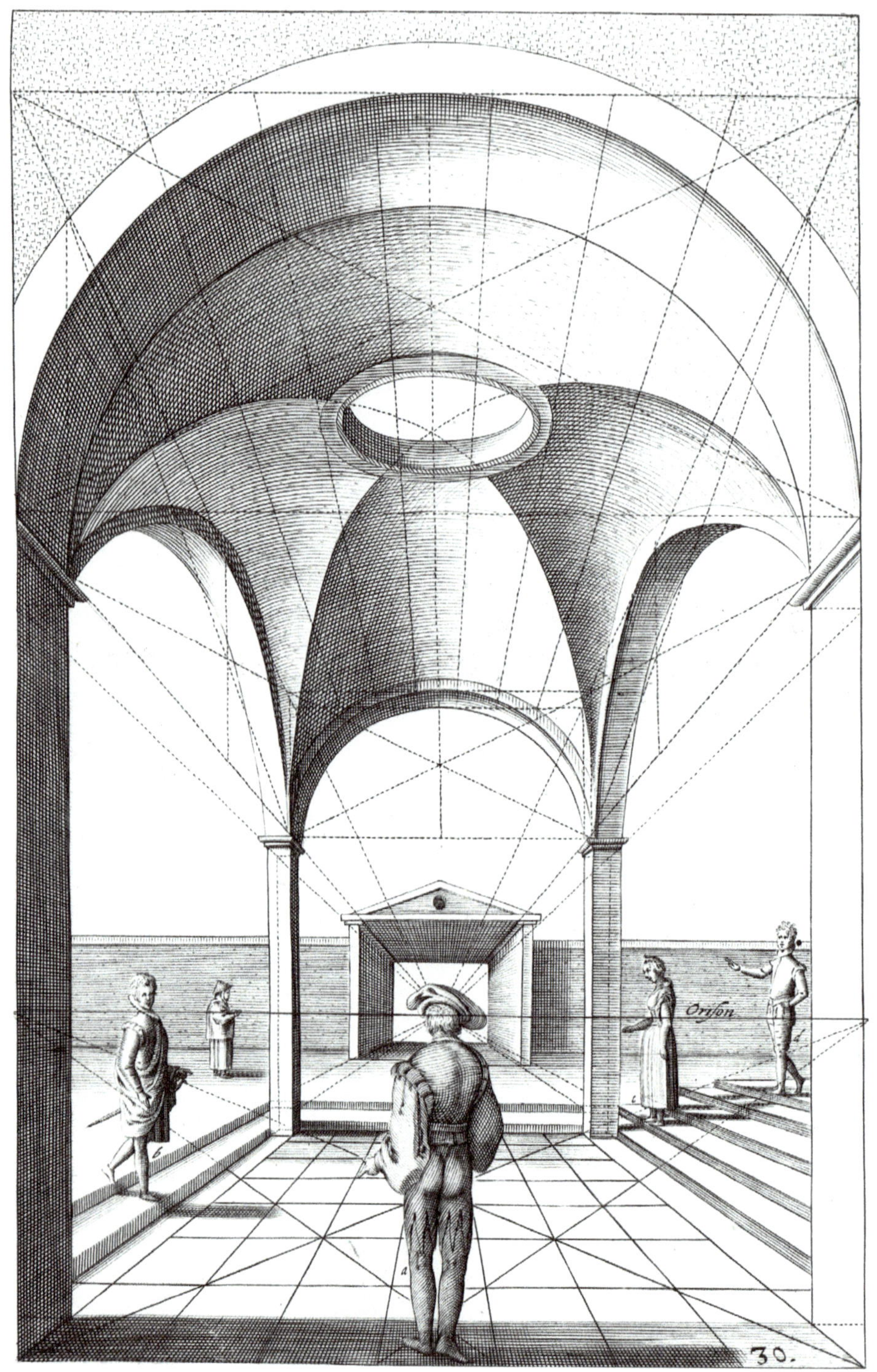

Plate from *Perspective* by Hans Vredemann de Vries 1604

Introduction

Our world is solid, it exists in three-dimensions. As we move around, we see the world from different viewpoints. We tentatively explore this world from an early age and, by trial and error, learn how to perceive depth and judge size and distance, so allowing us to move around safely without harming ourselves or others.

By contrast with our solid, three-dimensional world, a painted canvas is flat, it is two-dimensional. When we look at a painting and close one eye, nothing changes. If we move around in front of the painting, nothing changes. Nevertheless, over the centuries, artists eventually succeeded in representing our solid, three-dimensional world realistically on a flat, two-dimensional canvas, creating an amazing illusion of depth and solidity.

How have artists represented our world over the centuries?

At what point did artists first represent the world in a realistic, natural-looking way?

What techniques did they use to help achieve realism?

We will explore these questions by illustrating art from early pre-history to modern-day hyperrealism. We will go on to explain the many depth clues used by artists in representing our world. Then we will describe how various mechanical and optical techniques can be employed to create an outline of a real scene, enabling the artist to complete the work in true perspective.

Lastly, we will explain the development and use of linear perspective as a technique to creating such a framework, enabling the artist to achieve realism in representational art and the creation of realistic but purely imaginative works. Modern-day computer games and movies rely heavily on this approach.

Along the way we will show the talent and dexterity of the masters with examples of their works, illustrating the creation of naturalistic depth and reality on a flat surface.

When we are finished, I hope that the next time you observe a painting, especially a famous one, you will appreciate even more *the genius behind the canvas.*

A Brief History

First, let's go back in time and look at some prehistoric art. Here is a splendid example of lions sketched during the stone age, some 30,000 years ago, on a cave wall in the Ardèche valley region of France.

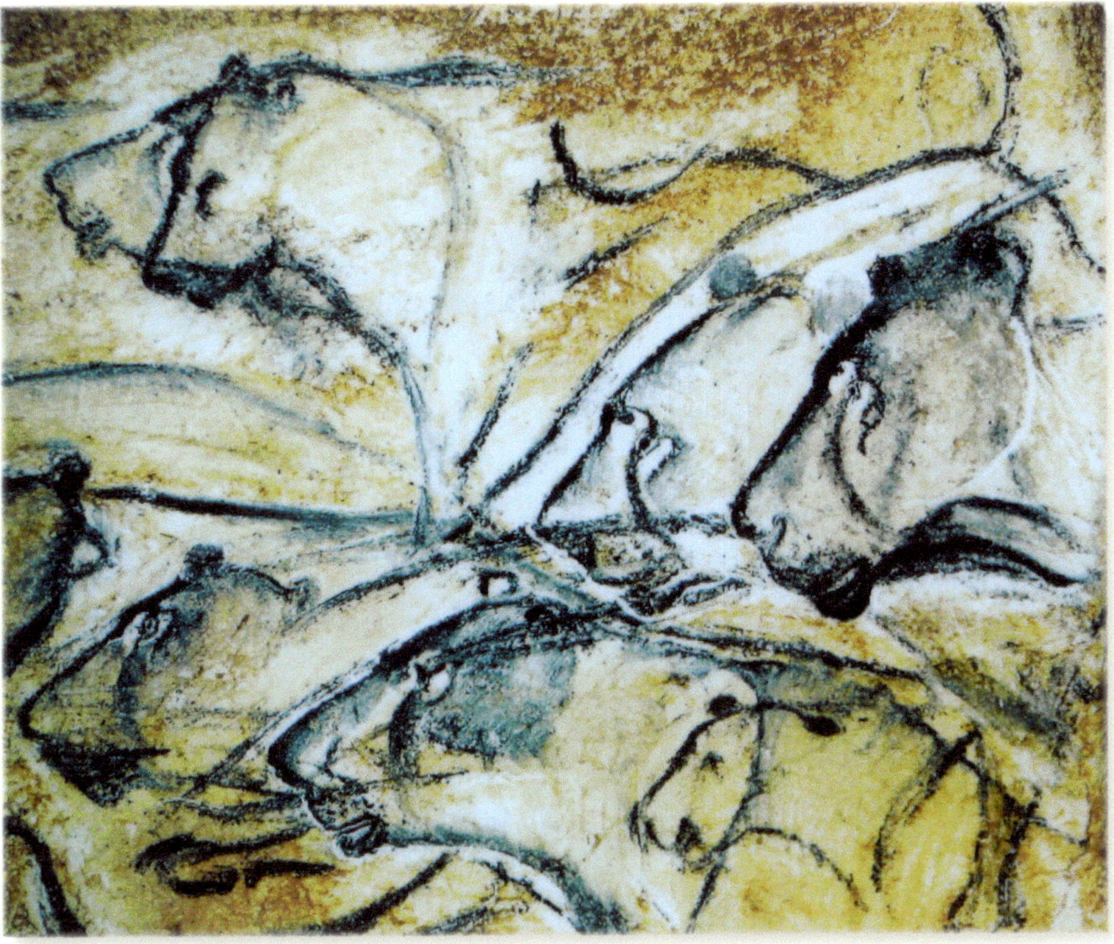

Fig. 1: *Lions painted in the Chauvet Cave*: a replica of the painting from the Brno museum Anthropos

A simple drawing on a cave wall, yet there is a clear sense of depth and movement in the scene, achieved by overlapping and offsetting their outlines. This is exactly what we would see if a herd of animals was passing us by. We don't know the relative sizes of the animals depicted, but the impression of depth works even if size does not diminish with distance from the viewer, as it would in reality if they were all of a similar size. We appear to be viewing the animals from their eye level, which suggests that we are perhaps sitting on (or hiding behind!) a rock as they pass by.

Moving on to a time around the Common Era, we can observe some first attempts at creating a sense of depth and realism in Roman wall paintings.

Here are two examples of frescoes from the *Villa of P. Fannius Synistor* in Boscoreale, Naples, dating from 43-30 BCE.

The fresco in Figure 2, opposite, presents some basic notions of perspective - notice the white columns on the left and right becoming smaller with distance. At the same time the tall gold columns in the foreground partially overlap the more distant columns so enhancing the sense of depth in the scene.

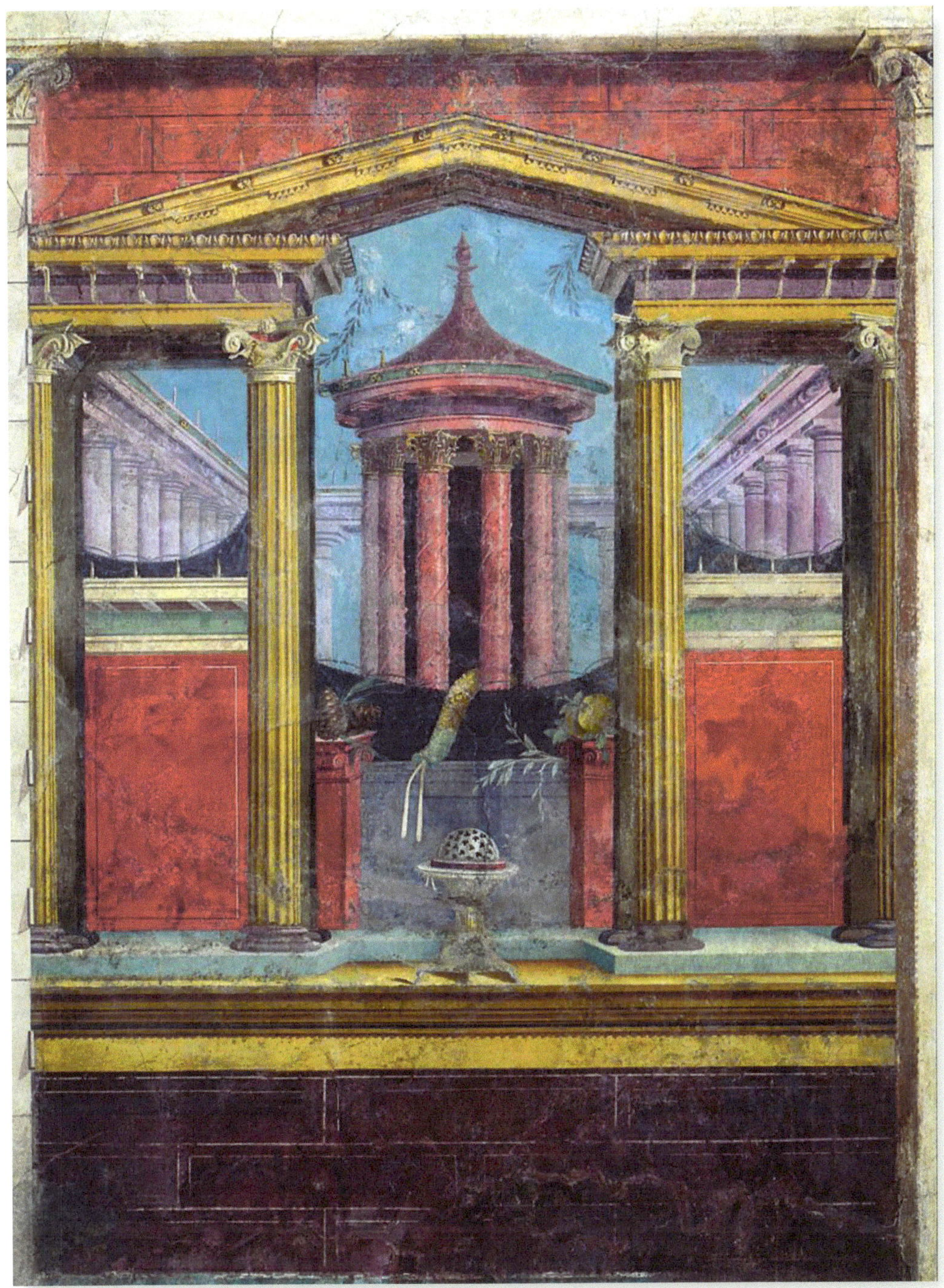

Fig. 2: Fresco on the *Villa of P. Fannius Synistor* in Boscoreale, 43-30 BCE showing primitive use of vanishing points

The second fresco presents a rather curious collection of buildings.

A fresco is a type of wall painting using dry pigments mixed with a little water and placed directly onto a thin layer of freshly-laid wet plaster. After some hours the pigment is absorbed into the plaster and becomes a part of the wall.

Again there are notions of perspective and overlap, together with some attempts at light and shadow, all of which combine to provide a sense of depth. Well preserved, the villa was entombed in the eruption of Mount Vesuvius in 79CE and not excavated until just before the First World War.

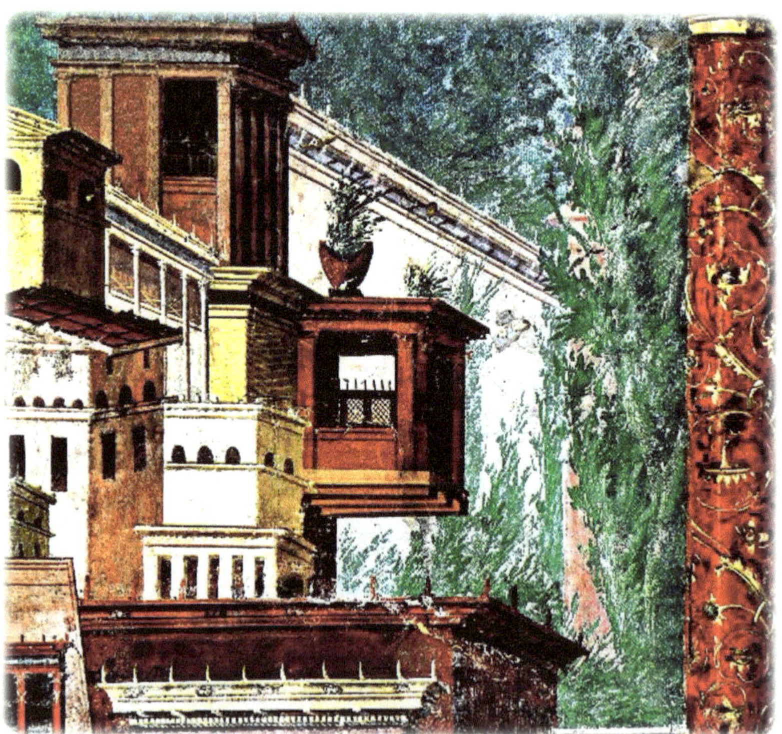

Fig. 3: Detail from another fresco on the *Villa of P. Fannius Synistor* in Boscoreale, 43-30 BCE

Moving on to the Early Middle Ages, from the fifth to the tenth centuries, much art was religious and symbolic in nature.

By way of example, one of the oldest known icons in existence shows *Christ and Abbot Mena*, an encaustic (hot wax) painting on a fig tree panel, dated perhaps to the 7th century. Now in the Louvre, the icon was brought from the Apollo monastery in Bawit, Egypt.

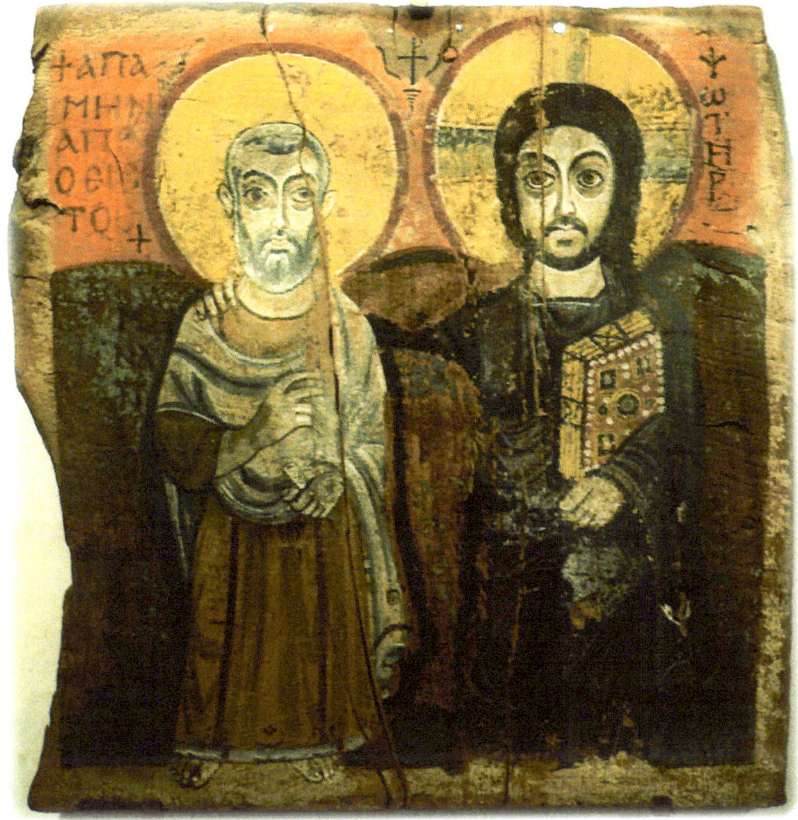

Fig. 4: *Christ and Abbot Mena*, 6-7-8th century, Fig tree wood panel

These early paintings often told a simple story and were plainly illustrated, showing saintly figures based on biblical accounts. There was no intention of providing a sense of depth or realism, although the book in the hand appears solid, but with problems of perspective that we shall explore later.

Let's move on a few hundred years to the High Middle Ages, encompassing the tenth to the thirteenth centuries. The figure opposite is an extract from the Saint Albans Psalter, an English illuminated manuscript, and one of several psalters known to have been created at, or for, the Saint Albans Abbey in the twelfth century. Produced on vellum (calf skin), it shows Mary Magdalen announcing the resurrection to the apostles, and is dated to approximately 1120.

Again, the topic is religious, telling a simple story through an illustrated picture. While splendid in its own right, the scene is quite flat and not realistic. There is some attempt at providing context – notice the crenellated wall and the partially overlapped buildings in the upper background of the picture.

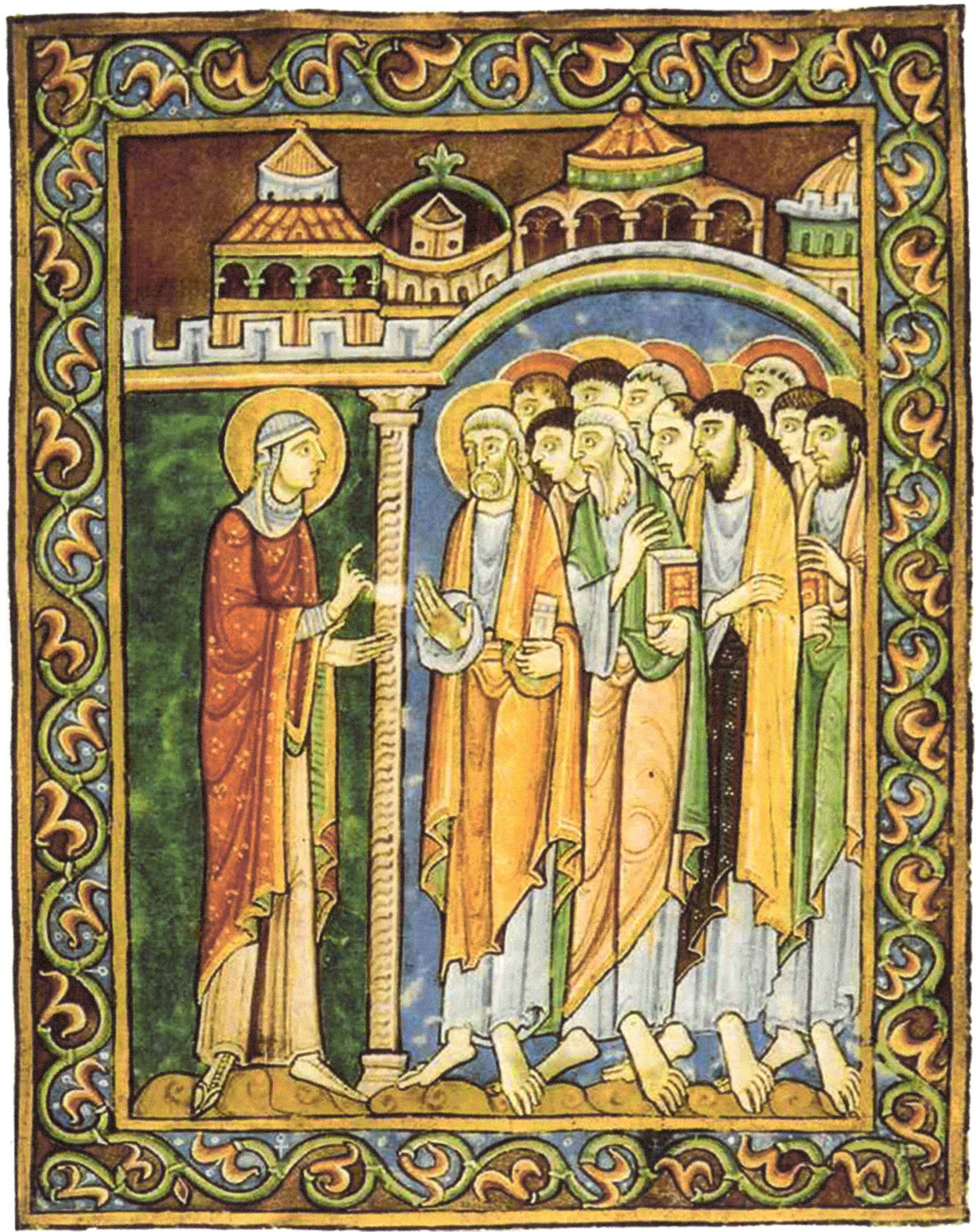

Fig. 5: *Mary Magdalen announcing the resurrection to the apostles,* 1120
(St. Albans Psalter, St Godehard's Church, Hildesheim)

Moving on a further two hundred years to the Late Middle Ages (fourteenth to fifthteenth centuries) we can find non-religious art.

This next example is entitled *King Otto IV of Brandenburg playing chess with a woman*. It dates from around 1320, and is taken from the Manesse Codex, a book copied and illustrated between 1305 and 1340 in Zürich. This impressive manuscript contains songs and poetry, and was produced for the Manesse family.

You may notice how the scene is more realistic, showing figures engaged in normal human activities. However, there is little representation of depth: the artist primarily follows what is termed a hierarchical convention. This approach places the important figures higher up in the scene, and makes them larger. Conversely, the lowly court musicians are painted smaller in size and placed at the bottom of the picture.

Notice that the figures are all viewed from the front, the king and partner playing chess dominating the scene. The chessboard, however, is shown as though we are looking down onto its top surface. This is not to say that the artist was trying to represent the scene naturally and realistically, but rather to tell a story.

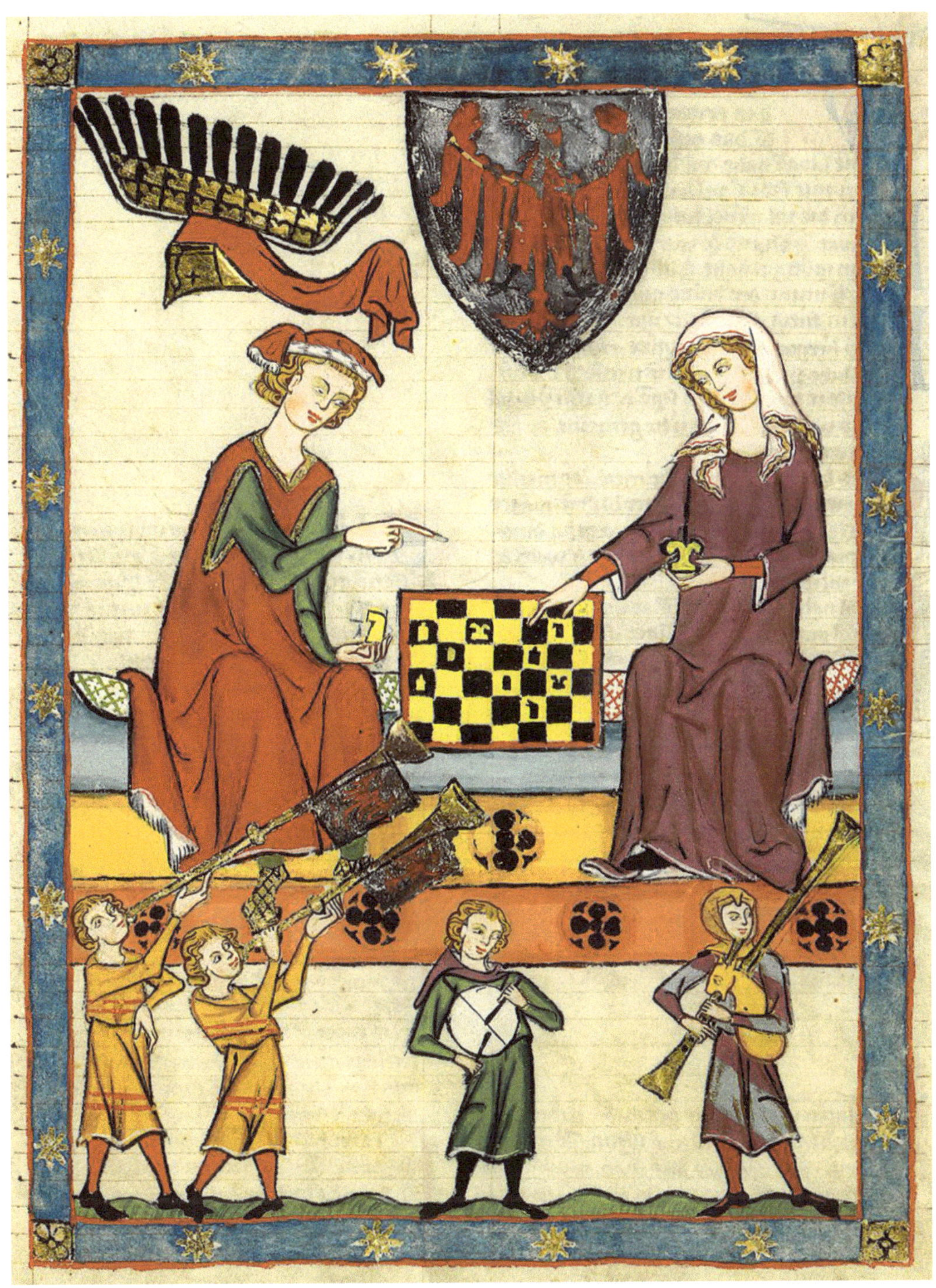

Fig. 6: *Meister des Codex Manesse,* Manessische Liederhandschrift c.1305–1340 (water colors, parchment, Heidelberg Universitätsbibliothek)

The overall effect is of a painting that appears rather flat, and does not draw us into the scene. However, the artist clearly communicates what is going on: the important figures, the king and woman, are playing chess, on a fine blue, silk-covered bench, while being serenaded by lowly musicians.

At the same time, representing the chess board from above makes it abundantly clear what game is being played, something that would not have been so obvious if it had been drawn end-on, as it would have appeared in reality. No ambiguity of message here.

We might ask why the musicians appear in front of the king and chess partner. This overlap would imply they were actually in front of the key figures. But their size implies their being more distant. I would argue that this ambiguity is simply an artefact of what the artist wanted to convey. Better to ask the question how else could the artist have portrayed the musicians and their instruments serenading from a lowly position?

Not above, since this would break the hierarchical convention of the key figures being higher up. Not behind, because that would obscure their instruments. If the musicians were truly in front then of course they would appear larger than the key figures but this approach would again break the rules of hierarchical convention. So, by placing the musicians below and smaller, albeit in front of the key figures, the artist precisely conveys their lowly situation without obscuring their function.

Of course, the artist could have drawn the musicians much smaller and avoided any overlap. Aside from the aesthetic question of balance, we would most likely lose the impression of the musicians being associated with the key figures.

Let's look at another painting from the Late Middle Ages, see Figure 7, over the page. This example was completed around 1410 by an unknown artist, about a hundred years after the previous codex. It is entitled *Paradiesgärtlein (The Garden of Paradise)* and is painted in oil, on an oak wood panel. The work is currently in the Städel Museum, Frankfurt (on loan from the Historisches Museum, Frankfurt).

We seem to be viewing the scene from outside the garden, a little higher up, perhaps from an upstairs window. This time there is a good attempt at creating the illusion of depth and realism on the flat surface. But there are several aspects of the scene that look odd or wrong to our modern-day eyes. The artist still places the most important figure, Mary, the lady in blue reading a book, higher up and larger. So, the artist continues to follow the hierarchical convention, at least in part. In reality since the lady in blue is farther back in the garden, to appear natural she should be painted somewhat smaller. Also notice the small basin bottom left. It appears to our eyes a little misshapen.

Let's now look at the white stone wall surrounding the garden. You may notice how the sidewall, on the left, isn't painted smaller with distance either, and the back wall is painted the same size as the side wall even though it is farther away. If you focus your attention on the corner of the wall upper left, you might get the impression that the wall is coming out towards you and not receding into the distance as it should.

If you don't see this ambiguity immediately, just let your eyes focus on the top left corner for a few seconds and you will see the effect.

Of course, I am not trying to say what the artist should or should not have done. He may quite deliberately have painted the scene

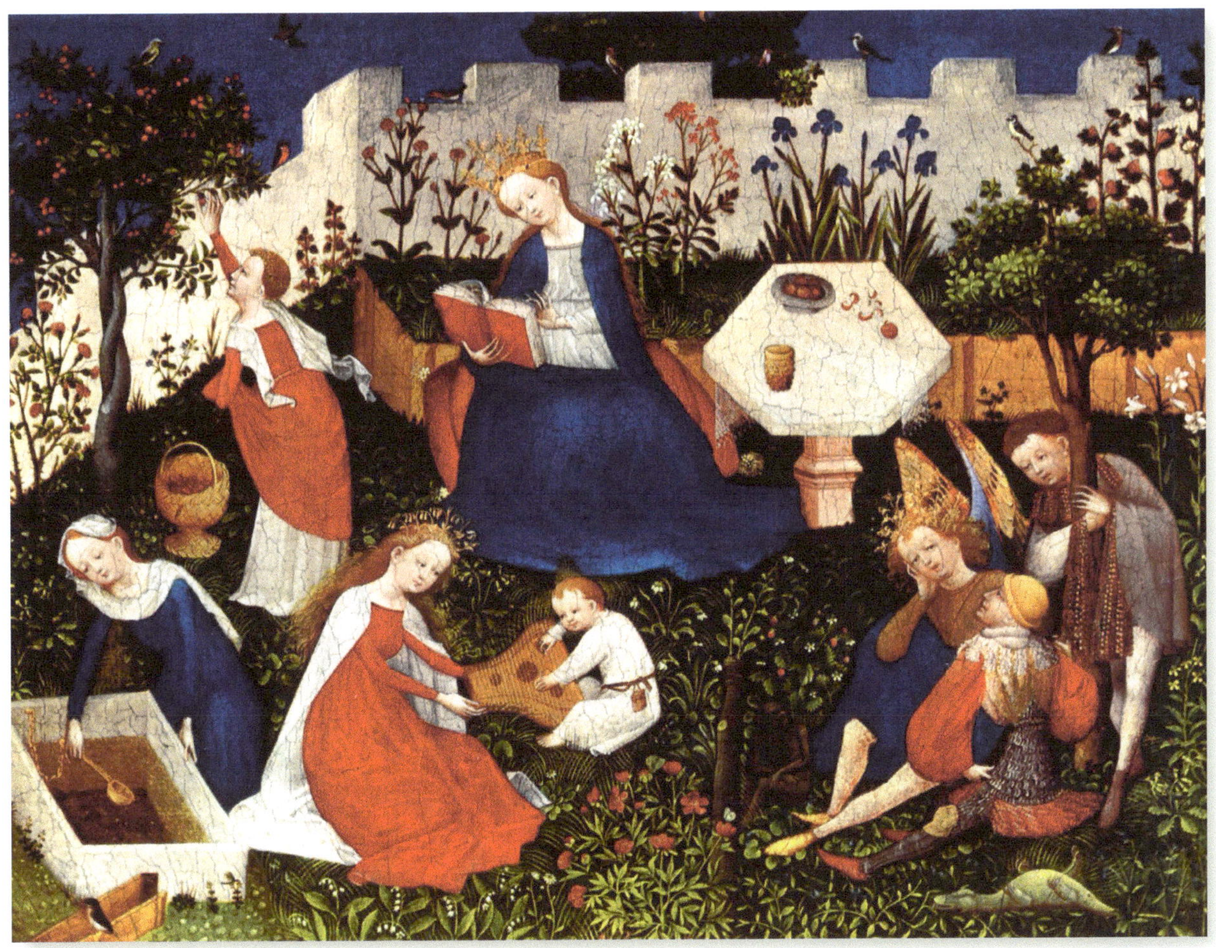

Fig. 7: *Paradiesgärtlein*, Upper Rhenish Master c.1410-1420
(Egg tempera, oak, oil paint, Städel Museum, Frankfurt)

thus. I am simply explaining why the scene appears odd to us today. The key point is that these anomalies are all errors of perspective.

In summary, the artist has painted some areas of the scene, the most important perhaps, in symbolic, hierarchical style, and surrounded them with some elements of depth and realism. Was this mixture of styles deliberate, or was it simply that the artist had little knowledge of how to accurately represent our solid world on a flat canvas? We will never know of course. The overall effect here is one of confusion. We are nicely drawn into the scene by the depth clues, but we are confused on entering the picture because of the mixed depth messages.

As an aside, this painting is considered to be one of the earliest to depict flowers and plants naturally – notice the beautifully painted varieties all along the garden walls and in the garden itself. A few examples are reproduced below:

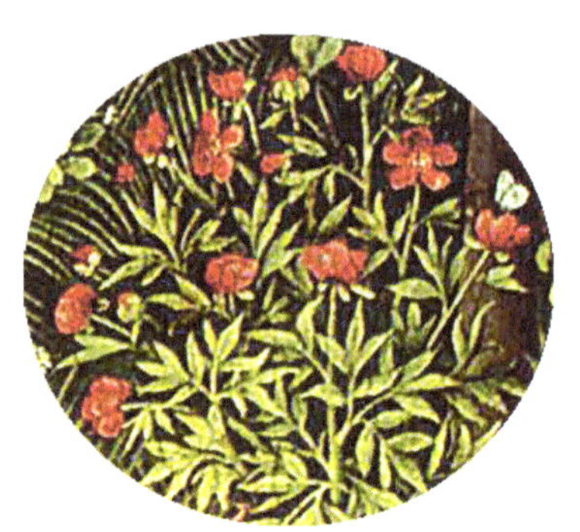
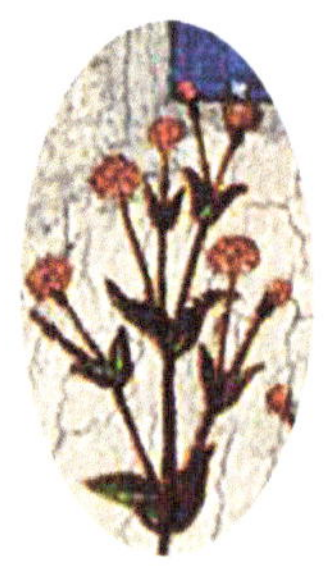
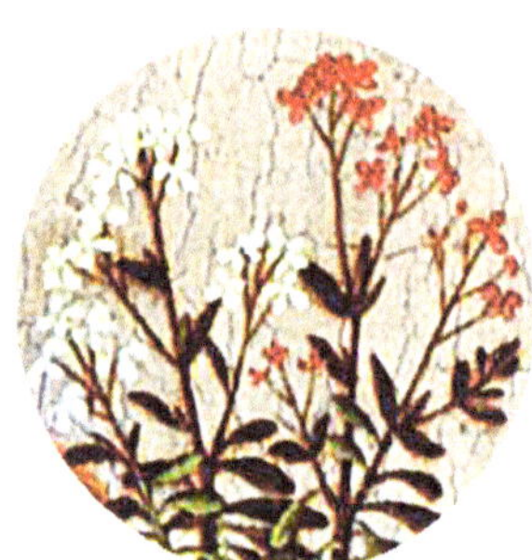
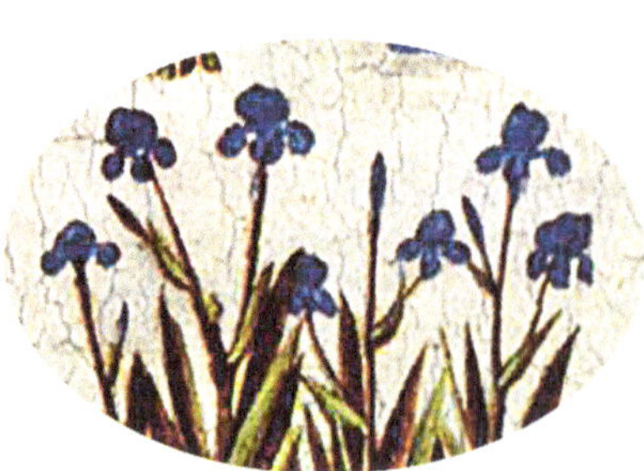

Now let's draw our attention to the garden table. The artist has drawn the table support viewed from the front, as is the view of the overall scene. However, the table top is drawn as though we are looking from above. This might remind you of the chess board viewed from above in the previous painting. In each case, the artist clearly wants to show us on his flat canvas what is on the chess board or what is on the table. But since each artist has already chosen his viewpoint – looking into the scene from outside – in reality, we wouldn't be able to see either the top of the table or the top of the chessboard. In fact, each artist is providing multiple viewpoints on the same canvas.

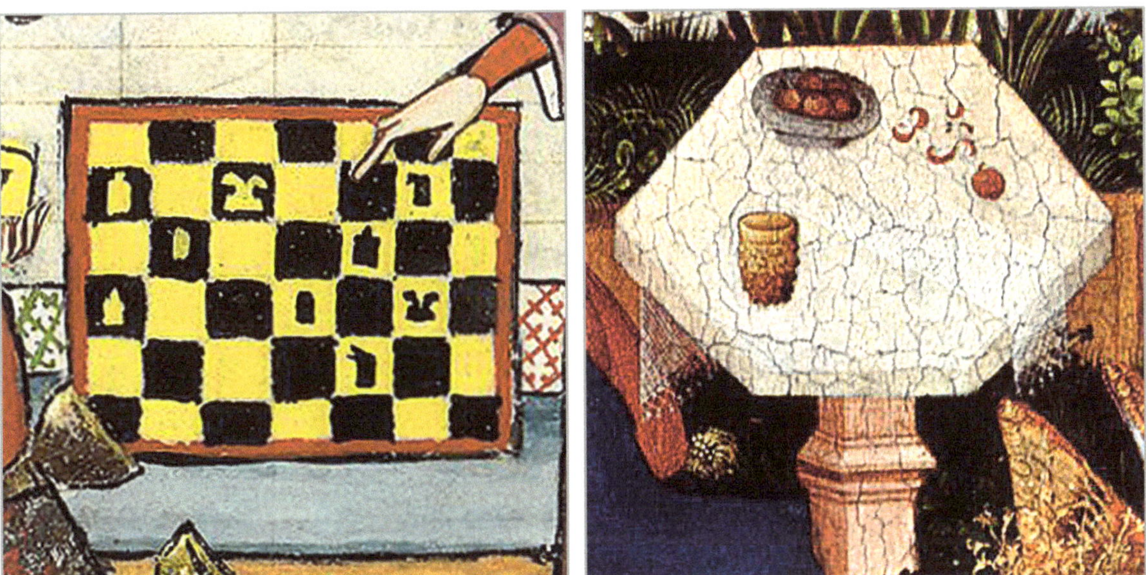

Fig. 8: Detail from *Meister des Codex Manesse and Paradiesgärtlein*, showing the view from on high

It is interesting to compare the multiple viewpoints offered in the previous two paintings with the cubist approaches considered avant-garde in the early twentieth century.

In a move away from realistic, single viewpoint art, cubist artists attempted to depict key elements in the scene from a multitude of viewpoints (simultaneity) rather than from a single viewpoint.

Opposite we have a good example of cubist simultaneity. Georges Braque, a co-founder with Picasso of the cubist movement, created *The Round Table* in 1929.

We see a round table in the corner of a room. The room and the table pedestal are clearly viewed from the front, while the table surface appears to be viewed from on high, laden with a whole collection of objects, with some viewed from the front, and some from above.

By way of comparison, the inset, opposite, shows the table from the *Paradiesgärtlein*, painted some 500 years earlier. Clearly multiple viewpoints have been around for a long time!

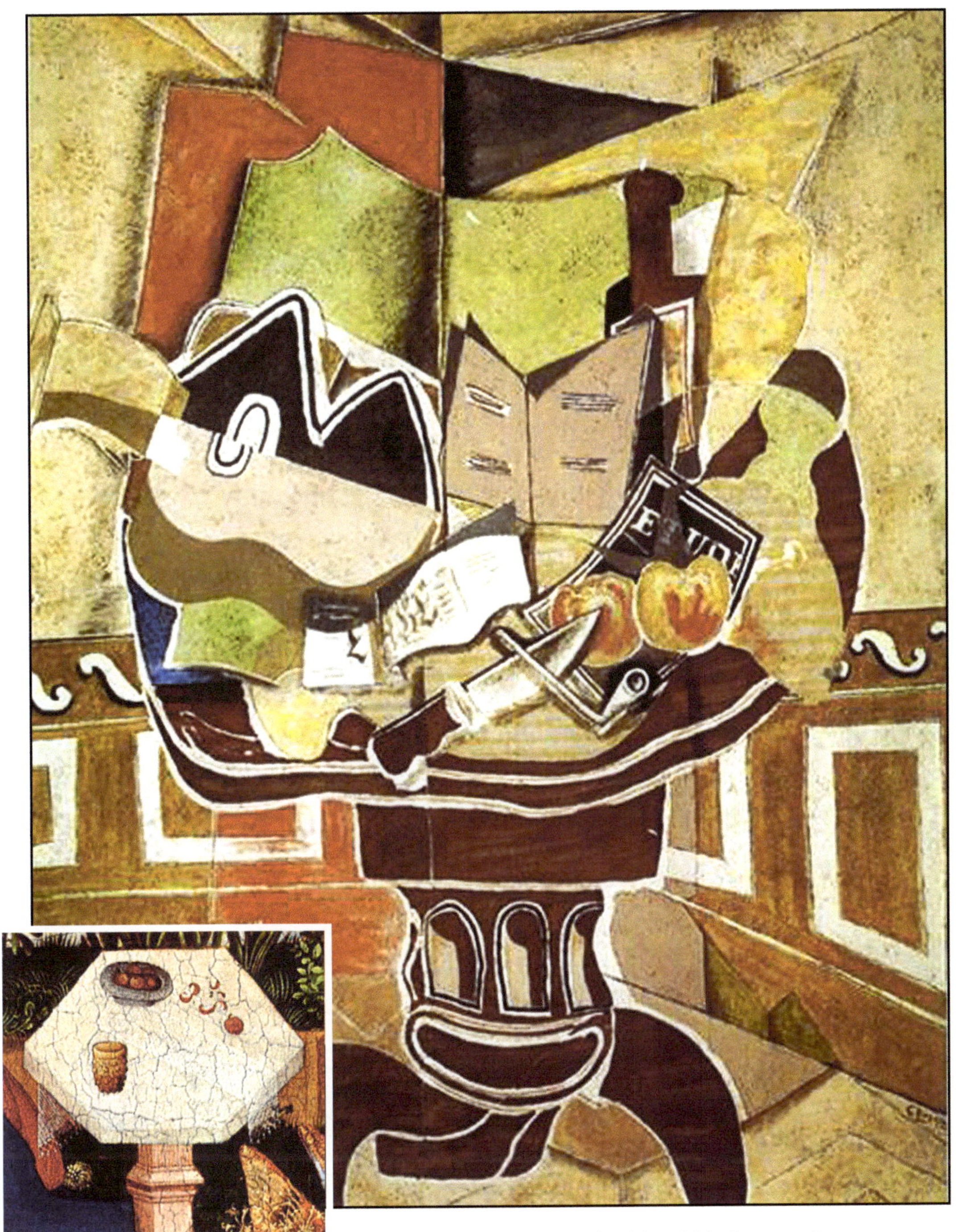

Inset: close-up of the table from the *Paradiesgärtlein*

Fig. 9: *The Round Table,* 1929, Georges Braque (oil, canvas, Philips Collection, Washington, DC, US)

Returning to our historical overview, let's move on to the early modern period, encompassing the Renaissance.

Just fifty years after the *Paradiesgärtlein* was created, observe the sudden transformation in imagined art towards an amazing impression of reality and depth. *The Delivery of the Keys* by Perugino was painted around 1482 on the northern wall of the Sistine Chapel in the Vatican City.

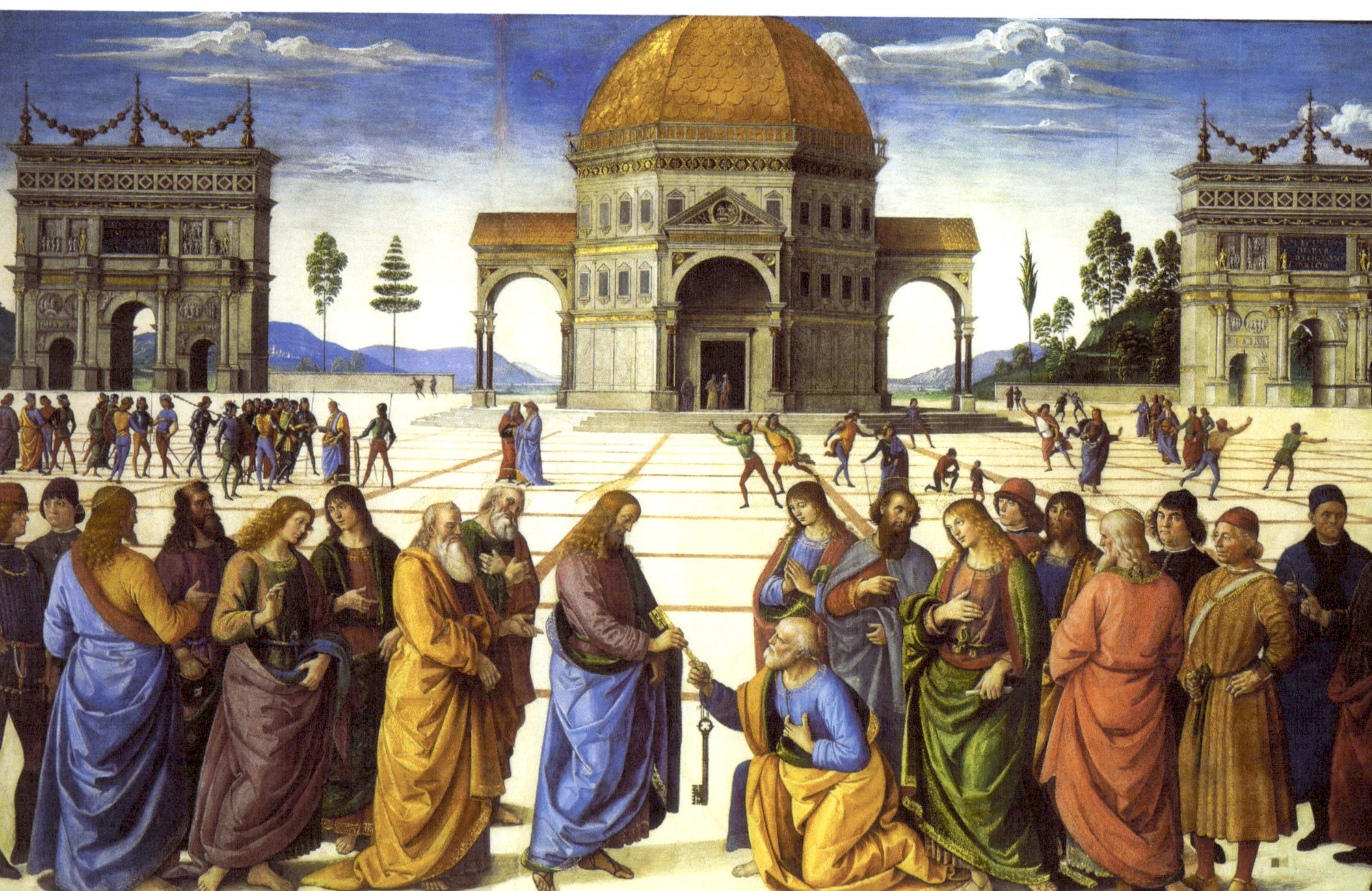

Fig. 10: *The Delivery of the Keys*, c. 1481–1482, Fresco, Perugino, Sistine Chapel, Vatican City

Here we have a religious topic drawn with life-like figures, although the most important figures are arranged somewhat curiously in a foreground line across the picture. The octagonal temple of Jerusalem with its porches provides a dominant solid-looking central background, while the tiled sandstone squares diminish in size with distance, giving a fine impression of depth. This style of representation became all the rage during the Renaissance.

Here is one more example, a fine oil painting by Raphael, dating from 1504. Entitled *The Marriage of Virgin Mary*, it was clearly inspired from an earlier Perugino painting of the same name. Again, we have a solid central background building with realistic figures in the foreground, and a sandstone tiled floor disappearing into the distance. All combine to provide a great sense of depth and realism, even though it is an imagined scene.

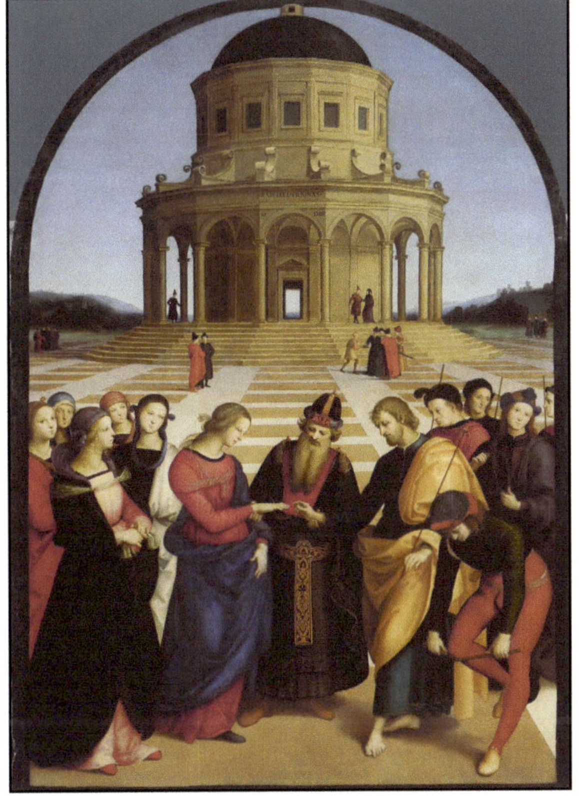

Fig. 11: *The Marriage of Virgin Mary,* Raphael, 1504, oil on roundheaded panel

If we compare the realism in these paintings with the *Paradiesgärtlein* painted around 1410, we could reasonably ask what suddenly changed in the fifthteenth century that enabled artists to create such an illusion of realism? We will answer this question in the following chapters.

Meanwhile, continuing our chronological survey, let's move on to the sixthteenth century and explore this painting by Pieter Bruegel the Elder, completed about 1560. The lively work illustrates children absorbed in some eighty games.

As an observer, we have a strong impression of viewing the activities from a safe distance, high up in another building. How an artist achieves this high viewpoint will also be addressed in a later section.

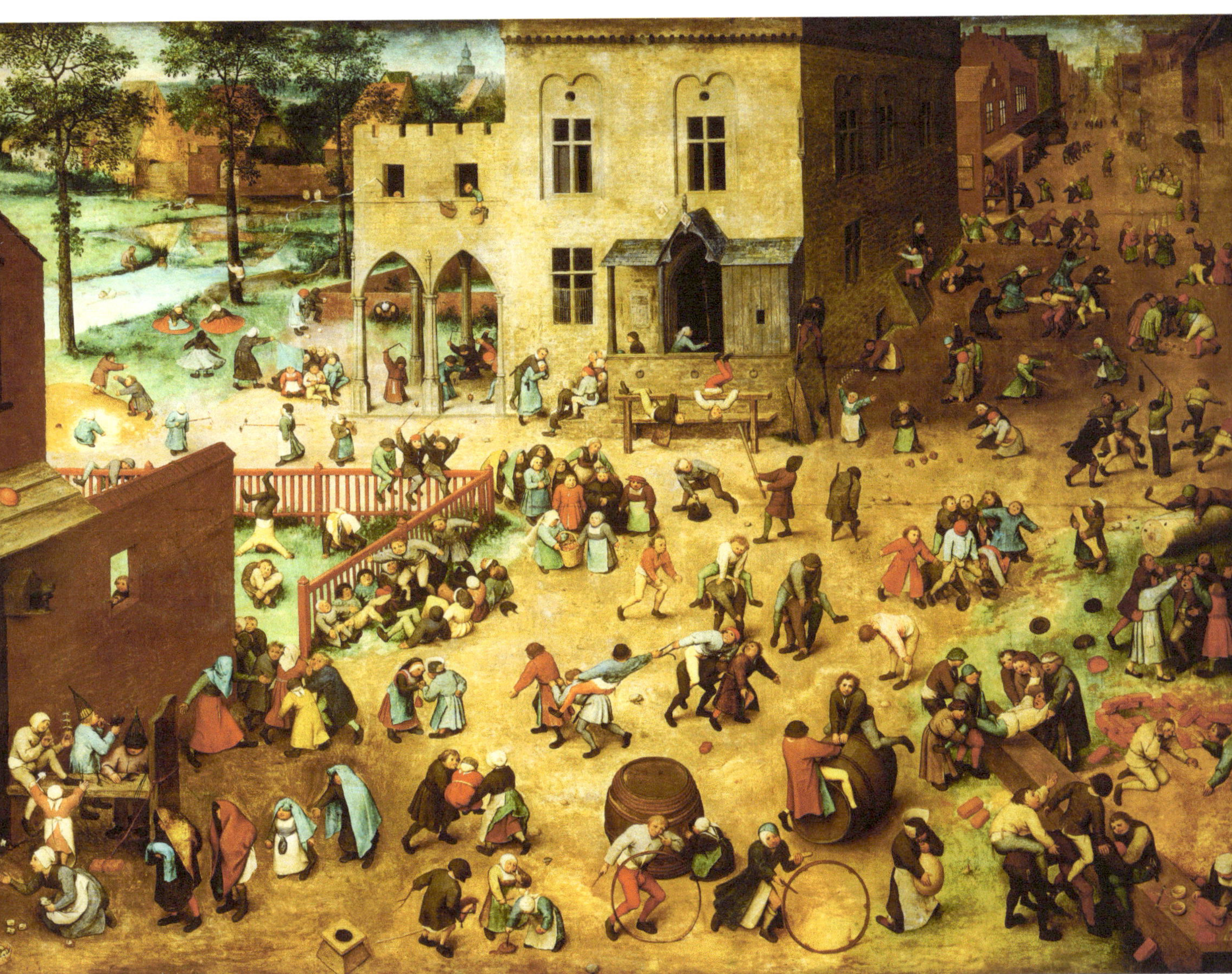

Fig. 12: *Children's Games,* Pieter Bruegel the Elder, 1560, oil on panel

Realism in art was now well established.

Observe this Venetian scene, entitled *The Piazzetta*, painted in oil on canvas by Giovanni Antonio Canal (Canaletto) around 1734.

Here the artist has translated our real world onto the flat canvas. There is a great sense of space and life. We are drawn into the picture, we feel part of the scene.

We could be standing right there in the piazzetta. Or could we?

Are we perhaps viewing the scene from somewhat higher up, maybe from a parapet? Again, we will discuss in a later section how this viewpoint may have arisen.

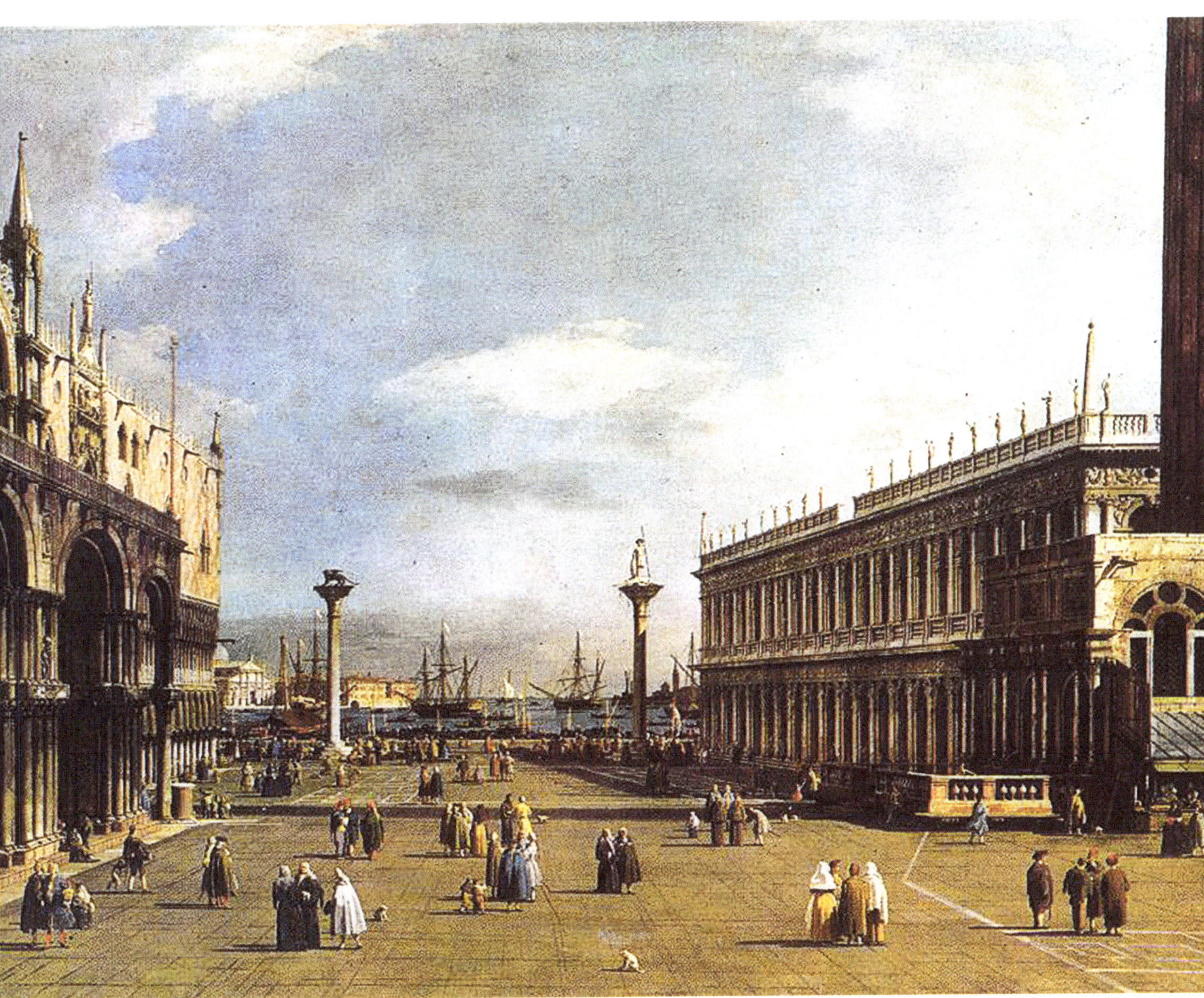

Fig. 13: *The Piazzetta,* Canaletto c.1734 (oil on canvas, Galleria Nazionale d'Arte Antica)

Here's another example from the eighteenth century, painted just twenty years after Canaletto's *The Piazzetta*.

Entitled *Interior of Saint Peter's in Rome*, by Giovanni Paolo Panini, it astonishes with its fine detail, and sense of depth and realism. We will return to this painting later to explore the techniques used. Like Canaletto's *Piazzetta*, this painting depicts what is considered to be a real scene.

So, we might ask, how did artists start to depict real scenes so realistically on a flat canvas?

Clearly these artists were highly talented. But was such realistic representation intuitive? Or did they use optical or mechanical aids to help achieve realism? Did artists use rules or techniques to achieve realism?

We will answer these questions in detail in the following chapters, so let's hold them for now and continue our historical overview.

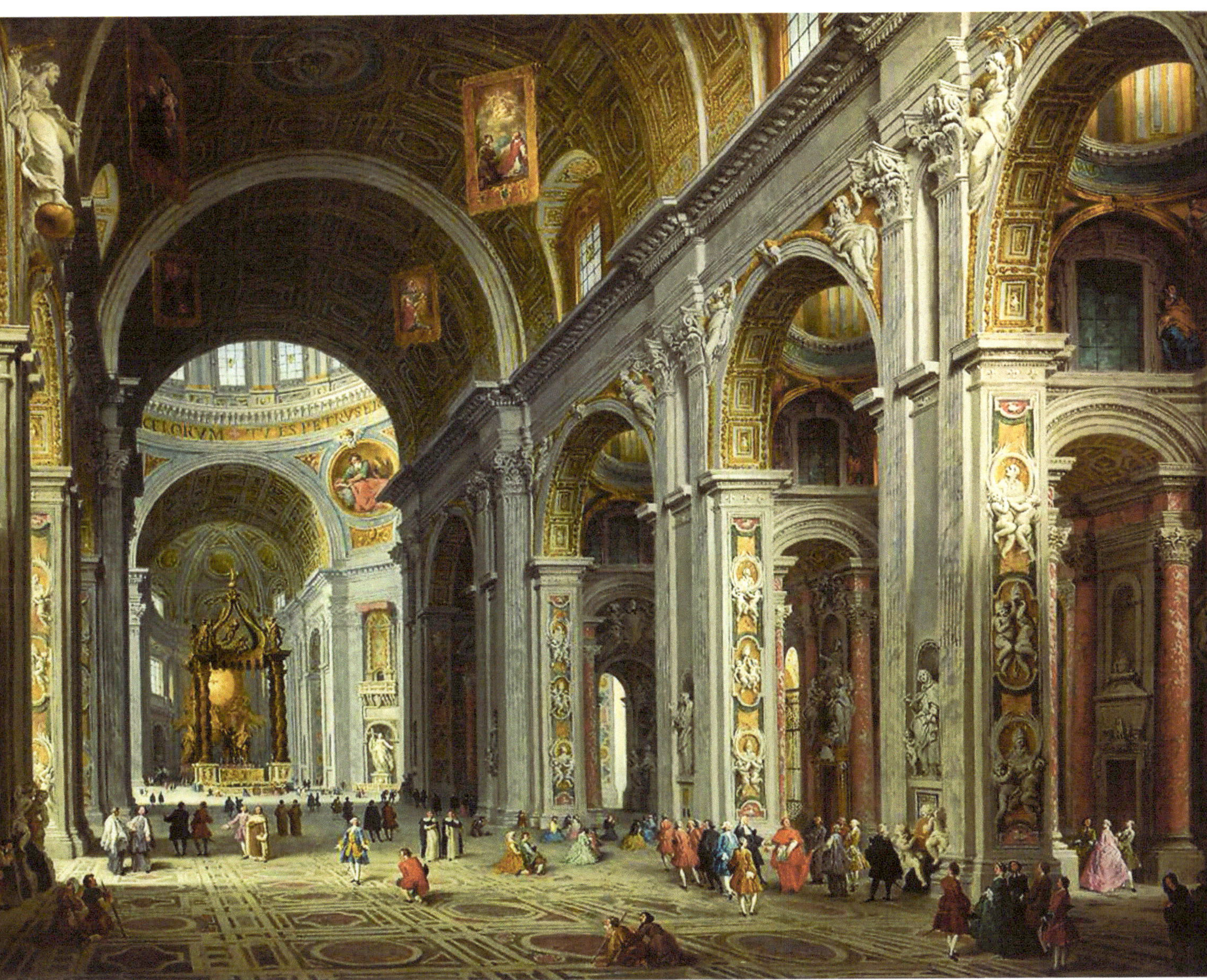

Fig. 14: *Interior of Saint Peter's Rome,* Giovanni Paolo Panini after 1754, oil on canvas

This next, intriguing scene is entitled *Lavaburst* and is an example of contemporary, illusory street-art created in 2008 by Edgar Mueller.

The artist has taken a real street, with real depth, that includes shops, houses, people, sidewalks and road. He has then overlaid onto the flat surface of the road an amazingly realistic but imagined scene of a gorge with a river torrenting through – all done in chalk!

When we first see this scene, we are taken aback by its apparent realism - we might think it a fake picture, a collage. But the artist has simply used rules of perspective, along with other well-known cues to depth such as light and shadow, to achieve this stunningly realistic visual illusion.

If we were to literally stand at the entrance to the street, we would have exactly the same impression of a gorge torrenting down the street towards us as we see in this photo.

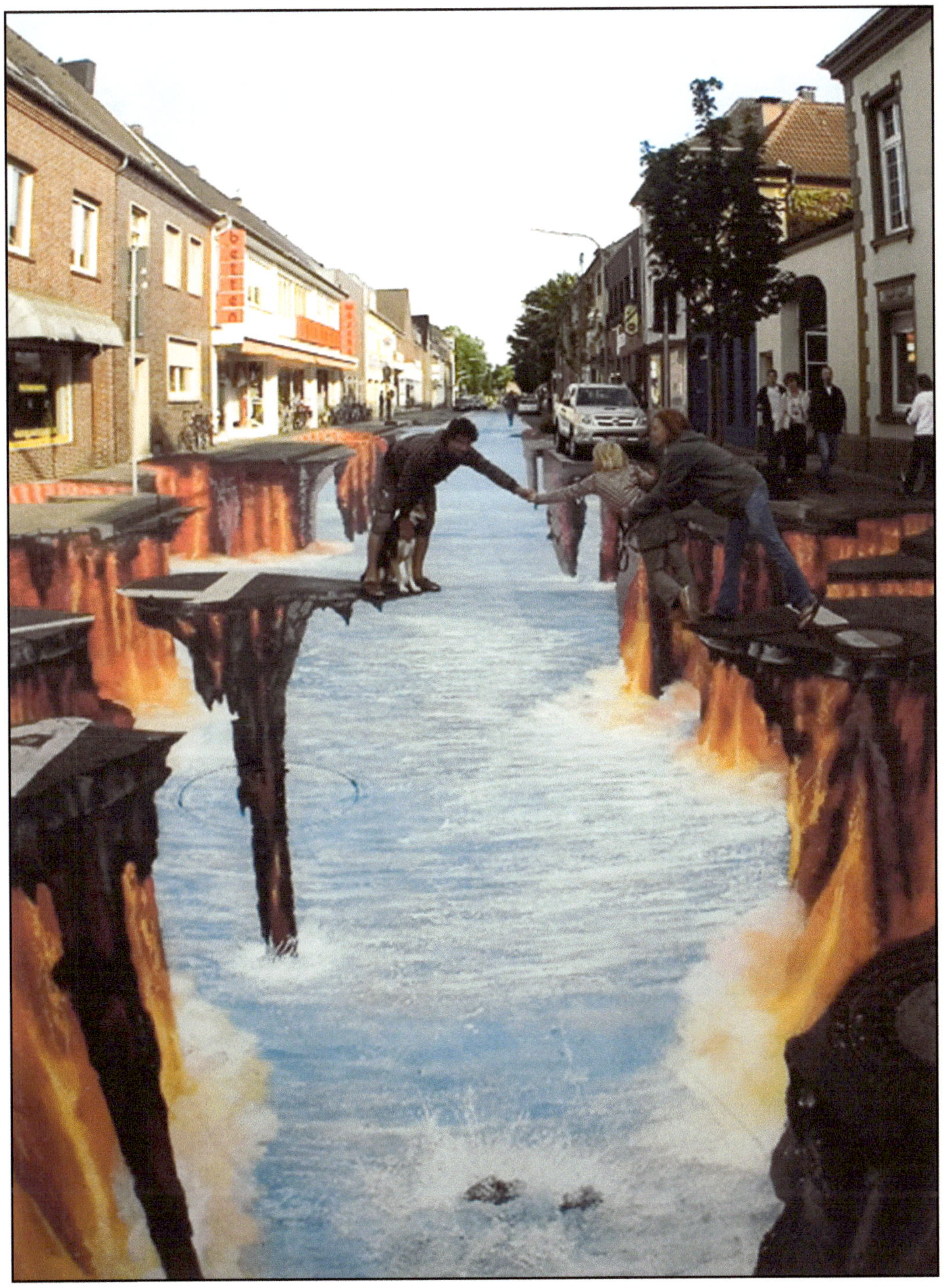

Fig. 15: *Lavaburst*, © 2008 Edgar Mueller, chalk on pavement

Finishing our brief historical overview, here is an example of contemporary, photo-realistic art painted by Richard Estes, entitled *Lunch Specials*.

Hard to believe perhaps, but this is an oil painting, created in 2001, almost three hundred years after the oil painting of *The Piazzetta* by Canaletto in 1734. This painting is so nearly photographic in quality and representation of our world that we could easily imagine being next in line for a tasty croissant!

In the following chapters we will describe the many clues to depth and realism in a painting, then go on to explore the critically important one of perspective and how over time artists came to create a set of rules to help achieve the illusion of depth and reality on a flat two-dimensional surface.

Throughout the book we will take examples of well-known paintings from over the centuries and illustrate how artists have achieved this sense of realism, how we feel drawn into the scene. We hope thus to provide you with an increased understanding of their techniques and so appreciate even more their masterly skills.

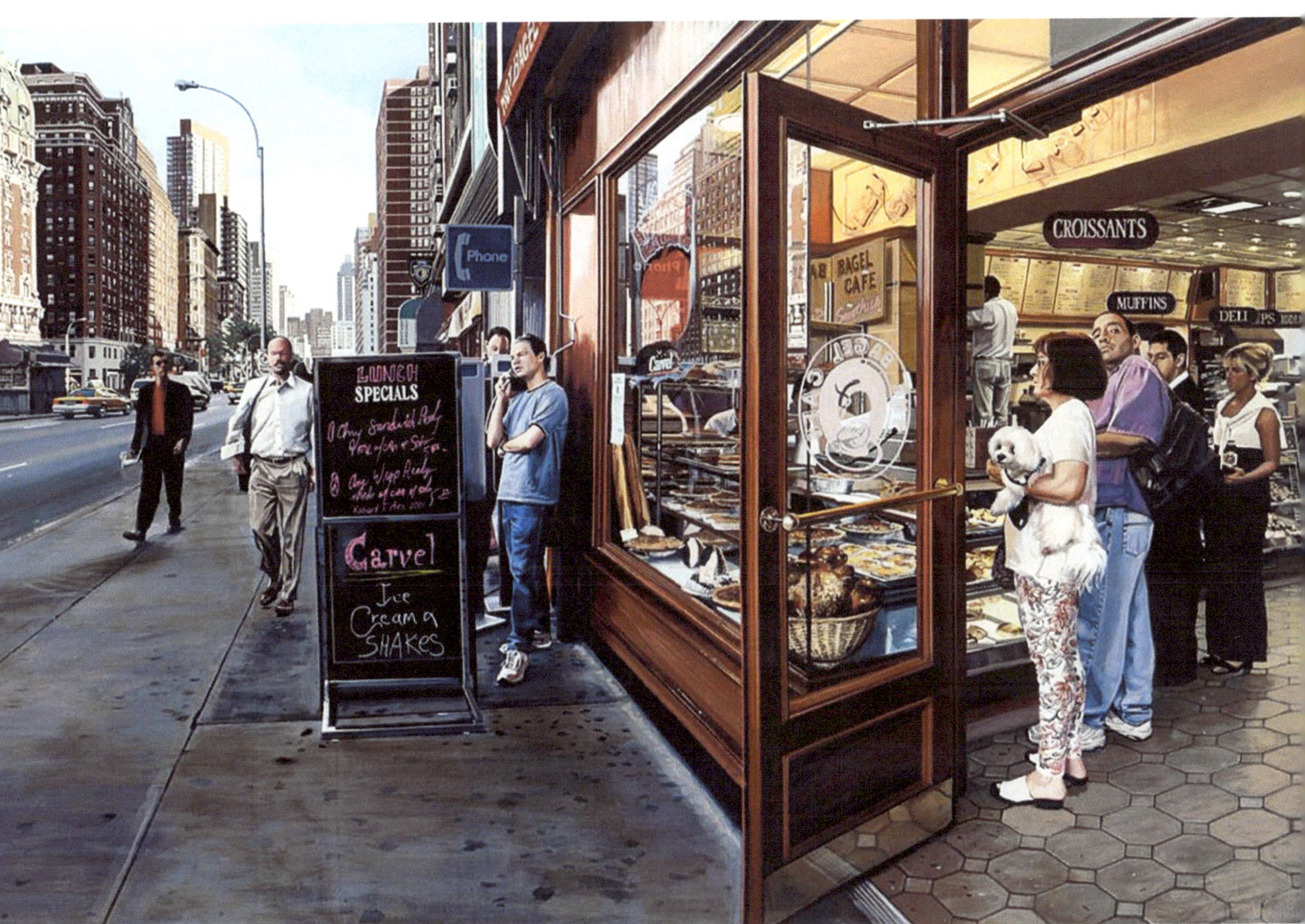

Fig. 16: *Lunch Specials*, © 2001 Richard Estes (oil on canvas)

Seeing Depth

Our world is solid, three-dimensional. As we move around, we see the world from different viewpoints, reinforcing our perception of depth, size and position.

Even standing still, with our forward-facing eyes giving us overlapping views of the same scene, we get two slightly different viewpoints of the world simultaneously, just as though we had slightly moved from one spot to another.

This stereo vision, from the Greek word *stereós* meaning solid, provides us with a superb sense of depth perception. As anyone who has been to the cinema and experienced a movie in 3D knows, the strength of our stereo vision can be spectacular.

However, having two eyes gives us no additional depth clues when looking at a painting on a flat canvas. Try looking at the real world with the left eye closed, then open the left eye and close the right eye, and so on, back and forth. Objects seem to move because we get a slightly different view from each eye. Now do the same in front of a painting and notice that nothing changes.

And yet we can readily perceive depth and solidity in a painting. How is this possible? Fortunately, perceiving depth does not require stereo vision, as anyone with a squint will tell you. There are many powerful depth clues available with a single eye.

With a picture, context and experience play important roles in our ability to perceive depth. When we are young and inexperienced in the real world, we lack the ability to interpret what we see on a flat picture.

Here's a simple example. Is this just a drawn picture or an image of a real scene?

In this case we're not easily fooled.

First, the man appears to be drawing the scene. Second, it is uniformly and unrealistically golden in color. Third, the stone blocks comprising the arch and pillars appear too consistent.

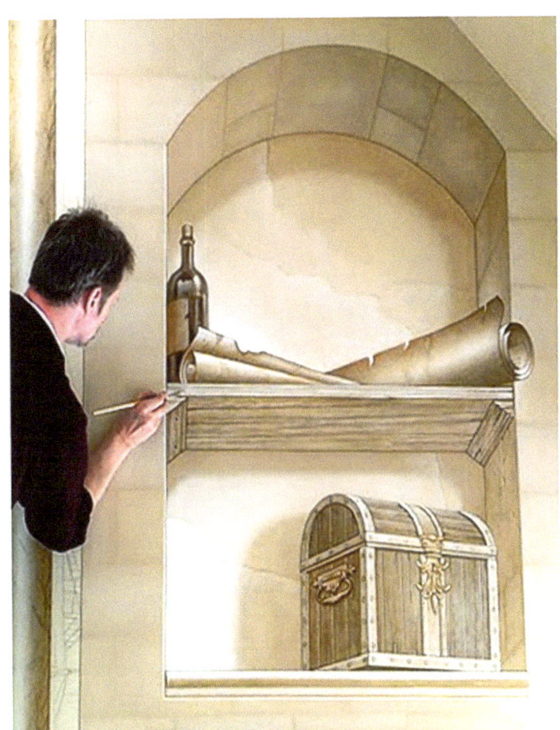

Fig. 17: *Just a drawn picture or a real scene?* (© Funatico.com, 2008)

On the other hand, *Lavaburst*, shown in Figure 15 of the previous chapter, combines a real street scene with a chalk drawing on the pavement and standing in the one place that offers a true perspective view it is hard to decide which parts of the scene are real and which are created. Below, we can see the artist at work creating the outlines, with the parking lines and curbs acting as powerful perspective aids.

So now let's explore the numerous depth clues available to an artist painting on a flat canvas (or on a flat pavement!), from a single point of view.

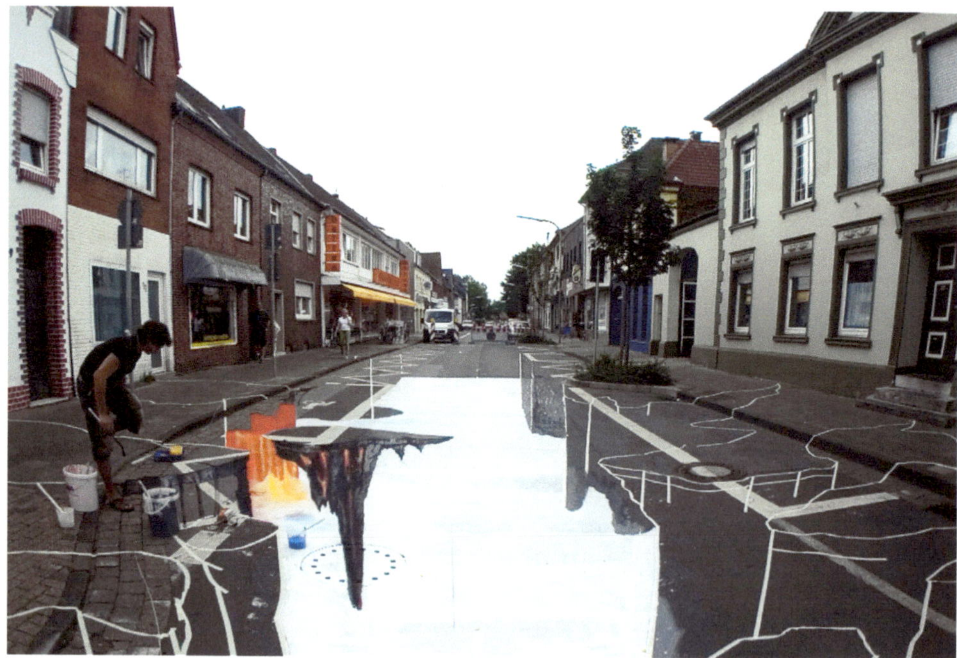

Fig. 18: Artist at work on *Lavaburst*, © 2008 Edgar Mueller

Overlap or Occlusion

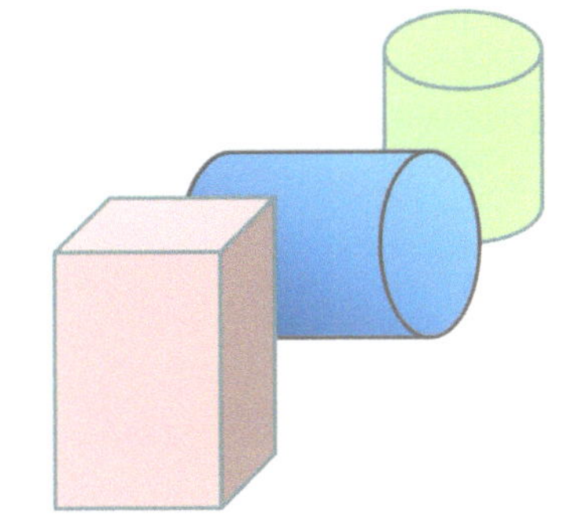
Fig. 19: Example of partial overlap

Sometimes also called interposition, overlap simply refers to the fact that a nearer item that partially or completely obscures more distant elements in a scene gives us a first, clear indication of depth.

Above is a simple example. The size of each object gives us no clue to positional depth. However, the pink cube is clearly closest to us since it partially overlaps the blue cylinder. The blue cylinder, in turn, partially overlaps the green cylinder which thus appears farthest away.

The animals painted on the cave wall in France some 30,000 years ago are excellent illustrations of partial overlap.

We can easily envision the herd of animals passing us by.

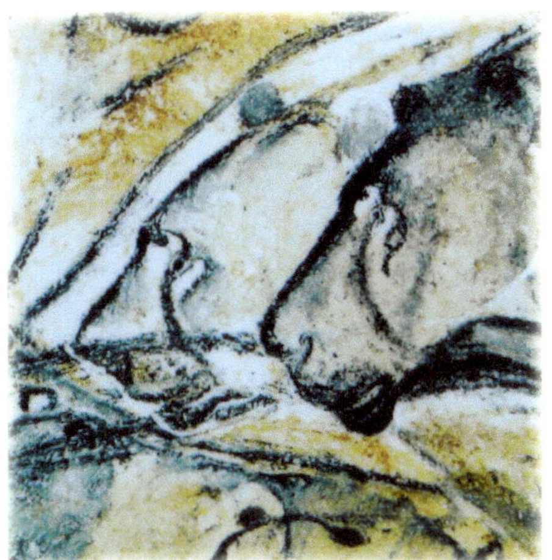
Fig. 20: Detail from the Chauvet cave art replica

In the pavement art example, there are many instances of occlusion - real and artificial. These include the people standing over the notional gorge and obscuring part of the notional water streaming below, and real people on the right sidewalk partially obscuring the real houses.

In the Mediterranean scene below, we have an immediate impression of depth.

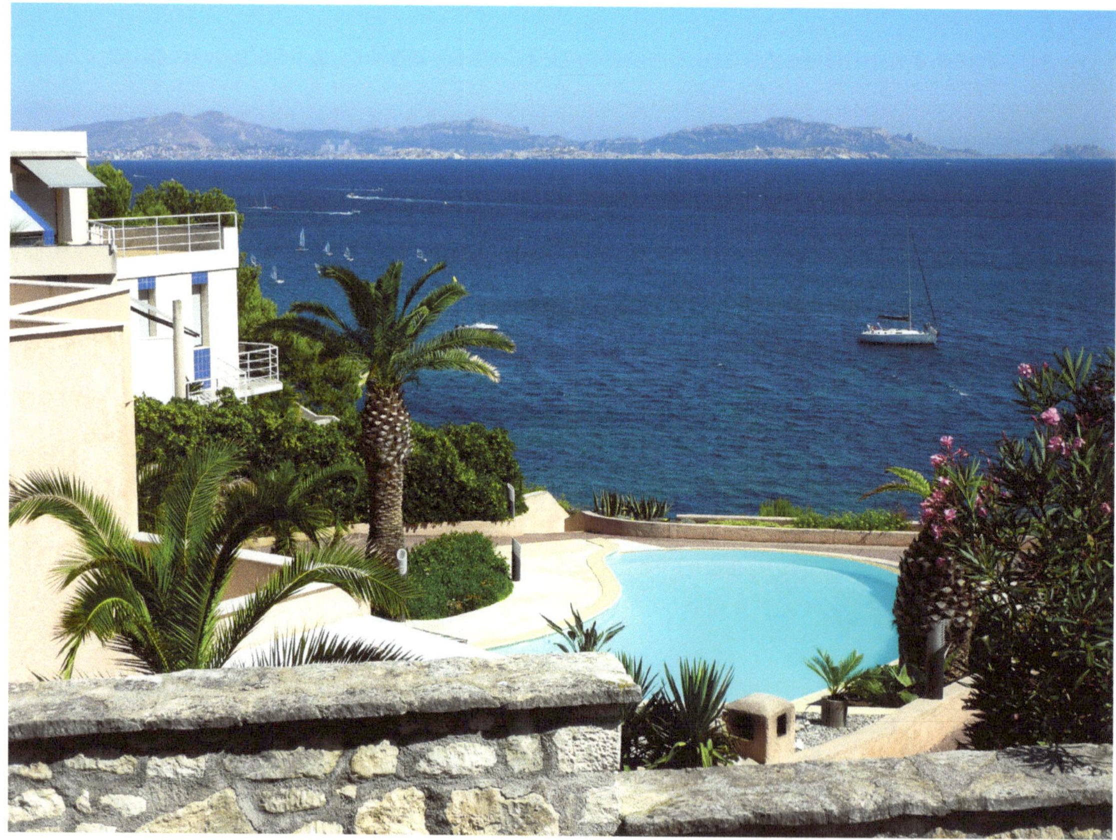

Fig. 21: A Mediterranean scene

There are excellent examples of partial overlap. The house is in front of, and partially obscures, the sea, the palm trees are partially in front of the house, and the stone wall in the lower foreground is in front of all the elements in the scene.

We shall return to this picture later to illustrate further depth clues.

Relative Size

If we see a flock of birds of the same species in the sky, the more distant birds will appear physically smaller to us.

However, we correctly perceive those apparently smaller birds as simply being the same size birds farther away, and not as smaller birds at the same distance as the larger birds.

There is a more than a two-to-one difference in the size of the birds in Figure 22, over, but we assume they are all of similar age and species and so simply perceive the smaller ones as the same but farther away.

We perceive this relative size change as depth in the scene.

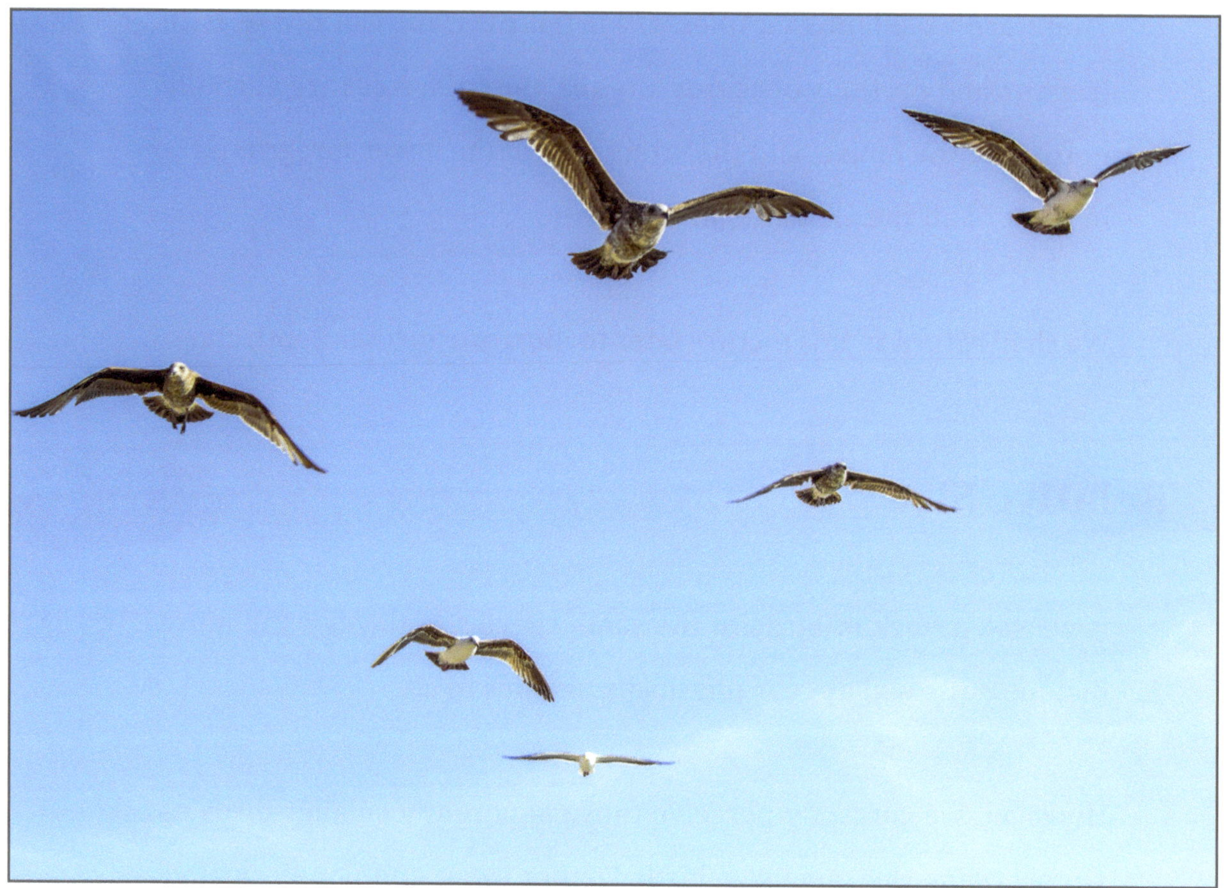

Fig. 22: *Brown birds flying in the sky,* Pikrepo

So relative size works well when we believe we are seeing similar items.

Consider this photograph opposite of Easter Island statues.

This time there is a three-to-one difference in height between the first figure on the left, and the last figure on the right, but we still

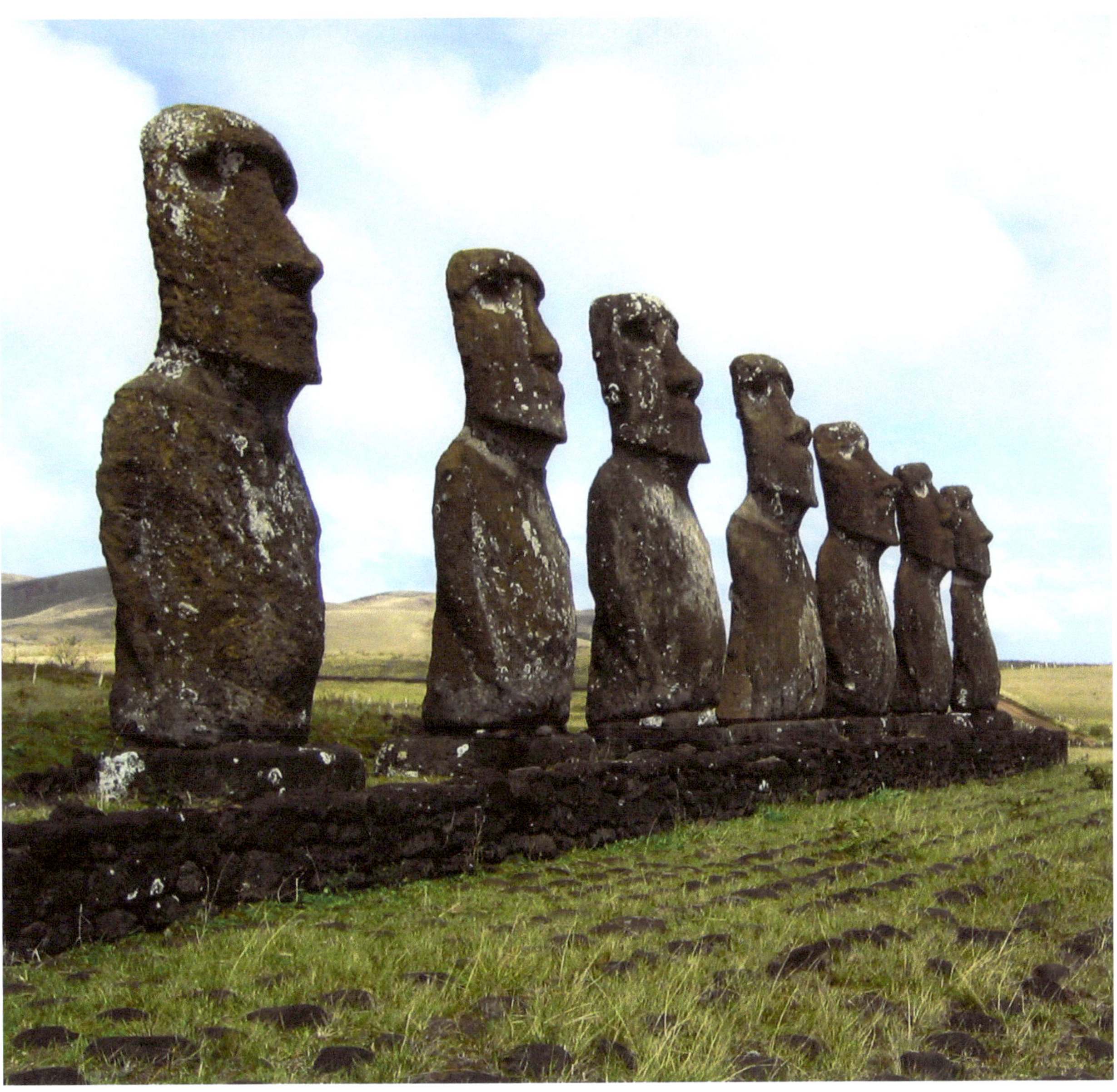

Fig. 23: Easter Island, © 2004 Phil Whitehouse

believe them to be of a similar size, with those to the right being much farther away.

Nevertheless, the eye can be fooled by a lack of other clues, or by the presence of contradictory clues. Consider this scene:

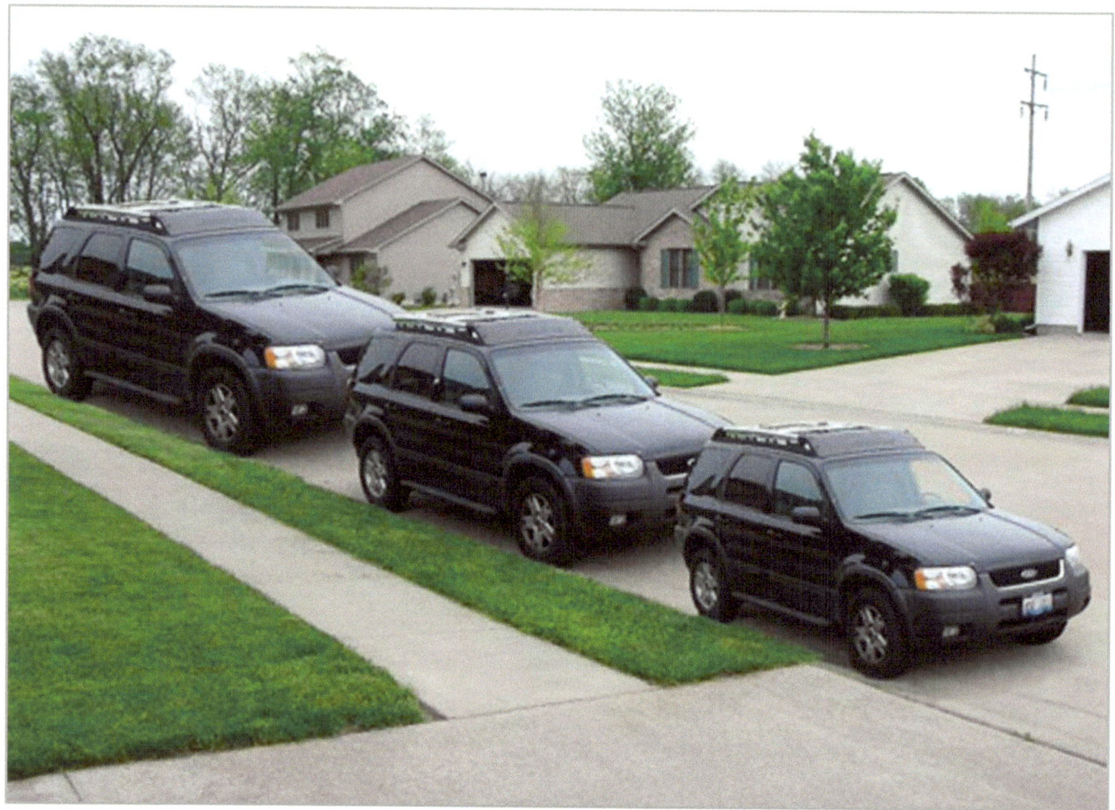

Fig. 24: *Three Cars Size Illusion* - all the vehicles are the same size (2009, earthguide.blogspot.com)

The three cars have been digitally replicated onto a real street scene, so, in fact, all three cars are exactly the same size. If you don't believe your eyes just measure them with a rule.

See the later section on perspective tricks for a detailed explanation of the contradictory clues causing this visual illusion.

Familiar or Absolute Size

Taking again our example of birds with which we're familiar, not only can we tell which ones are farther away, we can additionally estimate just how far the nearest bird is from us, because we are familiar with their real size. However, if we are not familiar with the item, or there is no familiar item in the scene, we can be easily misled.

Look at this statue of a Moai sculpture on Easter Island. Can you make an estimate of its height?

There is a good impression of depth in the scene, based on the relative sizes of similar objects, as we just have described.

However, we don't really have much by way of clues to estimate the true height of this particular Maoi sculpture.

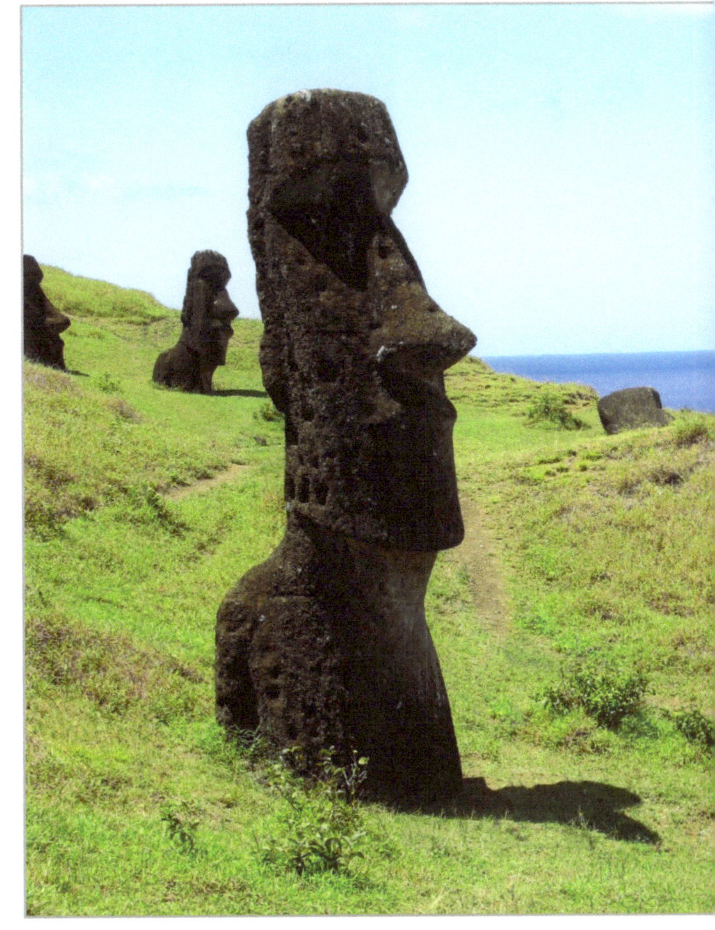

Fig. 25: Modified *Rano Raraku hillside*
© 2002 Robert Nyman

Now let's add in a familiar element adjacent to this sculpture. We immediately get a good impression of how tall the Moai sculpture really is!

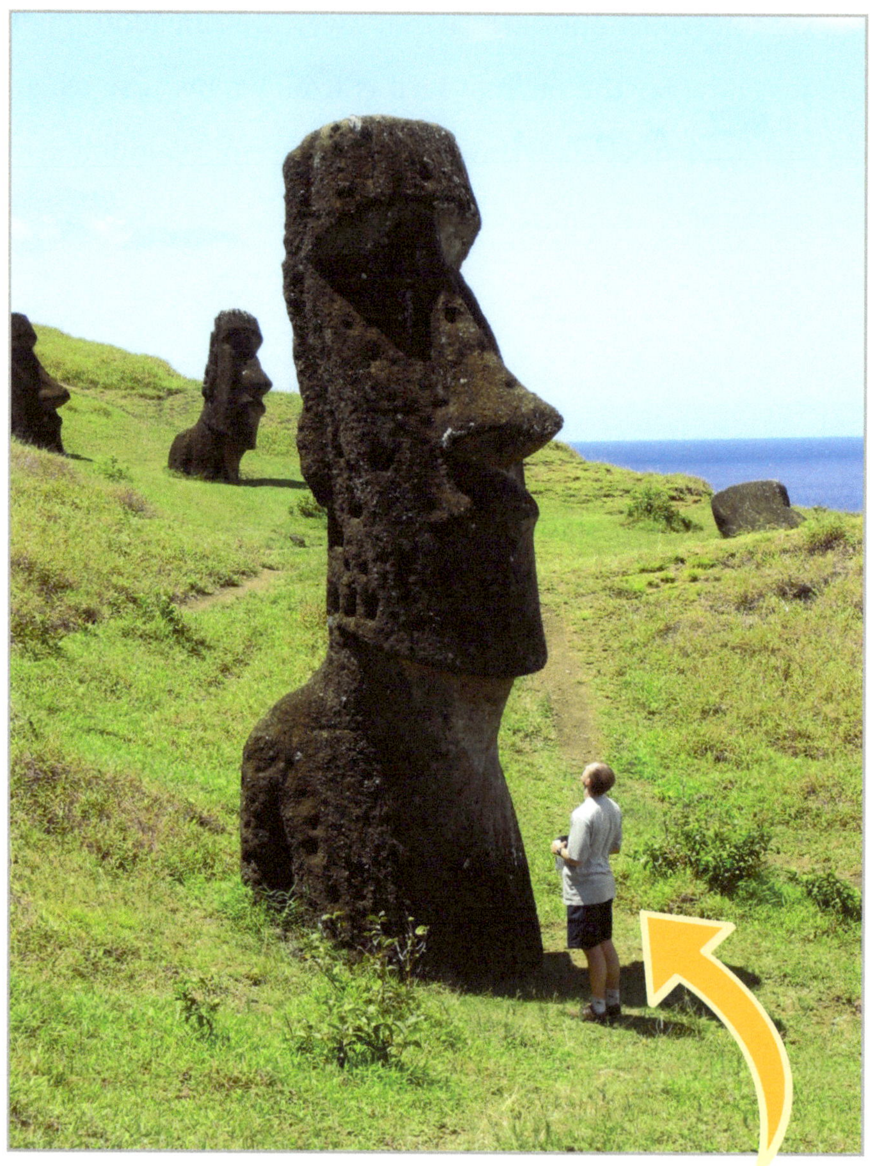

Fig. 26: *Rano Raraku hillside (original, with man added)*
© 2002 Robert Nyman

Having the familiar element of a person standing close by enables us to appreciate the significant size difference and then estimate the absolute height of the sculpture. It is more than three and a half times the height of a person.

Elevation or Relative Height

Visible elements in the scene located close to the horizon tend to be perceived as farther away, like the mountains in this picture. Of course, other clues may overrule this, such as the upper part of the house that is clearly nearby.

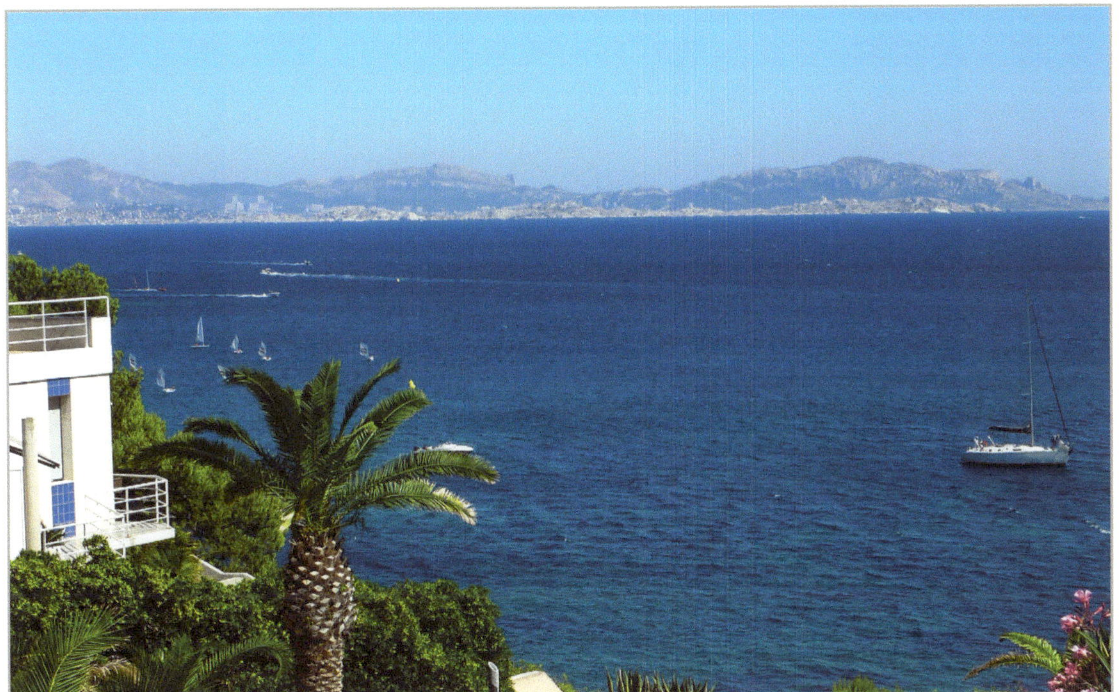

Fig. 27: Detail from a Mediterranean scene

Aerial Perspective or Haze

More distant items tend to appear lower in contrast, less sharp and slightly blue tinged. The air between us as observers and the distant item plays a major part in this effect. Notice in the scene below the change in color and contrast of the various mountain ranges as they disappear into the distance.

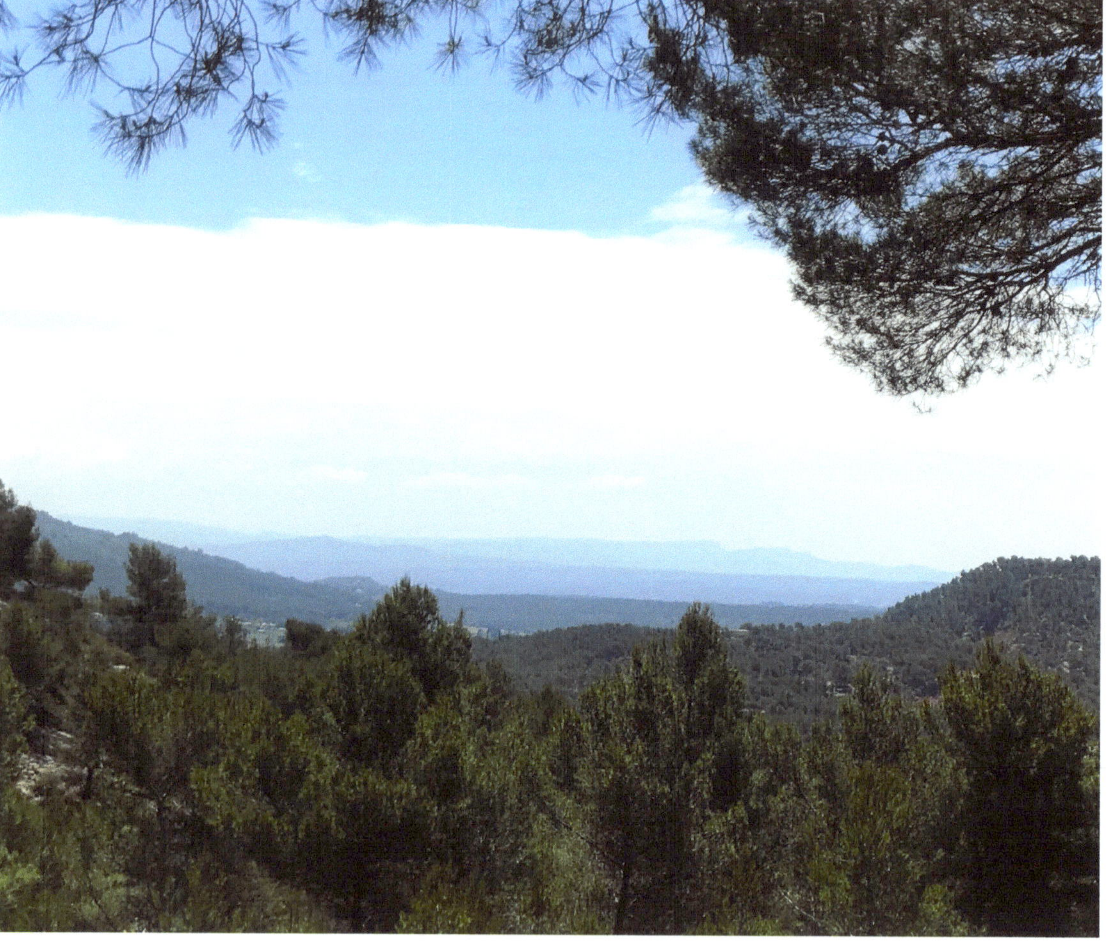

Fig. 28: Aerial perspective example, Provence, France

Light, Shade, Texture and Gradient

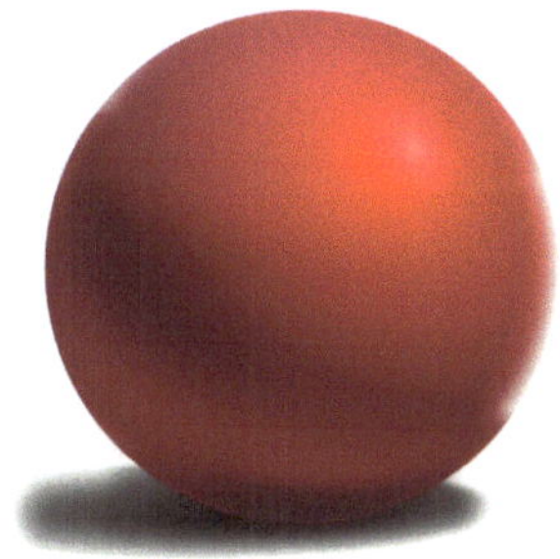

Fig. 29: Depth from light and shadow on a ball

Even a completely smooth, uniform item like a ball exhibits changes in appearance due to the play of **light** and **shade**, helping us gauge its three-dimensional shape. In reality, these clues can disappear on an overcast day, with no directional light, but are useful for an artist painting a fixed scene.

In general, the **texture** of an element in a scene is clearer and sharper in the foreground, and softer and duller with distance. There is a texture **gradient**.

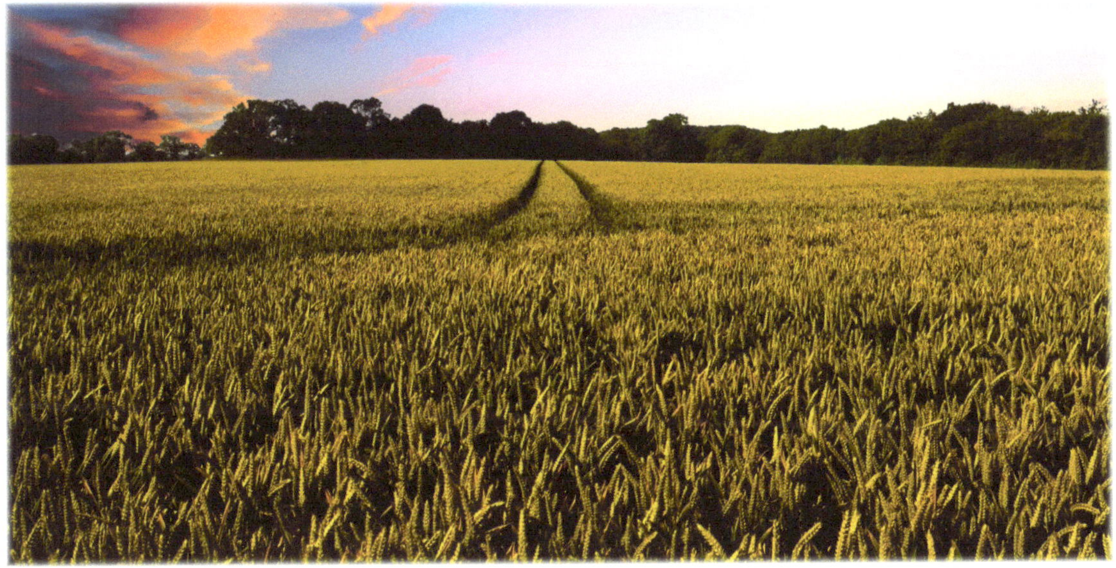

Fig. 30: Field of cereal crop showing the reduction in texture with distance

In the example above, the field of cereal is strongly textured from the foreground to the horizon. Close up we can easily distinguish the separate ears but they merge to a yellowish blur in the distance.

SUMMARY OF DEPTH CLUES

So far, we have described the following depth clues:

- ***Overlap or occlusion***
- ***Relative size***
- ***Familiar size***
- ***Elevation or relative height***
- ***Aerial perspective***
- ***Light and shade, texture and gradient.***

A talented artist can combine all these clues in a painting to great effect, without recourse to any special technique or optical aid.

However, implementing relative size (and shape and position) correctly for all the elements in a painting is quite difficult and time-consuming.

It is here we need to identify an additional, critical clue to depth in a scene, termed **perspective**.

This is completely independent of aerial perspective, which has already been described, and which simply leads to more distant elements in a scene appearing softer and with a blue cast.

The next chapter explains what we mean by perspective.

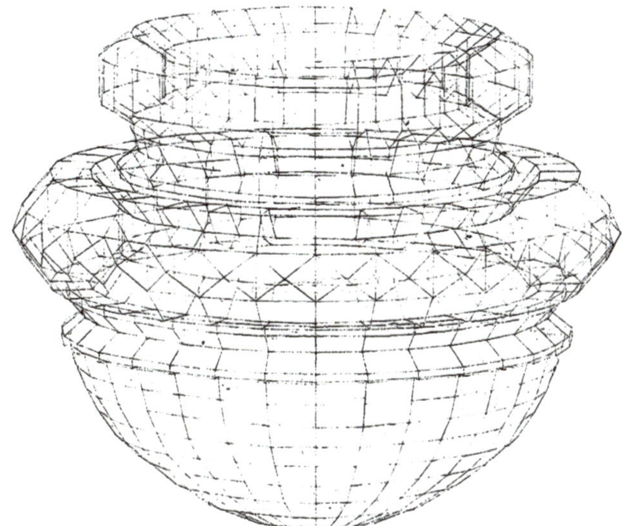

Fig. 31: Detail from *Vase in perspective*, Paolo Uccello, Pen on paper, 15th century

Perspective

If you stand in front of a window and paint on that window glass all the elements in the scene as you see them from that viewpoint, you would achieve a realistic representation of the scene. This would include size, shape and position, along with all the the aspects of sharpness, light, shade, texture and color.

Perspective is no more than describing how the size, shape and position of elements in a scene appear when viewed through that window. This sounds straightforward enough in principle, but in fact requires great skill and patience and begs the question of how to translate the scene from a transparent window onto an opaque canvas. Moreover, this window approach cannot be used if an artist wishes to create an imagined work where there is no real scene to copy. It is clear that perspective plays a critical role in creating the illusion of reality on a flat canvas.

For real scenes, as the famous painter David Hockney [1] stated in his book *Secret Knowledge: rediscovering the lost techniques of the old masters*:

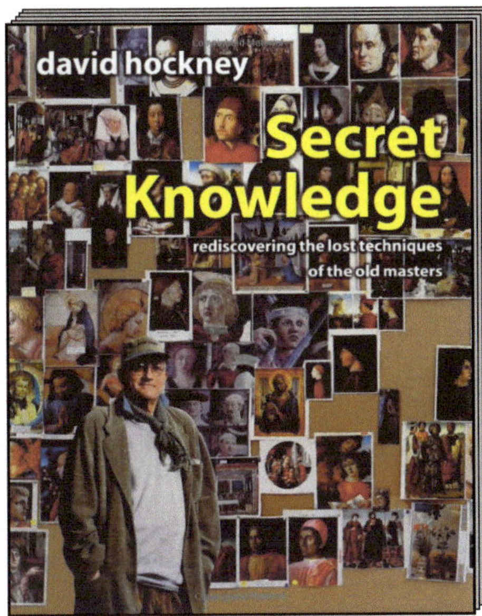

"At a certain moment in time, artists started to use optical aids and mechanical instruments to create a natural sense of depth."

Let's explore these optical and mechanical techniques first.

Fig. 32: Cover from *Secret Knowledge*
© 2001 David Hockney

Mechanical and Optical Aids to Realism

Figure 33 shows a classic example of an artist using a mechanical aid, illustrated in a woodcut by Dürer from 1525. It describes a simple but laborious technique to trace out the appearance of a lute onto a flat canvas. In this case, the artist wants to paint the lute as seen close-up and end-on.

Again quoting from David Hockney's book *Secret Knowledge*:

> *"Some of the most difficult things to paint with linear perspective are curved objects such as lutes."*

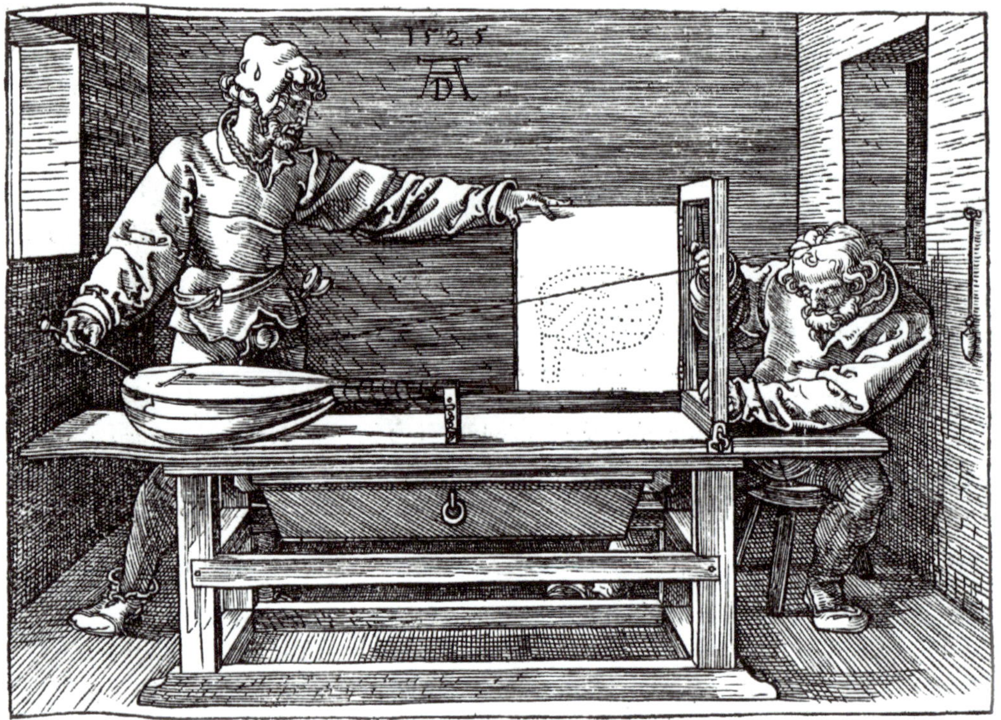

Fig. 33: *Underweysung der Messung,* Albrecht Dürer, 1525

The lute is laid in position on a table. Then the artist constructs an upright frame with a vertical and a horizontal string that intersect, and a hinged canvas. With the canvas out of the way, on the right-hand wall he attaches a cord from where the observer is expected to view the painting.

He then stretches the cord from that position to a point on the lute. He pinpoints where the cord passes through the upright frame by moving the two intersecting strings in the frame, like a crosshair. He then removes the long cord, moves the canvas back onto the upright frame and marks the crosshair with a dot. And so on. A simple but very laborious procedure! Once the artist has identified enough points on the canvas, he can dismantle the mechanical aid and complete the painting.

Here is an example from Holbein's *The Ambassadors* showing a lute painted beautifully, close-up and end-on:

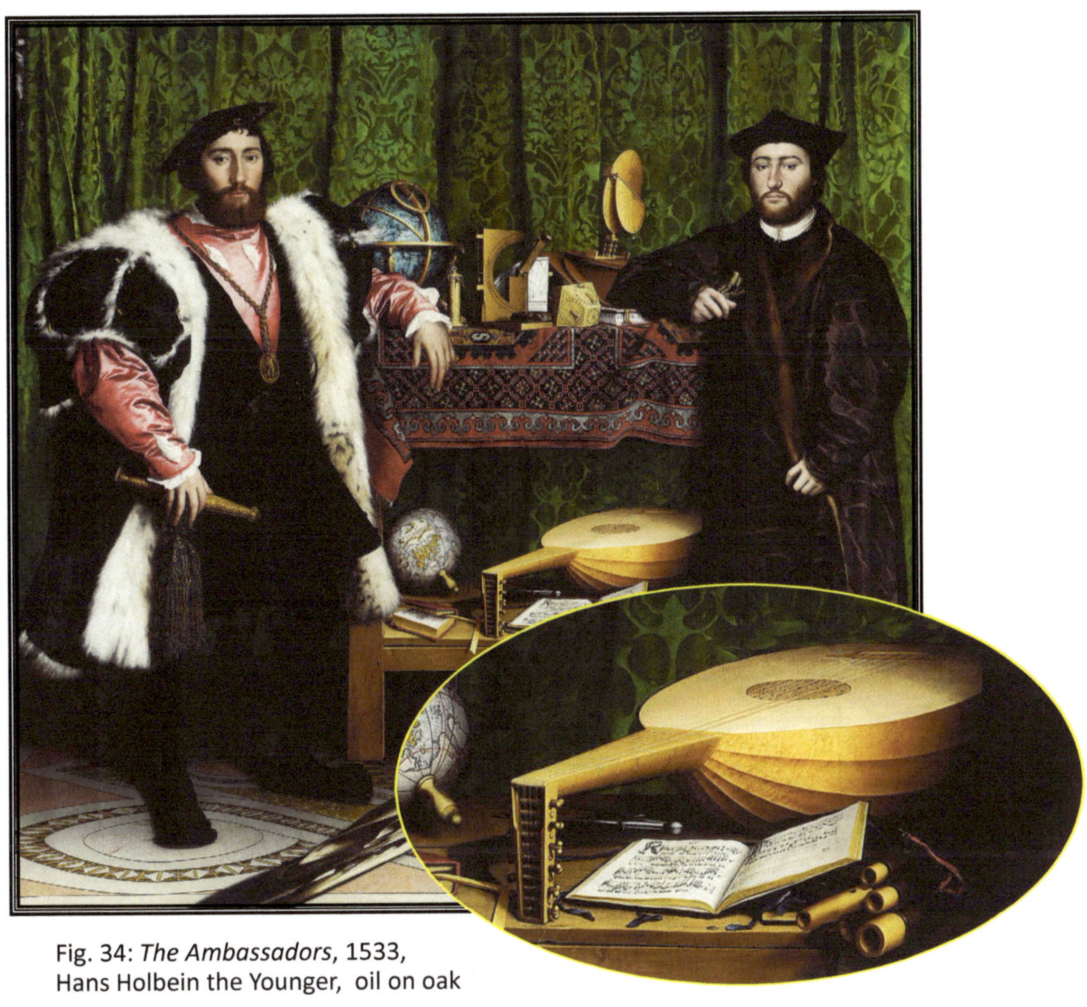

Fig. 34: *The Ambassadors*, 1533, Hans Holbein the Younger, oil on oak

Figure 35 presents another woodcut by Albrecht Dürer, perhaps created over the period 1510-1525, showing a second example of a mechanical aid.

The artist creates an upright frame, divided by threads into small squares. Next he divides his canvas into an equivalent number of squares. Then he sketches what he sees in each small square of the frame onto his canvas, taking care to keep his eye always in the same position with the aid of an upright pointer.

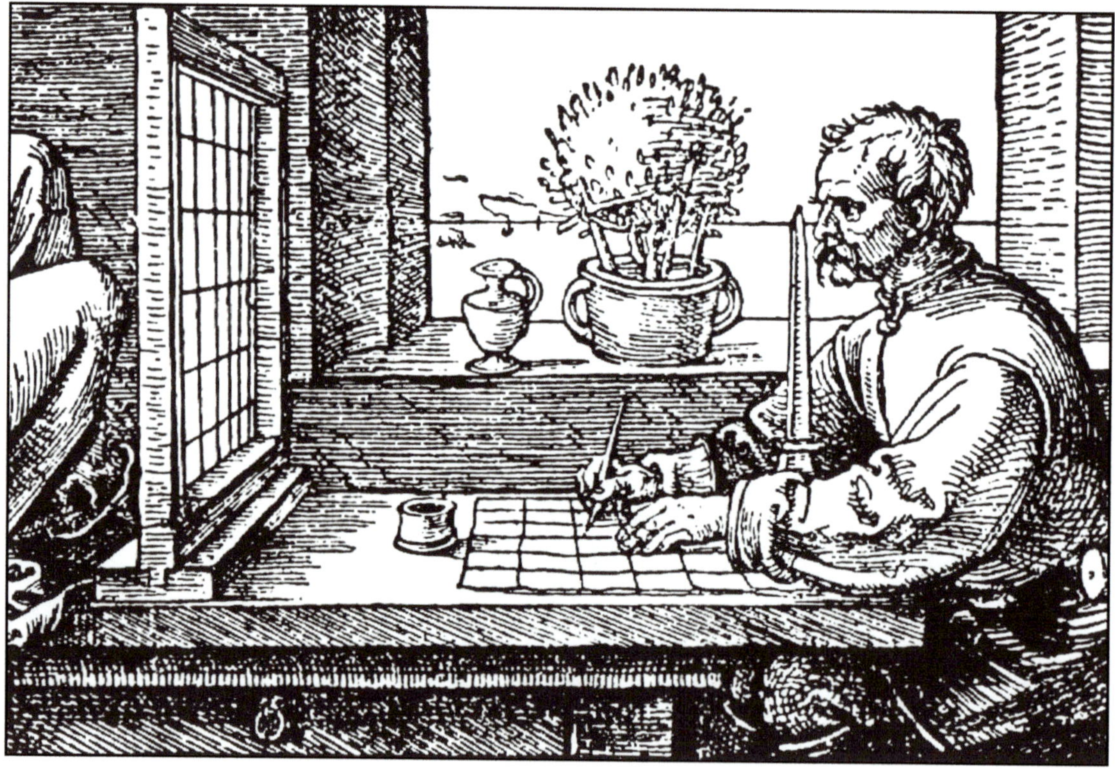

Fig. 35: *Der Zeichner des liegenden Weibes*, Albrecht Dürer 1510-1525

Brunelleschi is considered to have used this technique to paint real buildings in Florence. He then astonished his compatriots by demonstrating how life-like in depth and reality his paintings were by having his compatriots compare the real buildings with the painted ones via a special apparatus.

Figure 36 presents a third example of a mechanical aid. In this case however, the artist places a pane of glass in an upright frame and draws the outline of the scene directly on the glass, again always keeping the eye in the same position.

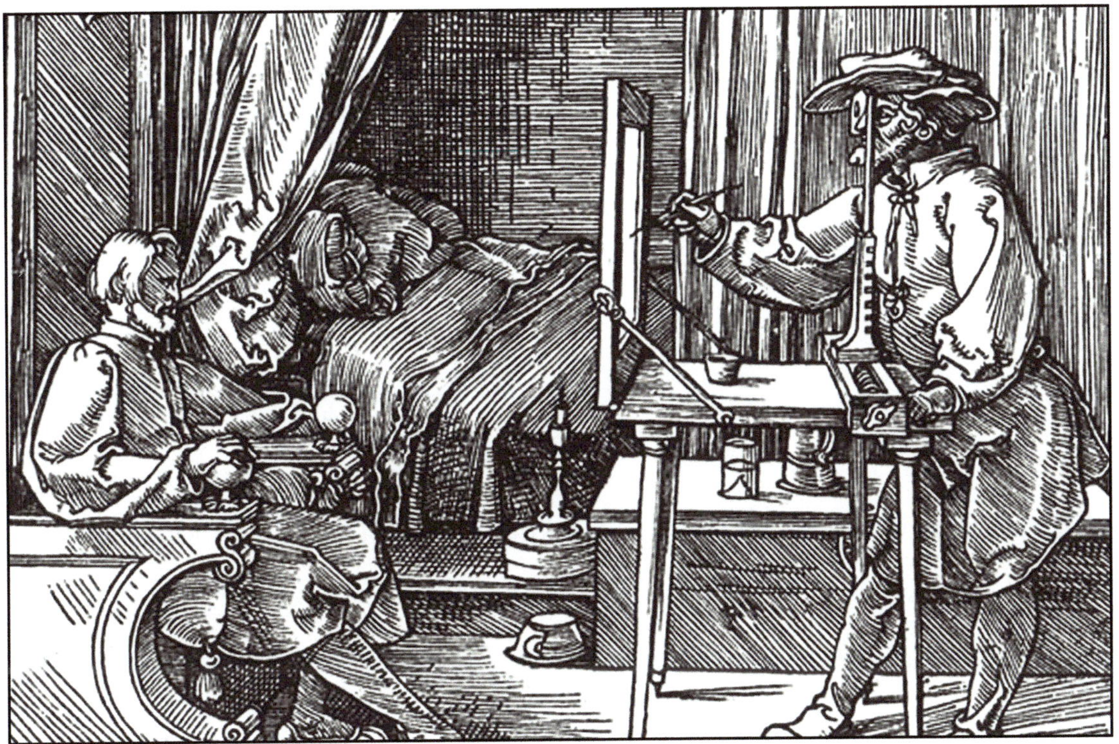

Fig. 36: *An Artist Drawing a Seated Man,* Albrecht Dürer, 1510-1525

A fourth, optical, approach, known by Aristotle as early as the 4th century BCE, is the *camera obscura* (Italian for dark room). In its basic form, it is essentially a dark room with a pinhole aperture in one wall. The oldest known published drawing of a *camera obscura* dates from the 1545 book *De Radio Astronomica et Geometrica*, written by Dutch physician Gemma Frisius who used it to study a solar eclipse. The image projected on the opposite wall is inverted (upside down) and reversed left to right, so not very useful for artists.

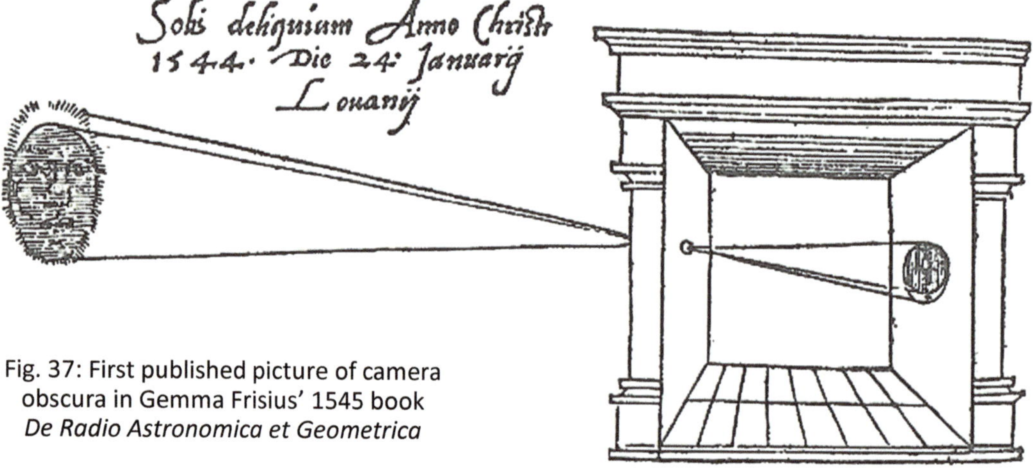

Fig. 37: First published picture of camera obscura in Gemma Frisius' 1545 book *De Radio Astronomica et Geometrica*

A much brighter image can be obtained if the pinhole is replaced with a convex lens. This is fundamentally how the human eye works, producing an inverted and reversed image on the back of the eye.

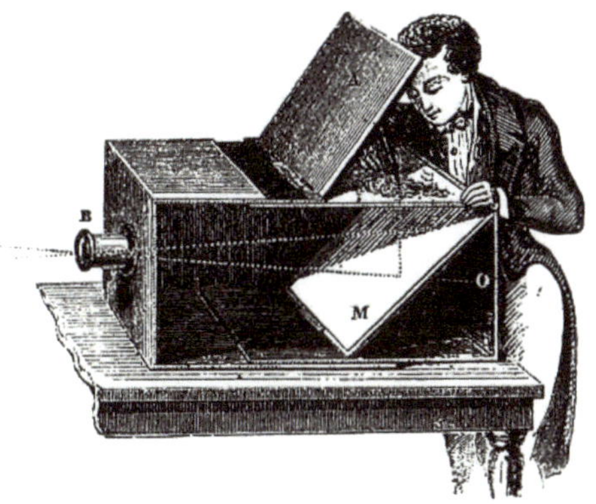

Fig. 38: *Camera Obscura box,* c.1850, 19th Century Dictionary Illustration

A portable version, similar to a box camera, comprises a lens and mirror projecting an image up onto a glass plate on which the artist can trace the scene. It is more useful for an artist since it produces an upright image but it is still reversed left to right.

An alternative version of the *camera obscura* used by artists outdoors comprises a tent and frame holding a mirror and lens to project the image onto a small table. Now the image is upright and not reversed left to right. According to Philip Steadman [2], by 1620 the astronomer Kepler was using a portable *camera obscura* tent with a modified telescope to draw landscapes. It could be turned around to capture the surroundings in sections.

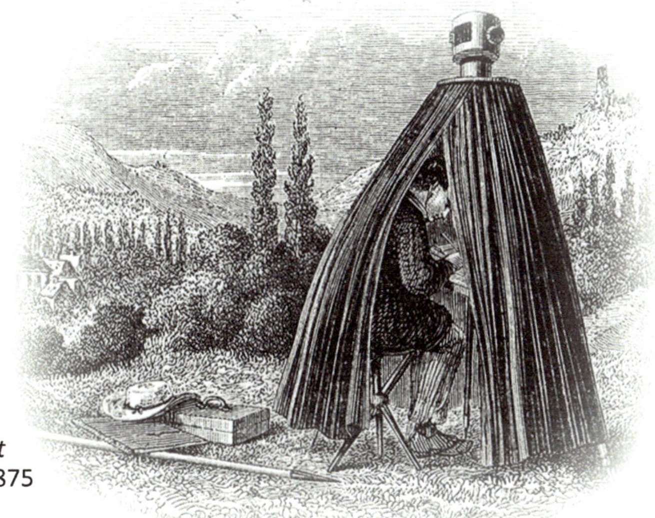

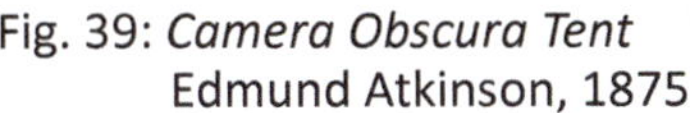

Fig. 39: *Camera Obscura Tent*
Edmund Atkinson, 1875

Camera obscuras were all the rage in 19th century Victorian England. Below is a fine example of a fully-working, building-sized *camera obscura* in Edinburgh, Scotland. You will notice the top of the building extends above the surrounding ones so as to have a clear 360 degree view, including to the coast in the distance.

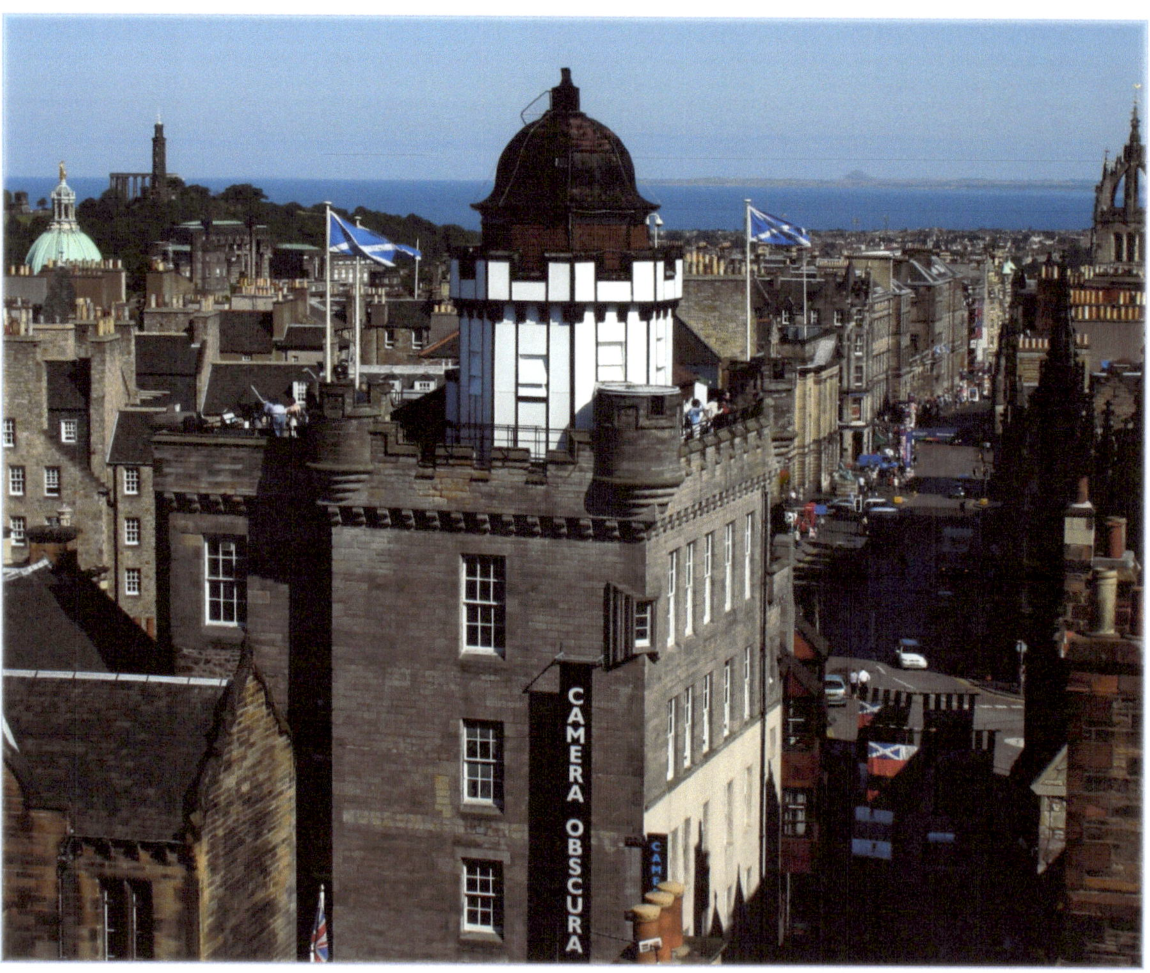

Fig. 40: *Camera Obscura*, Edinburgh, Scotland
(© Camera Obscura & World of Illusions, Edinburgh)

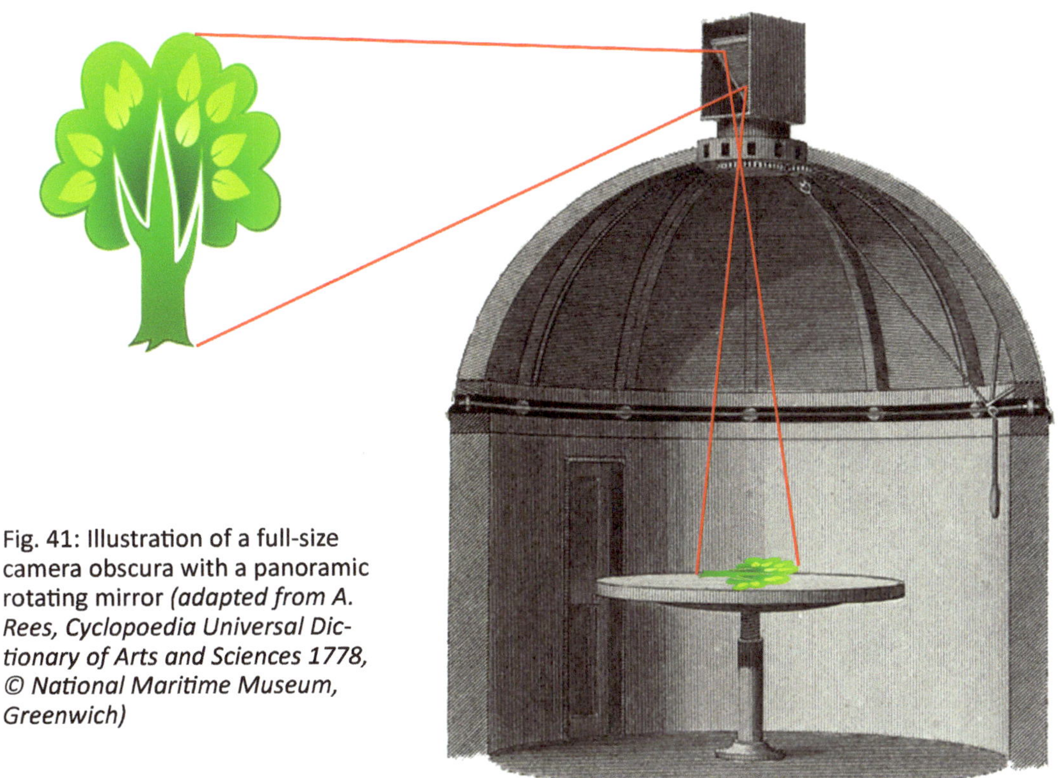

Fig. 41: Illustration of a full-size camera obscura with a panoramic rotating mirror *(adapted from A. Rees, Cyclopoedia Universal Dictionary of Arts and Sciences 1778, © National Maritime Museum, Greenwich)*

This *camera obscura* comprises a large, dome-shaped, windowless room with a simple mirror in the roof that can project the outside scene through a lens onto a horizontal table.

And in Figure 42, over, we have a sample view from this *camera obscura*, projecting a castle scene onto the table-top.

An artist can simply place his blank canvas onto the table and proceed to copy.

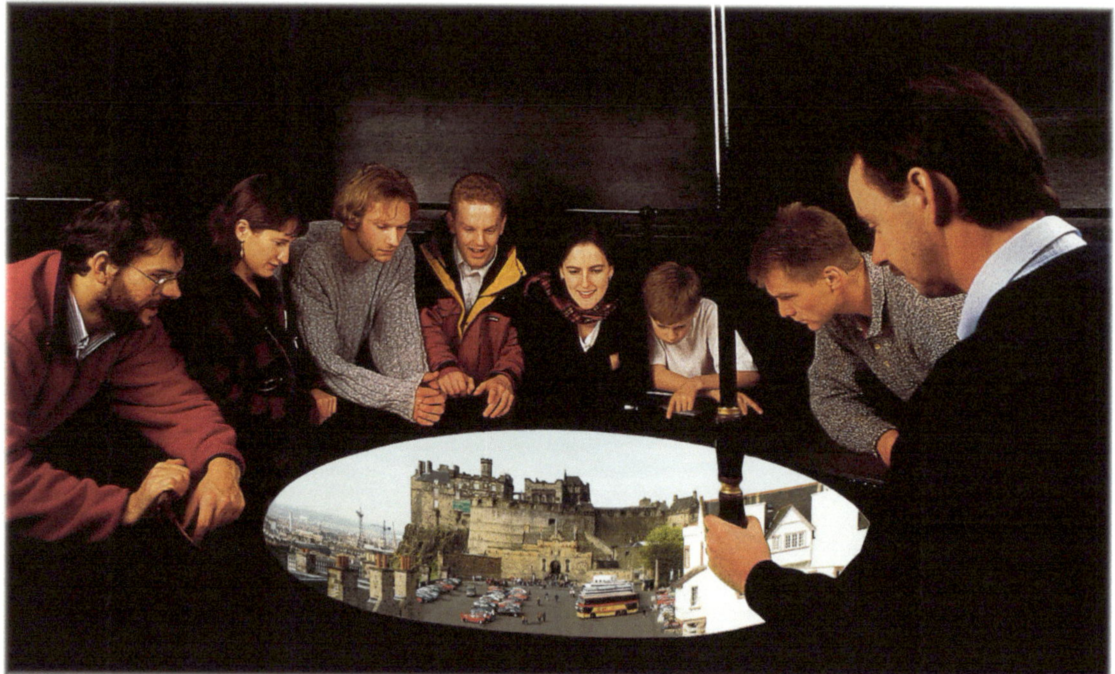

Fig. 42: A splendid view from inside, *(© Camera Obscura & World of Illusions, Edinburgh)*

It is generally thought that the *camera obscura* was used by famous painters such as Vermeer, and reputedly Canaletto. Philip Steadman's splendid book *Vermeer's Camera* [2] describes in detail how Vermeer may have achieved such realistic paintings.

Let's consider again the Canaletto painting of *The Piazzetta*, shown in Figure 13. You may recall that we seem to be viewing the plaza from above ground level.

Could Canaletto have used a form of *camera obscura* with a mirror placed on top of a portable cabin or tent acting as the dark room? If so, this could explain why the viewpoint is somewhat higher than that of a normal person standing at the entrance to the piazzetta.

A modern-day camera works on the same principle as a *camera obscura*. The outside scene is reproduced as a small image on a flat sensor.

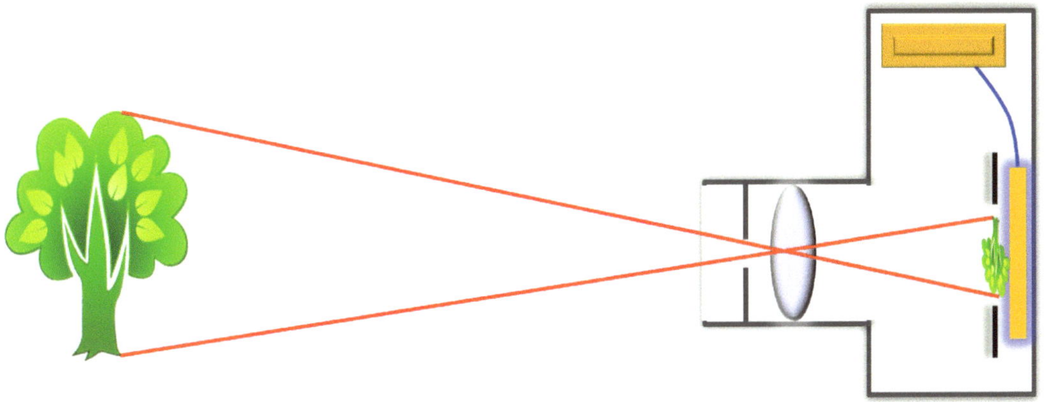

Fig. 43: Image capture in a camera

It is important to recognize that a camera *automatically* captures *all* the depth clues to creating a realistic representation of the scene onto the flat surface (sensor), from that one viewpoint. It is exactly like our earlier analogy of looking at a scene through a window and capturing the size, shape and position of all the elements, along with the usual aspects of sharpness, light, shade, texture and color, as they appear on that window. As mentioned earlier, the eye fundamentally works in the same way as a basic camera, see Figure 44 below.

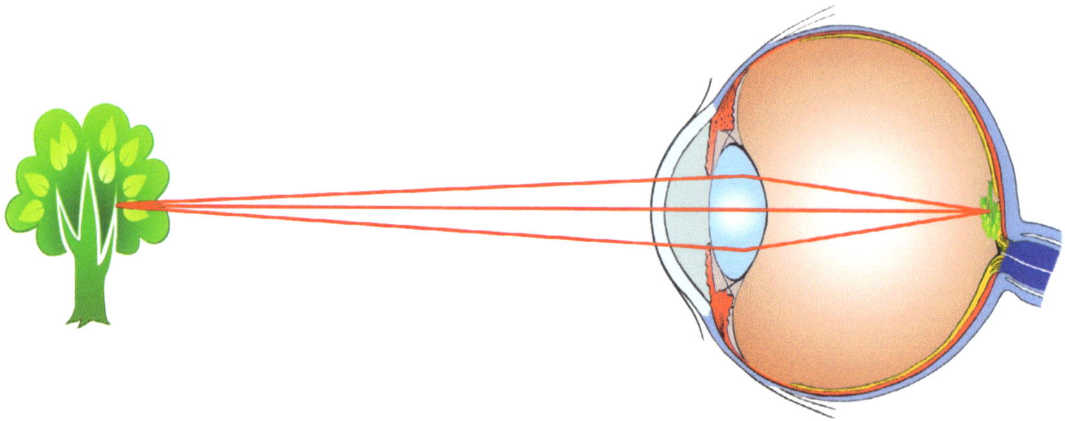

Fig. 44: Image capture in the eye

A much more recent optical device than the *camera obscura* is the *camera lucida* (Latin for *light chamber*). A version was patented in 1806 by the English chemist William Hyde Wollaston, although Johannes Kepler, the astronomer, described the principle in his *Dioptrice* of 1611.

Like the *camera obscura*, the *camera lucida* enables the artist to view the scene and the drawing surface at the same time. However, unlike the *camera obscura*, the *camera lucida* requires the artist to view the scene through an optical device, and the scene appears as a small, soft, virtual image overlaid on the drawing surface. The artist can then sketch key elements from the scene and so capture correct perspective, and go on to complete the artwork later.

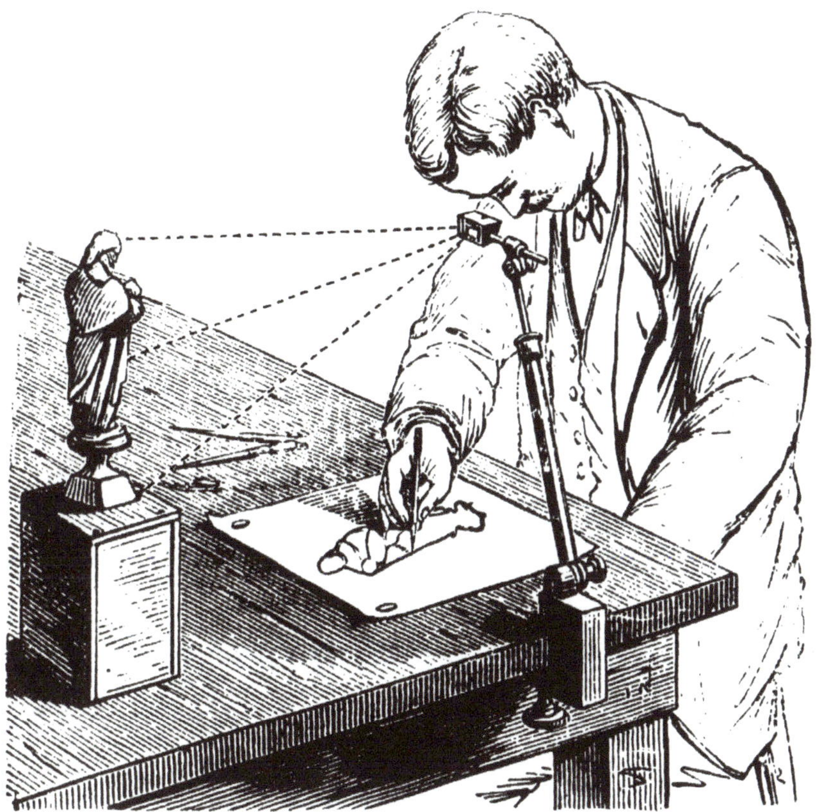

Fig. 45: A *camera lucida* in use

The device requires no special enclosure or lighting but the device is not easy to use. It must be firmly clamped so as not to move during the sketching process, the artist must keep the same viewpoint, and the drawing surface must be firmly fixed in place.

Several versions of the *camera lucida* exist. Wollaston's patented 1806 version comprises a prism with four optical faces that produces two successive reflections to ensure the scene appears upright and not reversed left to right. However, it is quite difficult to use, so a much simpler approach comprises a single half-silvered mirror angled at 45°. Unfortunately, the scene then appears reversed left to right. A better alternative comprises a glass panel, or half-silvered mirror, inclined at 45°, in conjunction with a regular flat mirror. This combination ensures that the scene is viewed upright, and not reversed left to right.

More sophisticated models include lenses to enable the distant scene and the drawing paper to be in focus at the same time, and neutral density filters to balance the brightness of the two images.

In summary, over the centuries, artists have been fascinated by optical lenses and mirrors, and it is thought many used them to help achieve a sense of reality and depth in their work.

The convex mirror in Jan van Eyck's 1434 *Arnolfini Portrait* is a superbly painted example, see the detail opposite. The artist has captured the whole reflected scene in curved perspective, showing

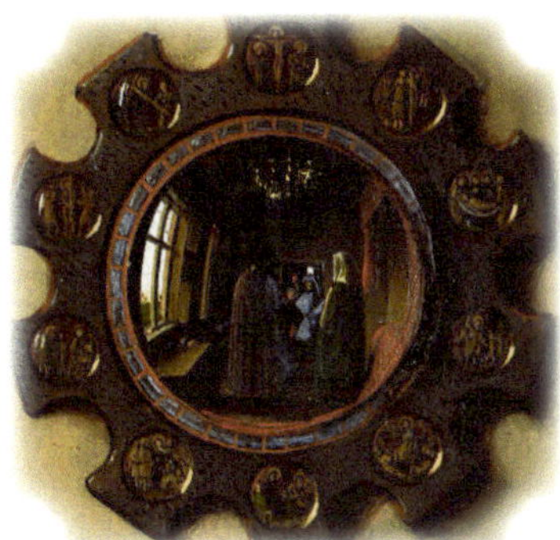

the room, the window, the chandelier, the backs of the couple, together with a front view of two figures appearing to come up into the room.

Fig. 46: The superbly painted convex mirror from Jan van Eyck's 1434 *Arnolfini Portrait*

So far then, we have described various mechanical and optical aids to achieving realistic perspective. All these aids require no knowledge or understanding of any rules. They are simply a means to copy a real, three-dimensional scene onto a flat canvas and create an illusion of depth and reality.

But without mechanical or optical aids, are there rules that could be applied to assist an artist in assuring realistic depth in real scenes? More importantly, how can an artist ensure realistic depth when creating imaginary scenes where there is no real scene to copy, even with the help of a mechanical or optical aid?

To answer these questions, we need to explore further what we mean by the term perspective and in particular the term linear perspective.

Linear Perspective

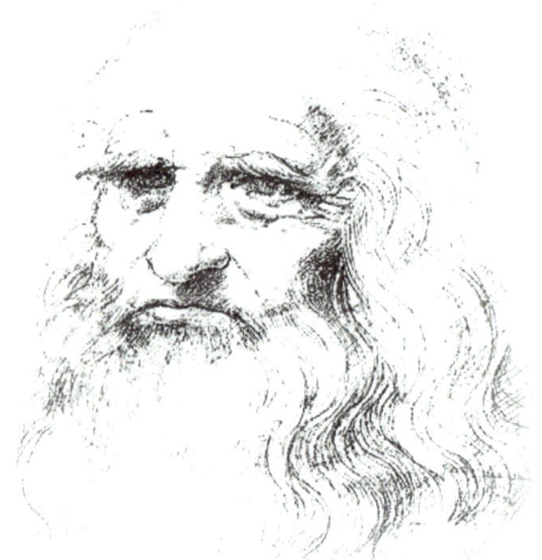

"The art of perspective is of such a nature as to make what is flat appear in relief..."

So wrote Leonardo da Vinci [3] who went on to say that:

> *"Perspective is the guide and the gateway; and without this nothing can be done well in the matter of drawing."*

As an aside, the word perspective derives from the Latin *perspicere* 'to see through'.

Linear perspective is a drawing technique that approximates how a scene appears to the eye. Essentially, elements in a real scene, when reproduced on a flat canvas, appear smaller with increased distance from the observer. This means smaller in width, in height and in depth, with smaller spaces between more distant elements. Parallel lines that recede into the distance appear to converge at one or more points on the horizon line called vanishing points. These parallel lines are often called orthogonals since they would be at 90 degrees to the picture plane, but for clarity in this book they are labeled as lines of perspective. Lines that are horizontal, across the picture plane, are termed transversals. A further key concept is that of foreshortening where an object's depth becomes shorter than its width with distance. More on this later. Although not directly applicable to recreating real scenes on a canvas, these concepts can be helpful in capturing the essential elements to ensure a realistic impression of depth.

While some early efforts were made to create the illusion of reality, it was not until the Renaissance that linear perspective became codified. The Italian Renaissance architect Filippo Brunelleschi developed drawings of various real Florentine buildings in correct perspective during the period 1415 to 1420.

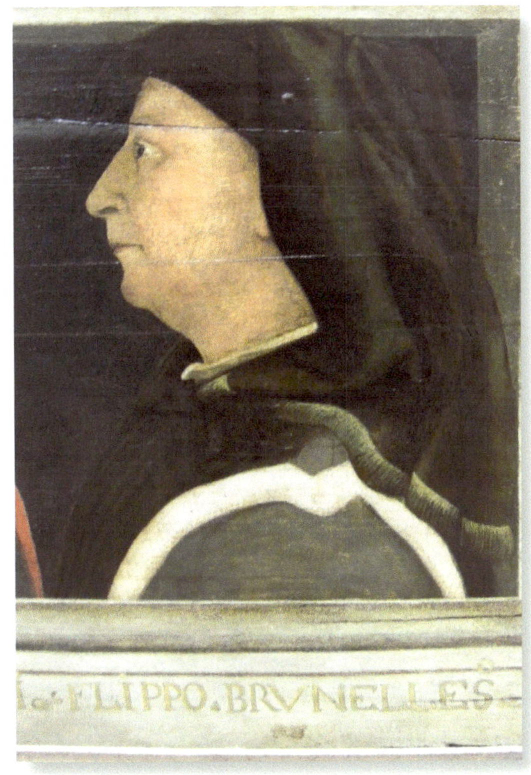

Fig. 47: Filippo Brunelleschi

According to Manetti, he used a grid or set of crosshairs to copy the exact scene square by square. You may recall we described a similar approach earlier. Whichever technique was used, the final result was a composition with accurate perspective, but as seen through a mirror. To compare the accuracy of his work with the real object, he made a small hole in the painting, and had the observer look through the hole in the back of the painting to observe the real scene. A mirror was then raised, facing the painting and so reflecting Brunelleschi's composition back through the hole, enabling the observer to see the striking similarity between reality and the painting.

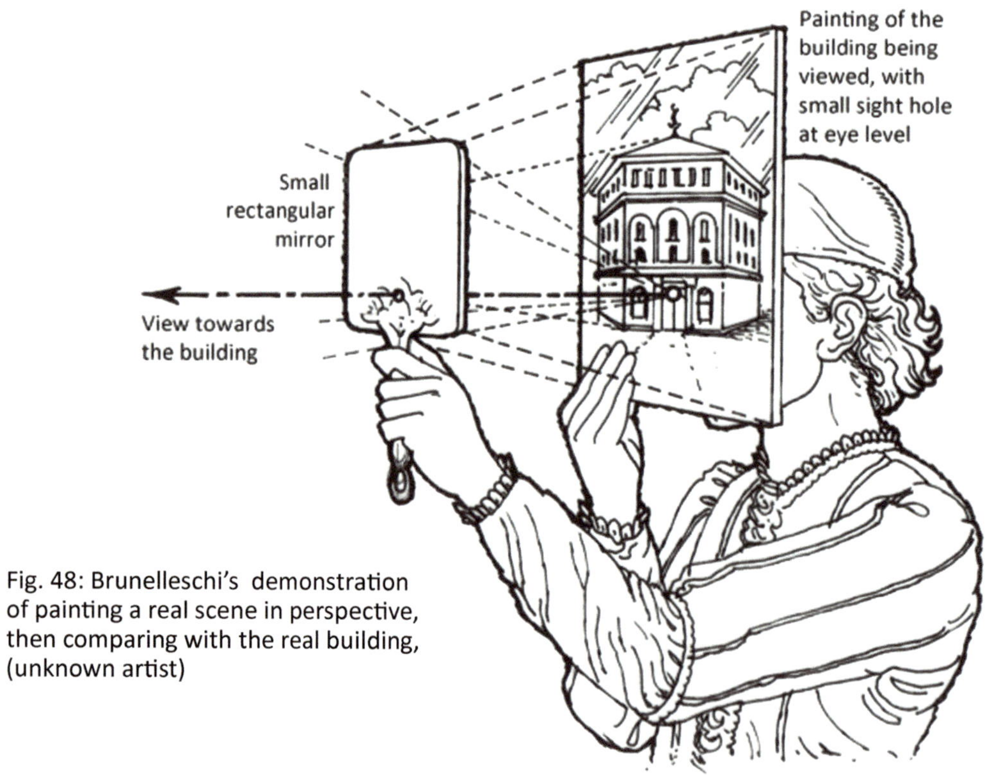

Fig. 48: Brunelleschi's demonstration of painting a real scene in perspective, then comparing with the real building, (unknown artist)

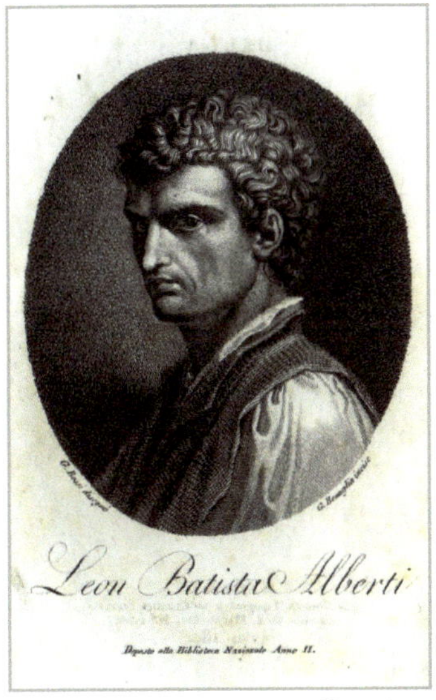

Fig. 49: Leon Battista Alberti

His friend, Leon Battista Alberti, a polymath who was also an architect, wrote *Della Pittura* (1435-1436), a treatise initially in Tuscan Italian, later published in Latin in 1450 as *De Pictura*. Alberti described, for the first time, methods for showing distance in painting. He cites Brunelleschi's experiments and dedicates the treatise to him. Here are sample pages from his work:

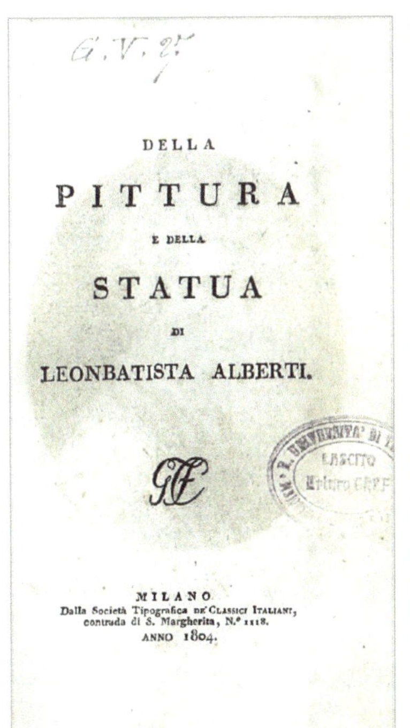

DELLA

PITTURA

E DELLA

STATUA

DI

LEONBATISTA ALBERTI.

MILANO

Dalla Società Tipografica de' Classici Italiani, contrada di S. Margherita, N.° 1118.

ANNO 1804.

Fig. 50: *Della Pittura*, Title Page Leon Alberti (later version)

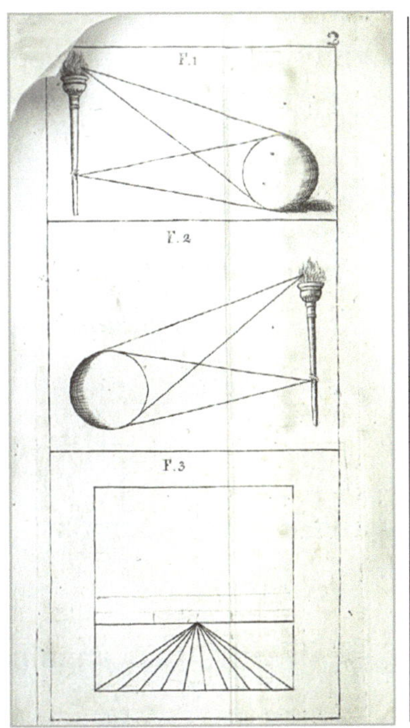

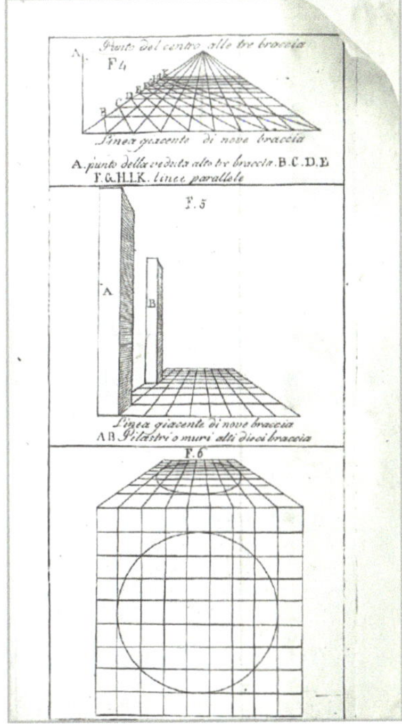

Fig. 51-52: Sample perspective pages from *Della Pittura*

Essentially, Alberti brilliantly described linear perspective. The example pages above illustrate how parallel lines recede to a single vanishing point, how the size of an object diminishes with distance, and how to construct columns and circles on a linear perspective grid.

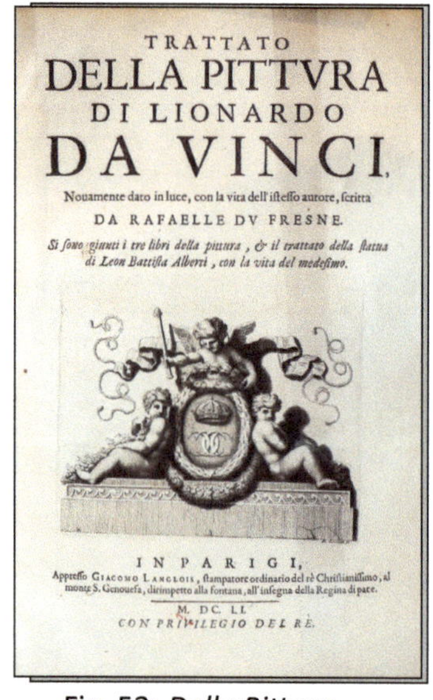

TRATTATO
DELLA PITTVRA
DI LIONARDO
DA VINCI,
Nouamente dato in luce, con la vita dell'istesso autore, scritta
DA RAFAELLE DV FRESNE.
Si sono giunti i tre libri della pittura, & il trattato della statua di Leon Battista Alberti, con la vita del medesimo.

IN PARIGI,
Appresso Giacomo Langlois, stampatore ordinario del rè Christianissimo, al monte S. Genouefa, dirimpetto alla fontana, all'insegna della Regina di pace.
M. DC. LI.
CON PRIVILEGIO DEL RÈ.

Fig. 53: *Della Pittura*, Leonardo da Vinci

Leonardo da Vinci rigorously studied form and perspective in great detail. He was born in 1452, just after Alberti's publication on perspective in Latin. Like Alberti, da Vinci was a polymath – both painter and engineer. The *Trattato della pittura* (Treatise on Painting) is a collection of Leonardo da Vinci's writings entered in his notebooks under the general heading "On Painting". The manuscripts were begun in Milan while Leonardo was under the service of Ludovico Sforza, from 1481, and gathered together by his heir Francesco Melzi. The cover of this version cites the earlier work of Leon Battista Alberti.

Now there was a clear set of rules that enabled artists to create realistic, imagined paintings. Let's explore these rules and how they are applied. Consider this image of a railroad track.

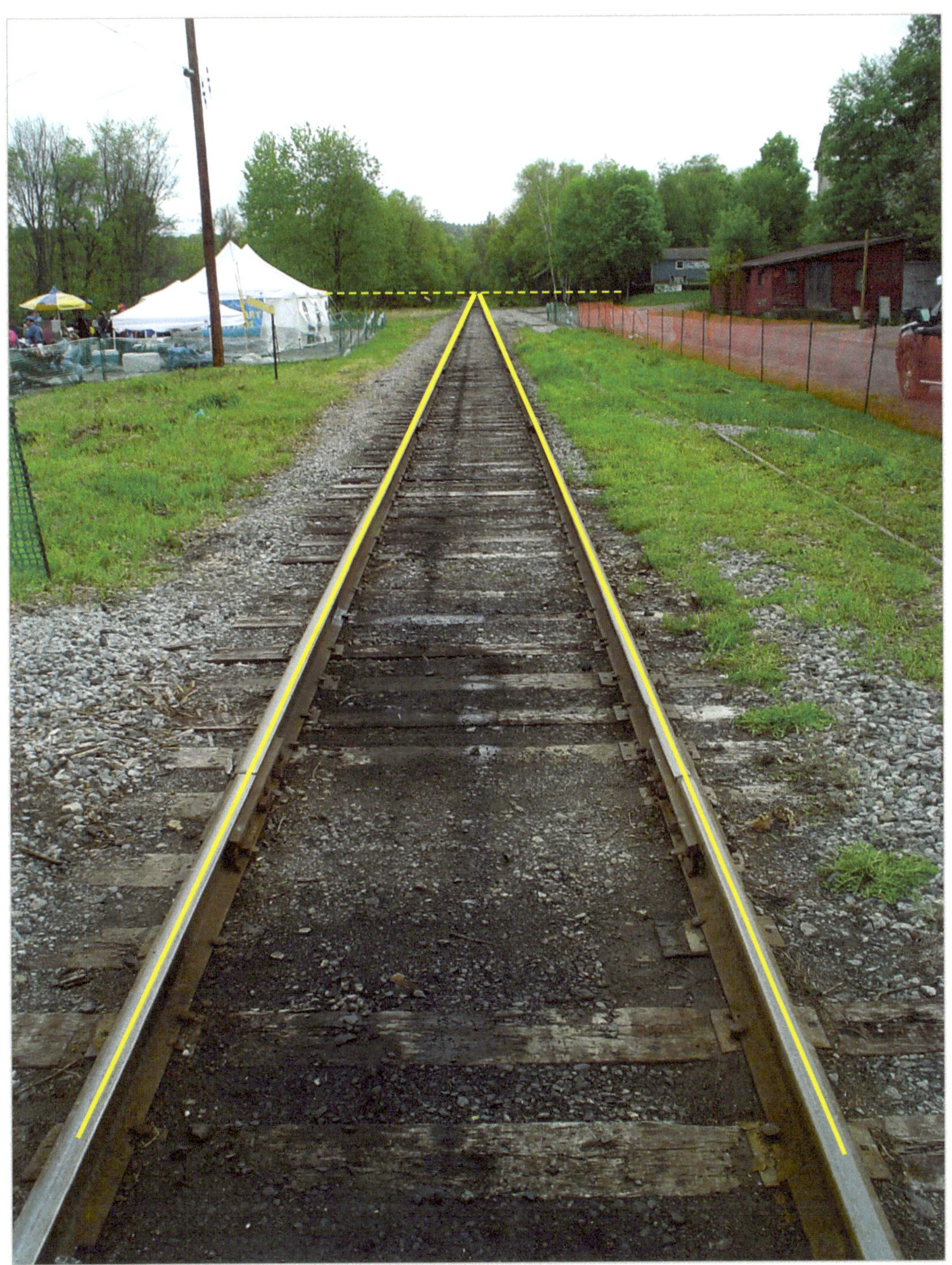

Fig. 54: Railroad Track Perspective

We appear to be standing centrally between the rails. The parallel rails themselves become thinner and closer together, eventually converging to a single point. The railroad ties appear narrower in width, thinner, and closer together, until they finally disappear into that same single point. We call this point the "vanishing point" for obvious reasons. In this particular scene we have a single vanishing point. This is often true for a scene containing parallel lines, for example roads, rail tracks, or corridors that are viewed from the front.

We can also identify a notional horizontal line through the vanishing point that represents the viewer's eye level, termed "horizon line" or "viewpoint". So-called one-point perspective contains only one vanishing point, usually on this horizon line. Finally, as mentioned earlier, we have a key concept termed foreshortening where elements in a scene appear much smaller in *depth* with distance than in *width*. More on this topic later.

Alberti understood and captured these key points, as is evident in this close-up view of one of his drawings shown here and illustrating single point perspective, along with foreshortening of a checkerboard floor pattern, with distance.

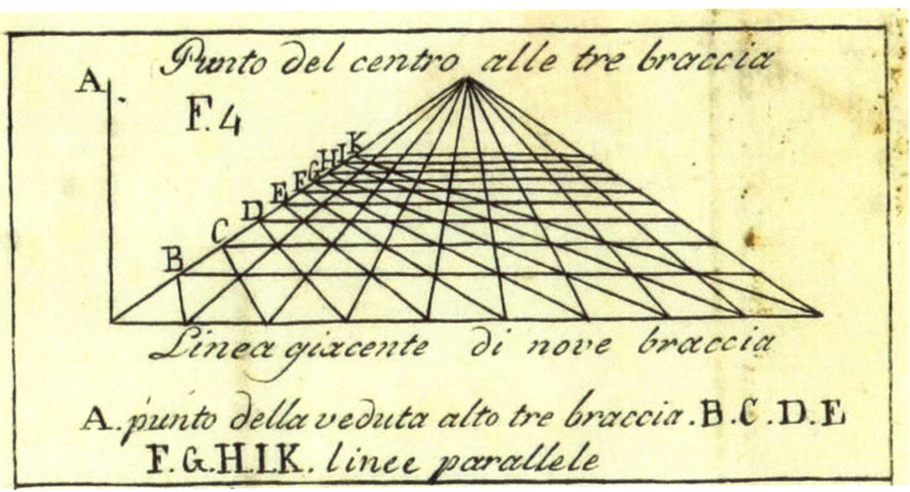

Fig. 55: Extract from 1804 edition of *Della Pittura*, Alberti, 1435-6

It was an amazing time for artists!

Now, with these newly-developed tools, an artist could paint imaginary landscapes and scenes with near-perfect three-dimensional realism. From this time onward, paintings quickly became much more realistic.

Even before Alberti's hot-off-the-press publication in 1436, the artist Masaccio used the same techniques to paint *The Holy Trinity*. Figure 56, over the page, shows his original framework. We can see his lines of perspective from the base to the top of the tomb, and from the splendid ceiling down to the same point at the top of the tomb, just below the base of the cross. The eye level is low and

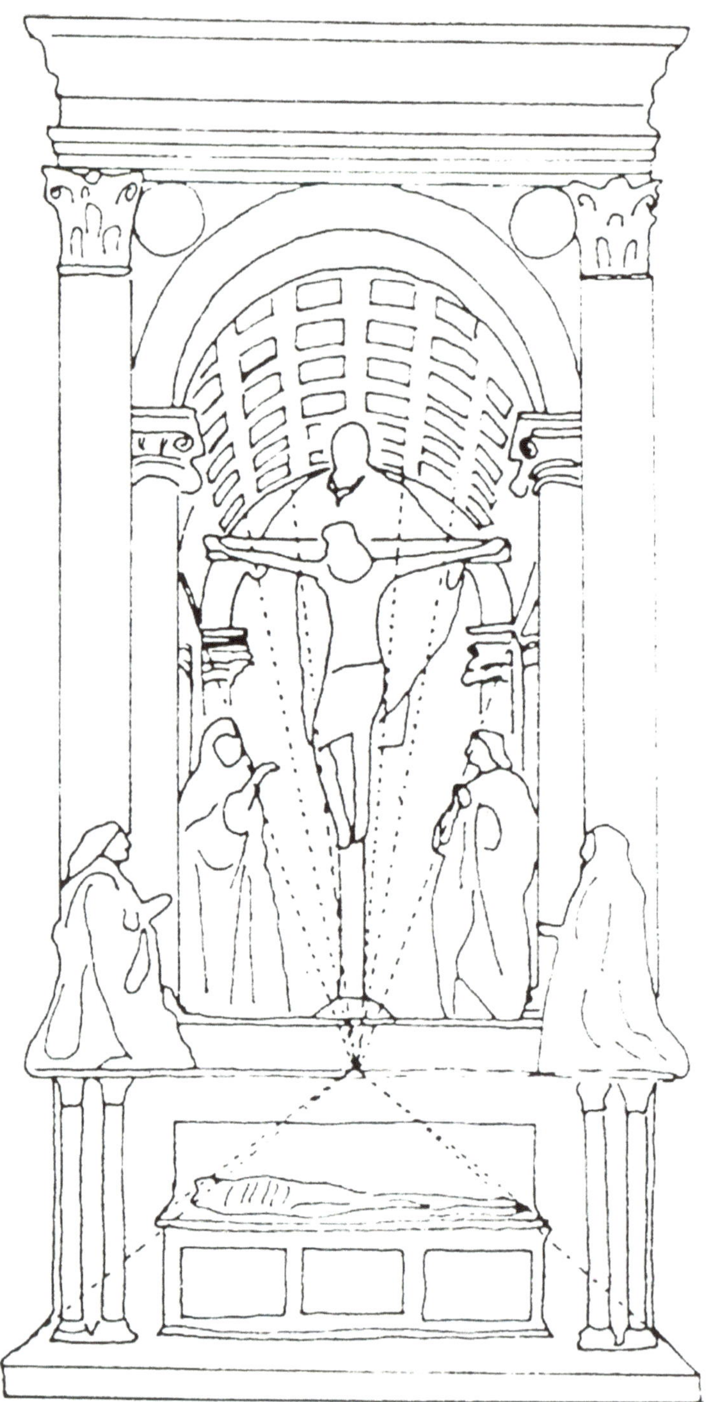

Fig. 56: Holy Trinity, his scheme of linear perspective, Masaccio c.1426-1428

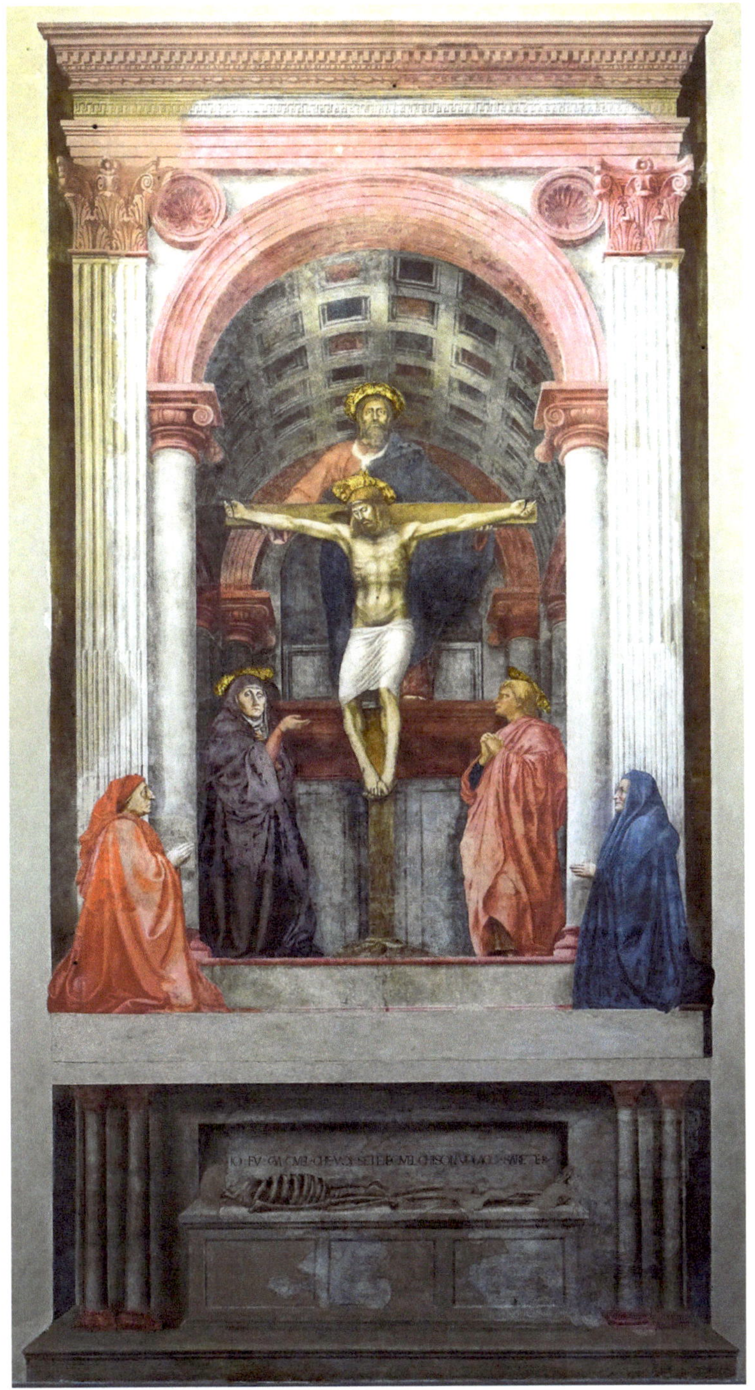

Fig. 57: Holy Trinity, the final fresco, Masaccio c.1426-1428

shows the artist expects us, as observer, to be perhaps kneeling in front the top of the tomb. Figure 57 shows his completed monumental fresco, produced over the years 1426-28, and situated in the Dominican church of Santa Maria Novella, in Florence.

Just a few years earlier, the artist Masolino da Panicale created a fresco illustrating *St. Peter Healing a Cripple and the Raising of Tabitha* (c. 1424) in the Brancacci Chapel of the Church of Santa Maria del Carmine in Florence. Illustrated opposite, it was probably completed by Masaccio and is the earliest extant artwork known to use a consistent vanishing point.

We can draw numerous lines of perspective that show the observer viewpoint to be central and at about the same height as the foreground people in the street, as though we, as observer, are standing just a short distance away. A classic example of single point perspective.

Nevertheless, the fresco does not have quite the same illusory strength of depth of later works, appearing rather flat and synthetic - notice the buildings in the upper background and the lack of strong shadows.

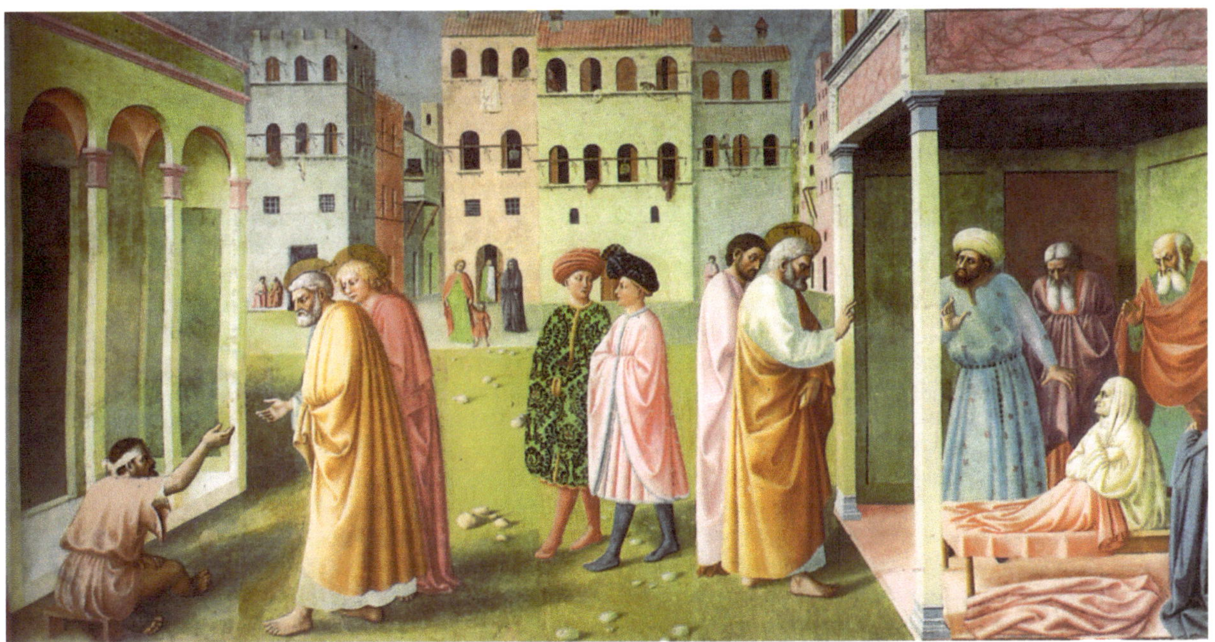

Fig. 58: *Healing of the Cripple and Raising of Tabitha*, fresco, c. 1424, Masolino & Masaccio

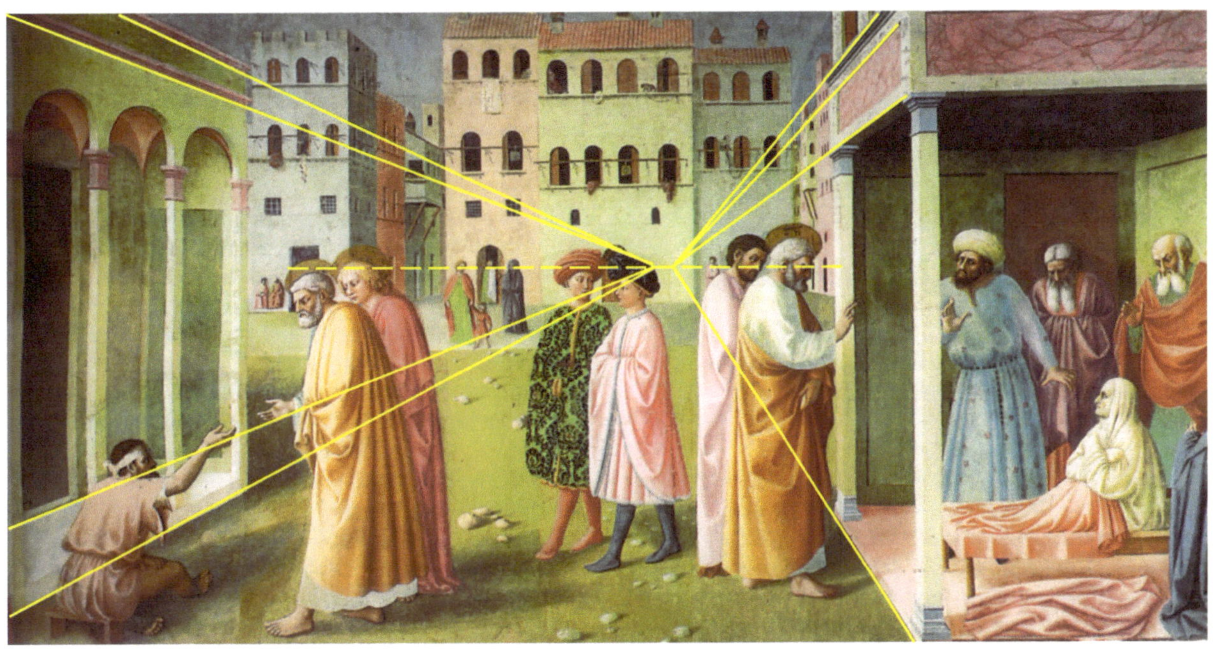

Fig. 59: *Healing of the Cripple and Raising of Tabitha* showing perspective lines

To further appreciate the notions of vanishing point and viewpoint, consider this 1658 painting by Pieter de Hooch entitled *A Woman Drinking with Two Men*. It seems authentically real. So how has the artist accomplished this?

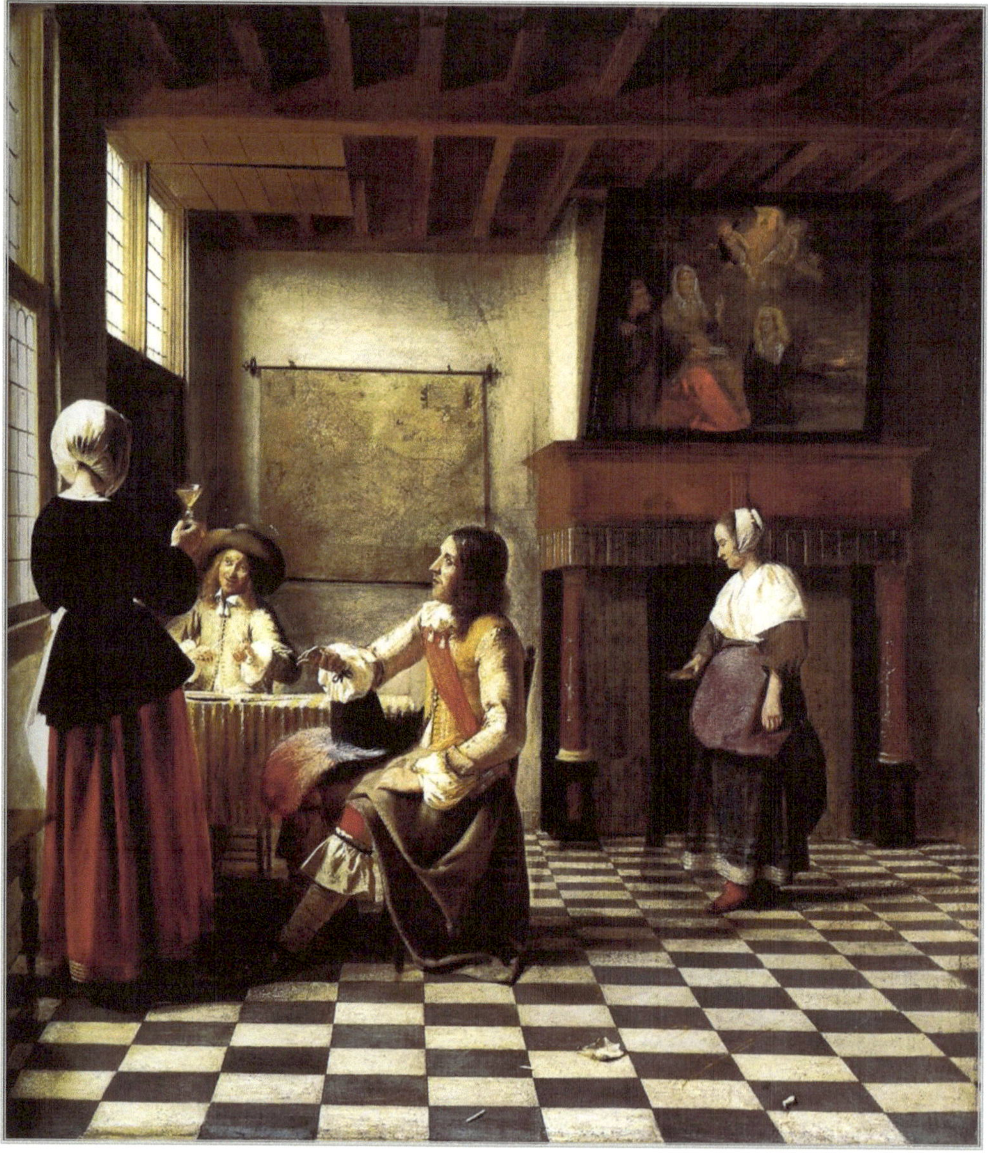

Fig. 60: *A Woman Drinking with Two Men,* Pieter de Hooch, c.1658, oil on canvas

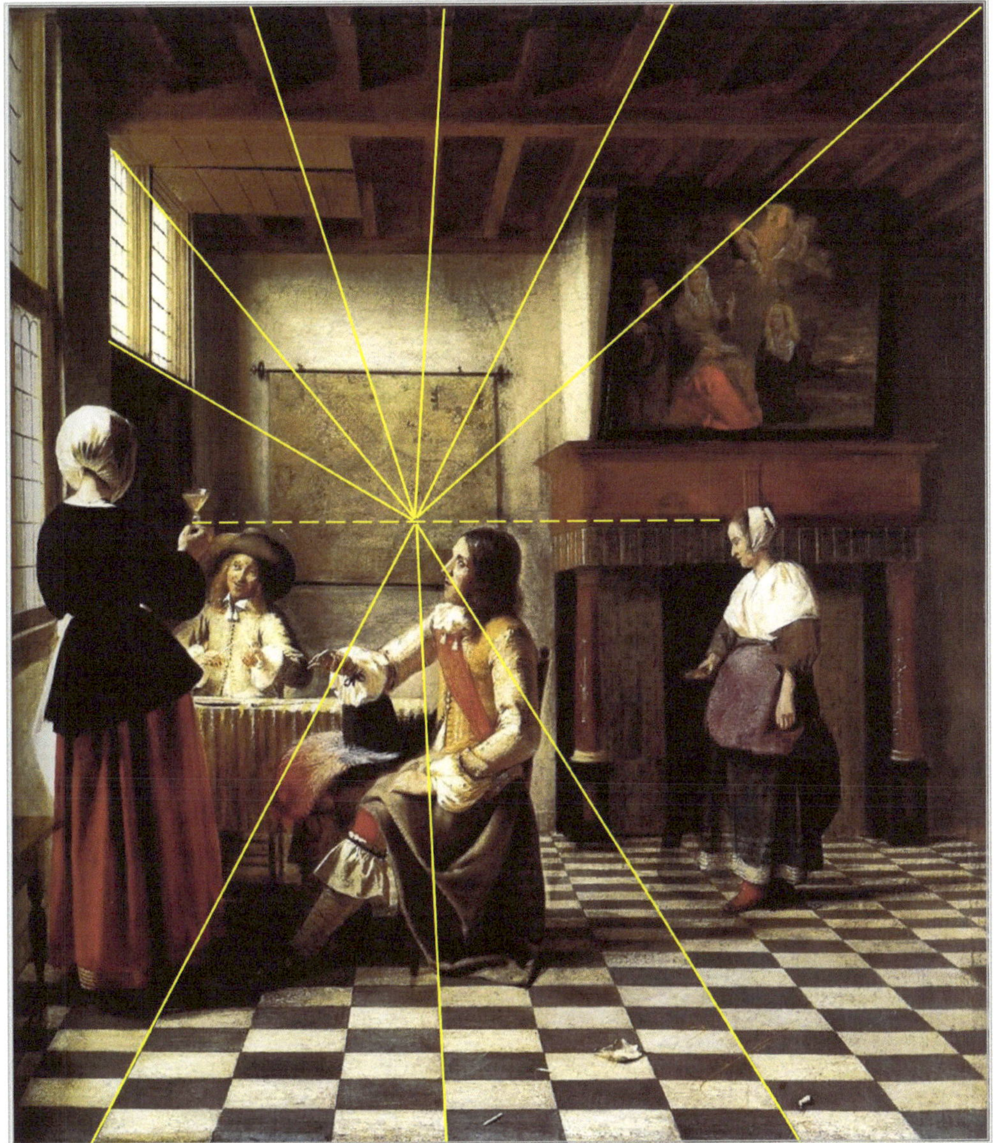

Fig. 61: *A Woman Drinking with Two Men,* showing perspective lines from ceiling, window and floor, together with horizon line

Let's overlay a few lines along the ceiling beams, the window frame and floor tiles. It is not obvious when looking at the original painting, but they all converge to a single point - the vanishing point. It is a good example of the perspective framework on which an artist can create naturalistic depth. Checkerboard style floors were often used by artists of the period to enhance the sense of depth and realism.

From the vanishing point, we obtain a viewer eye level just above the glass in the woman's hand, and a little below her eye level, suggesting we are looking slightly upward into the room, perhaps from a doorway one step down. The center of focus drives our eyes towards the group seated around the table.

Opposite is a fine example by Johannes Vermeer. *The Milkmaid* was painted about the same time as the previous de Hooch example, around 1660. There are no obvious roof beams or tiled floors to aid perspective, but there is at least a highly-structured, panelled window and windowframe.

By drawing some perspective lines from the panelled window and its frame, see over, we can immediately identify that the artist is asking us to focus around her right hand and the jug she is pouring from. The eye level suggests we are seated and perhaps admiring her skillful movements.

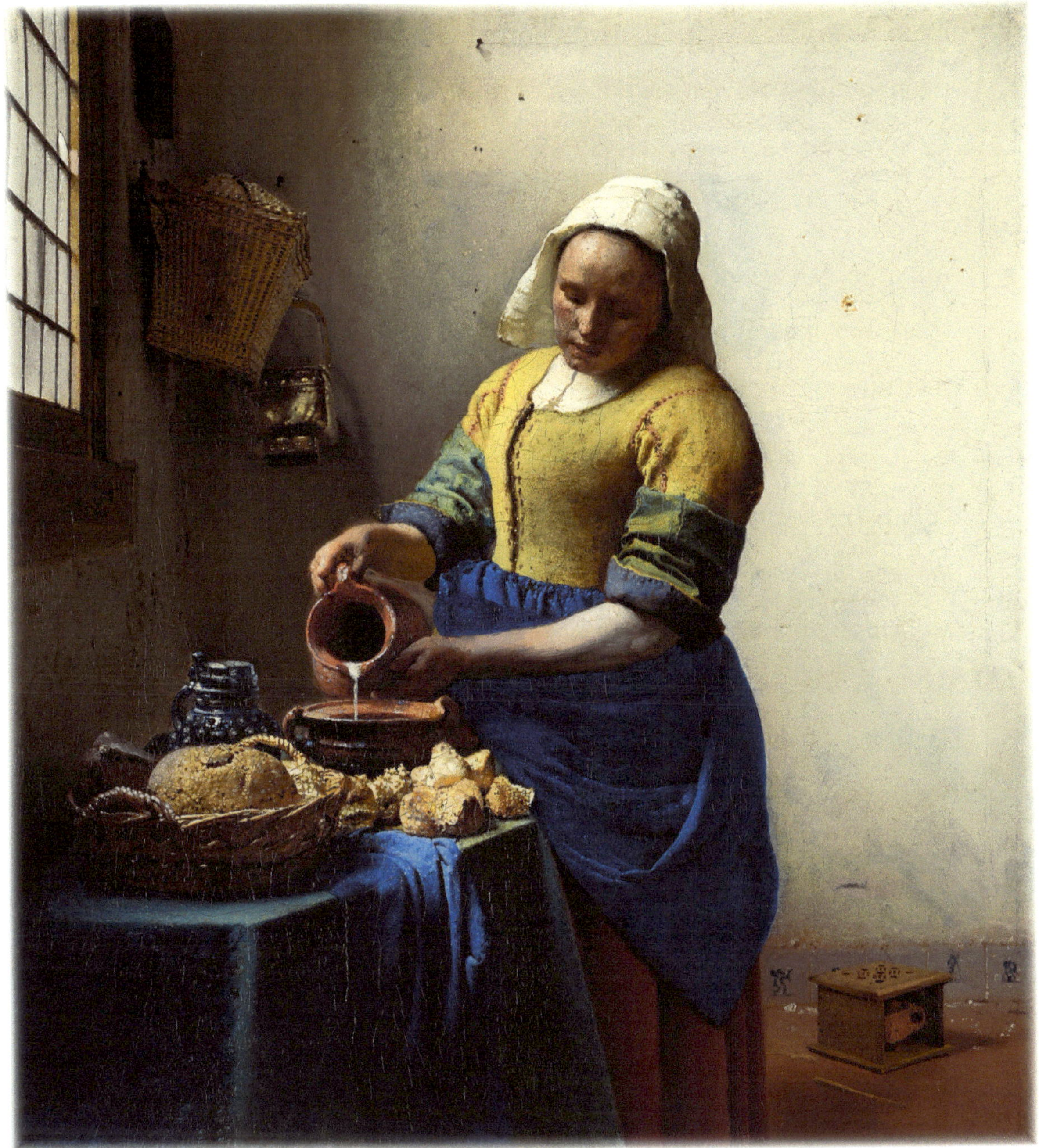

Fig. 62: *Het melkmeisje (The Milkmaid)*, Johannes Vermeer, c.1660
(oil on canvas, Rijksmuseum)

Even more amazing, evidence of pinholes at the vanishing point has been found in at least seventeen of the three dozen or so paintings by Vermeer.

Apparently, Vermeer used a pin and cord directly on the canvas to trace out lines of perspective. I quote from RKD, the Netherlands Institute for Art History [4]:

"While the camera obscura may have been used as a compositional aid and be responsible for many of the visual effects in Vermeer's paintings, pinholes found at the vanishing points of some seventeen of his paintings – as visible in X-radiographs – demonstrate that the artist used a mechanical procedure to construct perspective lines in his compositions.

First observed in 1949 by Karl Hultén in The Art of Painting (L26), Jørgen Wadum went on to show how the artist constructed the orthogonals of the tiles or furniture by placing a pin in the canvas at the vanishing point to which he attached a cord covered in chalk. By pulling the cord taut against the canvas the chalk would leave a thin line."

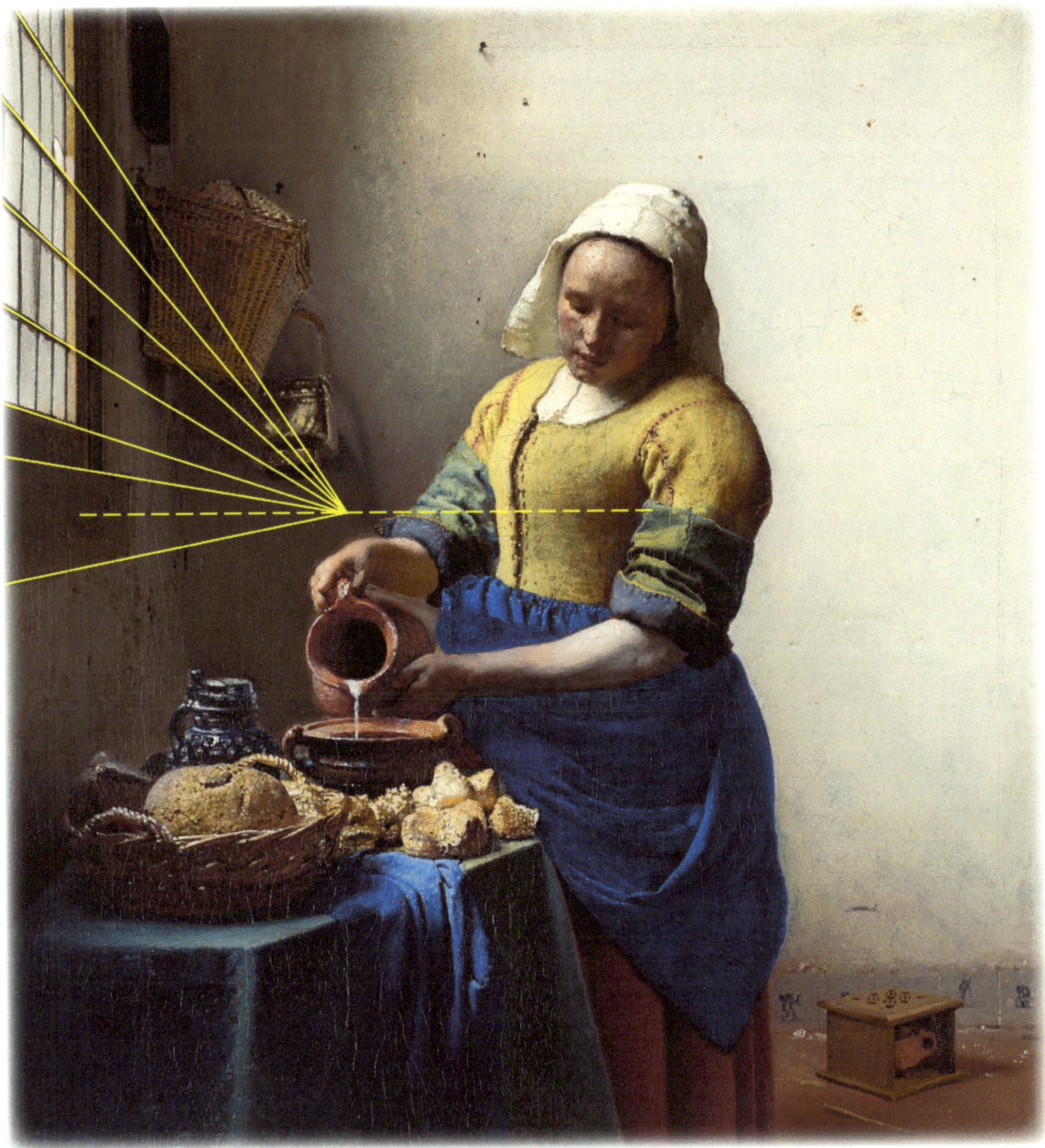

Fig. 63: *Het melkmeisje (The Milkmaid)*, Johannes Vermeer, c.1660 showing perspective lines and horizon line

Now let's return to our earlier example by Pieter Bruegel the Elder entitled *Children's Games* and painted in 1560, some one hundred years before Vermeer. Again, before drawing perspective lines or horizon line, we can pose two questions:

From what height do we appear to be viewing the scene?

Where is our attention being drawn?

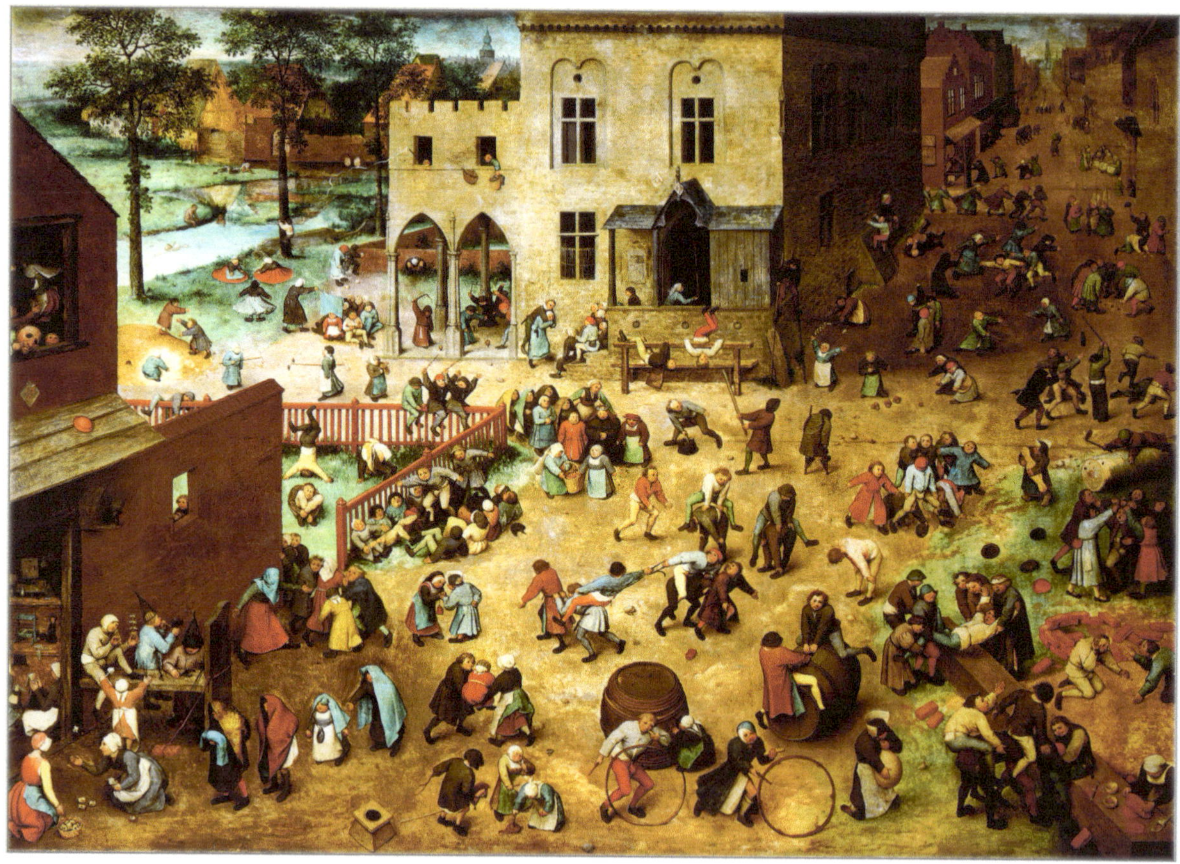

Fig. 64: *Children's Games,* Pieter Bruegel the Elder, 1560
(oil on wood, Kunsthistorisches Museum)

By adding perspective lines, we can clearly see that we are observing the scene from a high vantage point, from the safety of several floors up, a so-called high eye-level viewpoint.

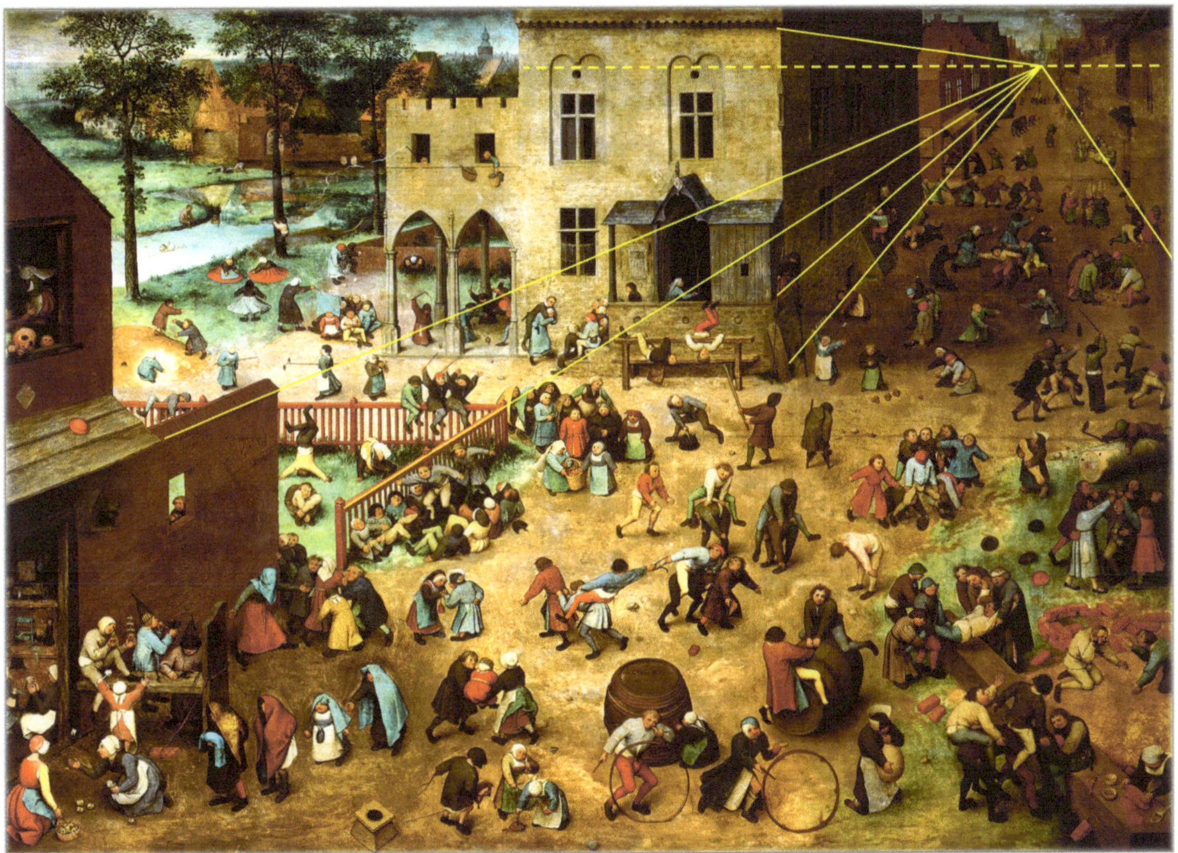

Fig. 65: *Children's Games,* Pieter Bruegel the Elder, 1560 with perspective lines added, together with the horizon line

And our attention is drawn from the foreground activities lower left in a grand sweep towards the top right, the most distant part of the scene.

By way of contrast, let's go back a hundred years to the time of the Renaissance and Alberti's treatise on perspective. Here we have the magnificent Van Eyck painting entitled *The Arnolfini Portrait*, a 1434 oil painting on oak panel.

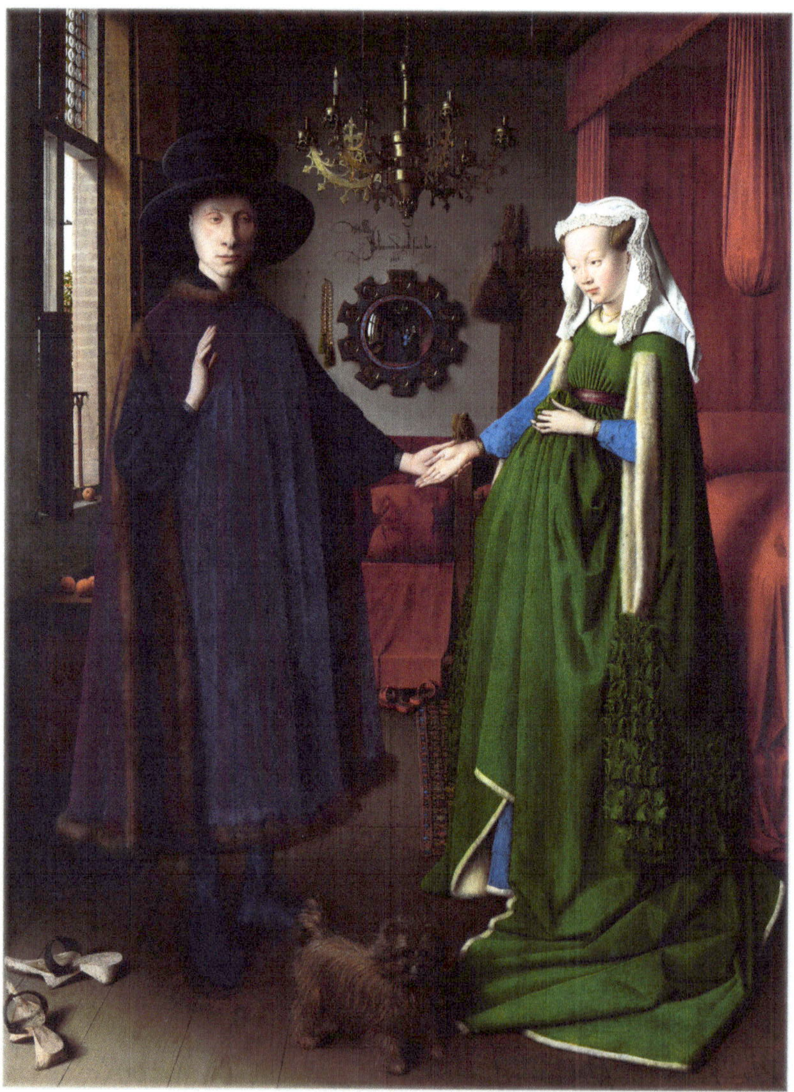

Fig. 66: *The Arnolfini Portrait,* Jan van Eyck, 1434 (oil on oak panel, National Gallery, London)

It is thought unlikely that Van Eyck would have known of the advances taking place around the same time in Italy related to the rules of perspective. Nevertheless, his painting is remarkable for its realism.

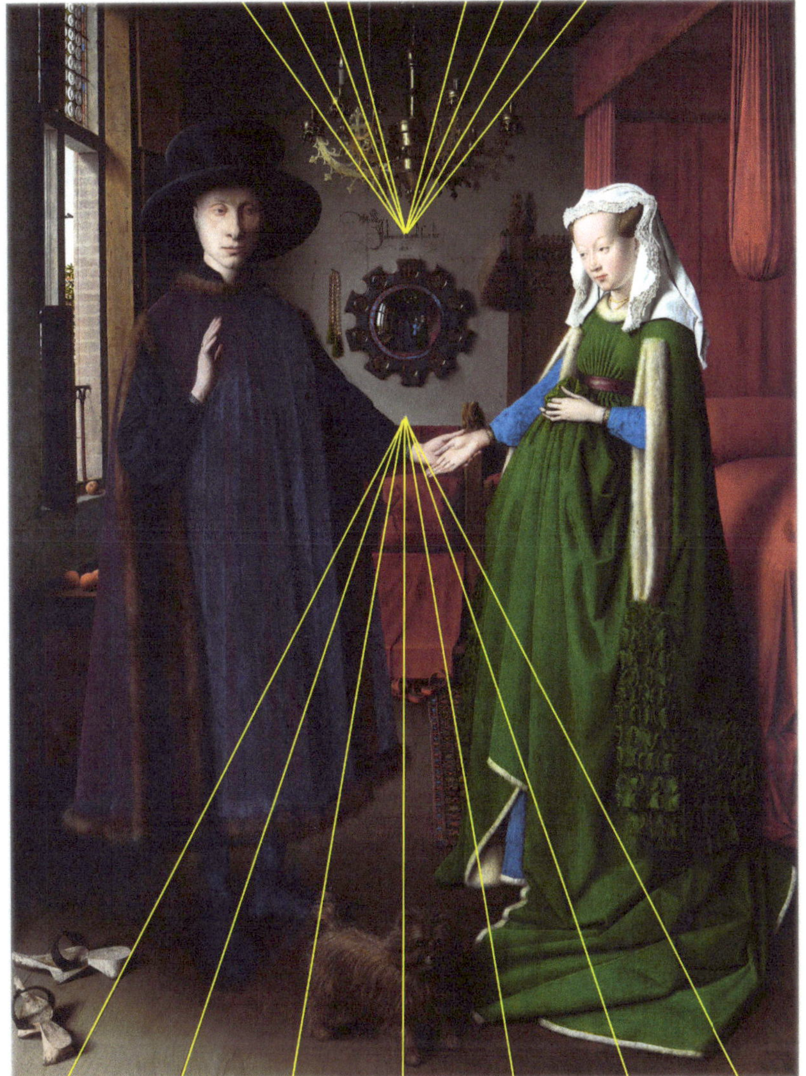

Fig. 67: *The Arnolfini Portrait,* Jan van Eyck, 1434 with ceiling and floor perspective lines added

When we overlay perspective lines, we discover that the ceiling beams, window glass and bed frame provide one very nice vanishing point, and the floor panels another. They don't coincide but they are not very far apart, they lie on the same vertical axis and they draw the viewer's attention towards the central convex mirror – an enigma in its own right.

There is much wide-ranging debate about this painting and Van Eyck's possible use of a perspective system that is beyond the scope of this book, but the interested reader can explore the topic further if desired [5]. The point here is that exact linear perspective is not necessary to create a magnificent, realistic work of art.

As identified earlier, Leonardo da Vinci knew of Alberti's treatise and made many notes himself on perspective. Here is a famous example of da Vinci's work: *The Last Supper*, a mural completed between 1495 and 1498. Similar to other works of the period, the main figures are assembled together and across the foreground.

At first sight, the scene appears relatively flat with little depth. But we can pose some key questions:

Where is our attention being drawn?

What key elements has da Vinci included to achieve a sense of depth?

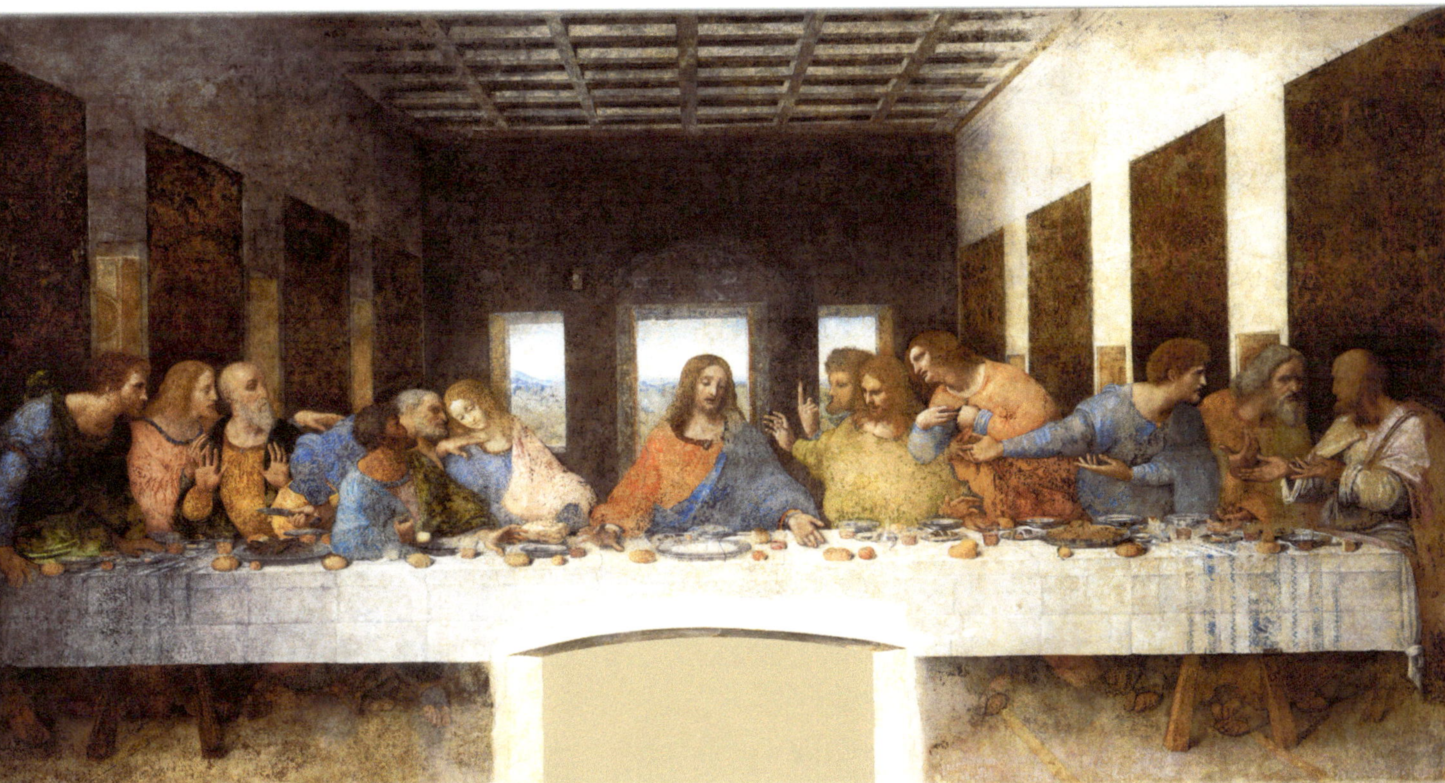

Fig. 68: *The Last Supper Restored*, Leonardo Da Vinci, 1495-1498 (painted on the refectory wall of Santa Maria delle Grazie, Milan)

Before responding to these questions, we need to understand the background to the work. *The Last Supper* was commissioned by Ludovico Sforza, the Duke of Milan, for the refectory wall of the Dominican Convent of Santa Maria delle Grazie, which was completed in 1497.

Here is a view of the refectory exterior, followed by a view of the interior, showing the placement of *The Last Supper*:

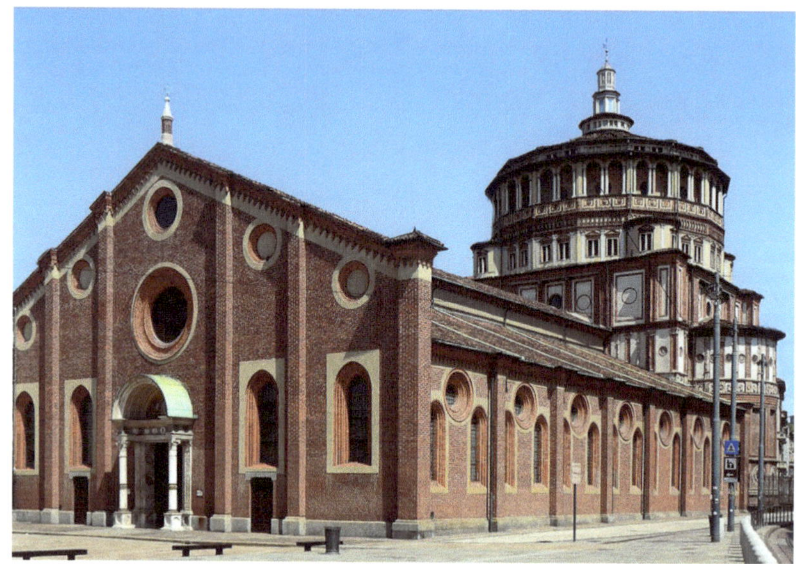

Fig. 69: Refectory view from the outside

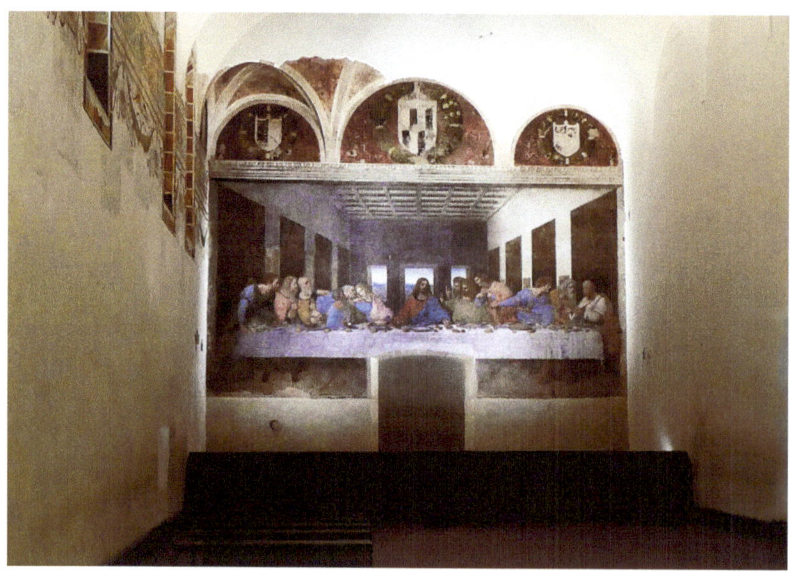

Fig. 70: Refectory view from the inside showing the illusion of perspective

Figure 70 illustrates the interior view as it appears today. We can immediately admire the painting's powerful illusion of an end wall extending beyond the building, and of light streaming in from the windows behind.

And when we draw in key perspective lines from the ceiling beams and the side walls of the painting, we can clearly see da Vinci's genius in creating that illusion of light and depth, while focusing our attention firmly on Jesus himself.

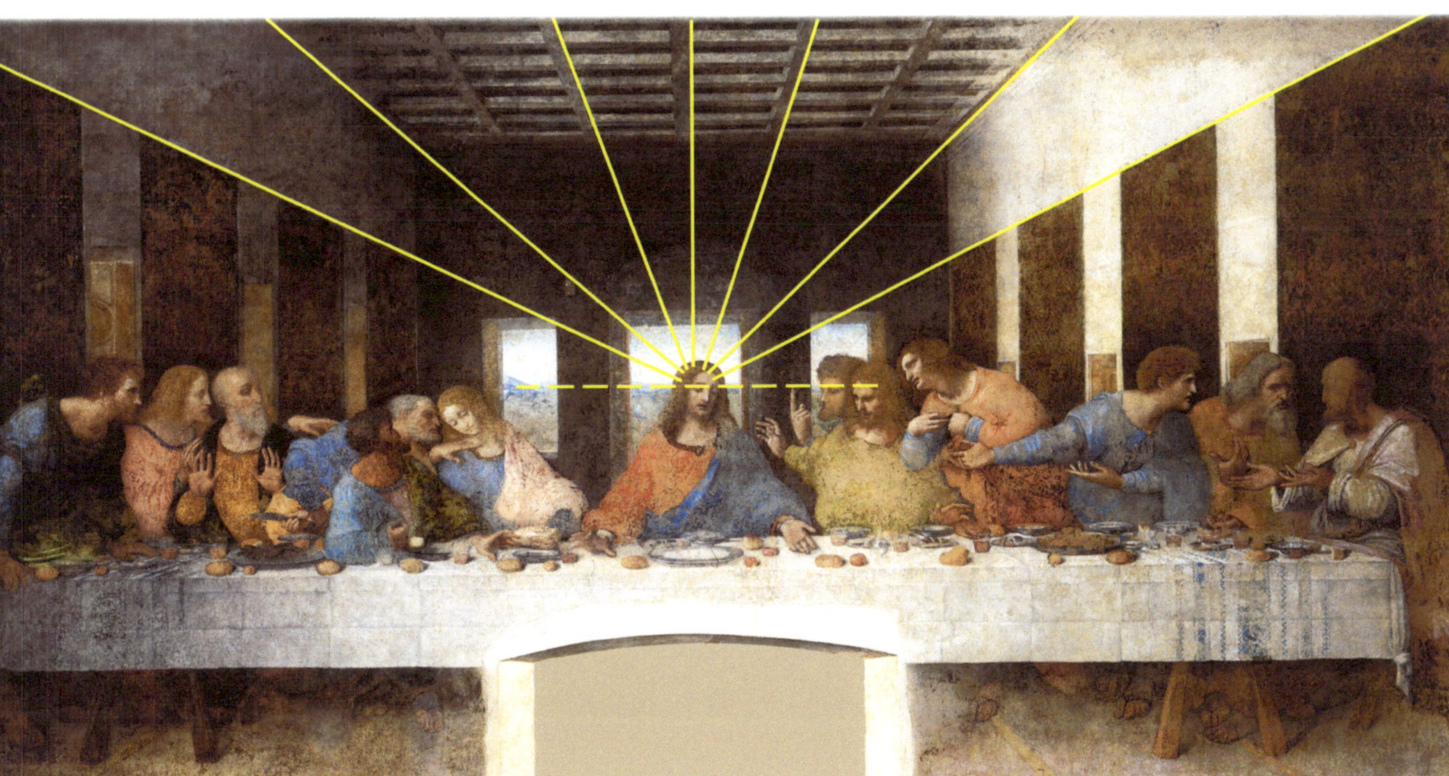

Fig. 71: *The Last Supper Restored* with perspective lines and horizon line

Let's return to this example of an eighteenth-century painting entitled *Interior of Saint Peter's Basilica in Rome*, one of about 30 such scenes painted by Panini. It impresses with its soaring arches and gorgeous decoration.

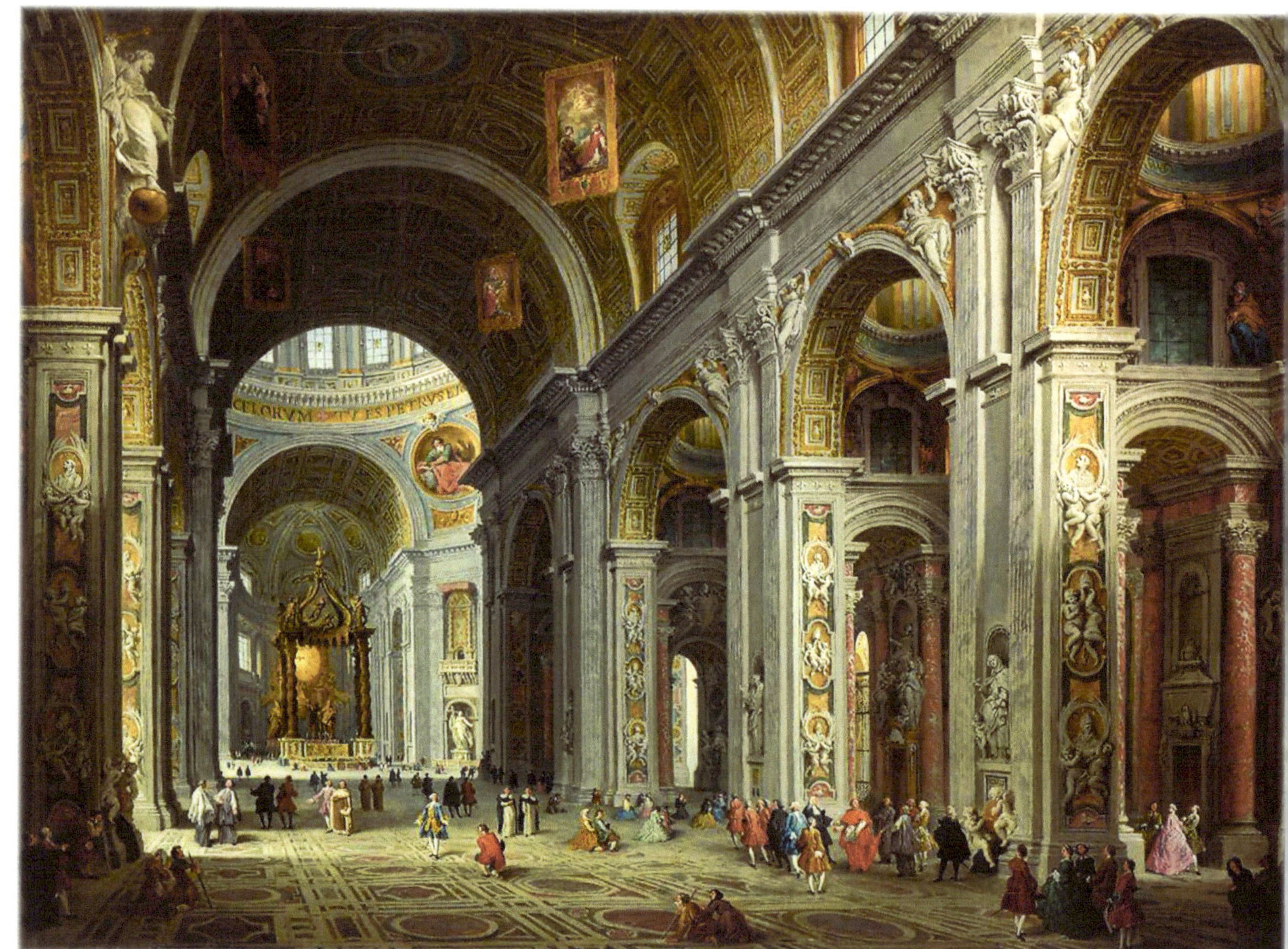

Fig. 72: *Interior of Saint Peter's Basilica, Rome*, Giovanni Paolo Panini, after 1754, oil on canvas

Adding key perspective lines shows how our eye is drawn into the scene, sweeping from the upper right towards the tomb of St Peter on the lower left, a viewpoint well above the figures at floor level, as though we are viewing from a raised gallery.

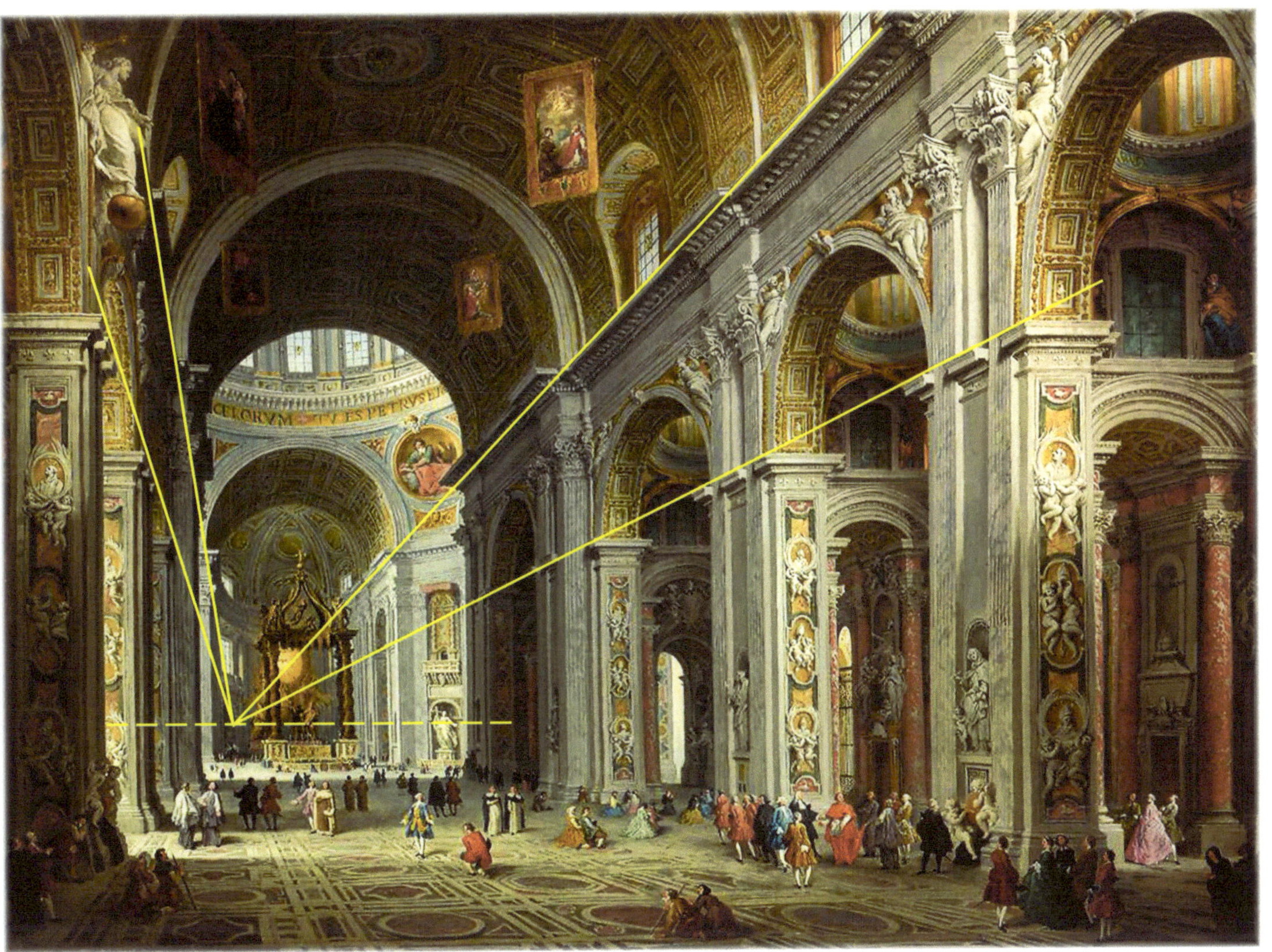

Fig. 73: *Interior of Saint Peter's Basilica, Rome* with perspective lines and horizon

Now consider this example of late nineteenth century art. While we do not usually think of Van Gogh as an artist providing clear structure in his paintings, on observing his *Bedroom in Arles,* painted in 1888, we feel immediately drawn into the room.

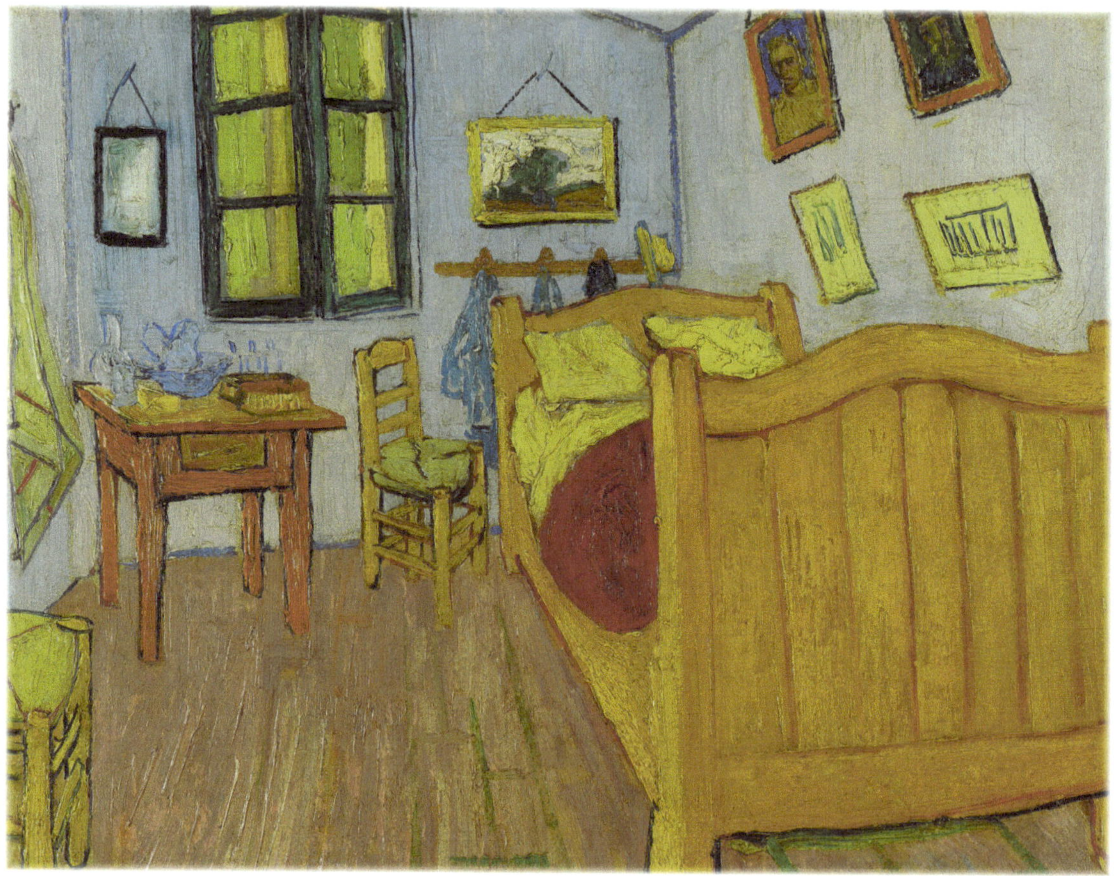

Fig. 74: *Bedroom in Arles,* 1888, Vincent van Gogh, oil on canvas (first version)

Key perspective lines, while by no means perfect, illustrate why we are so drawn into this captivating scene!

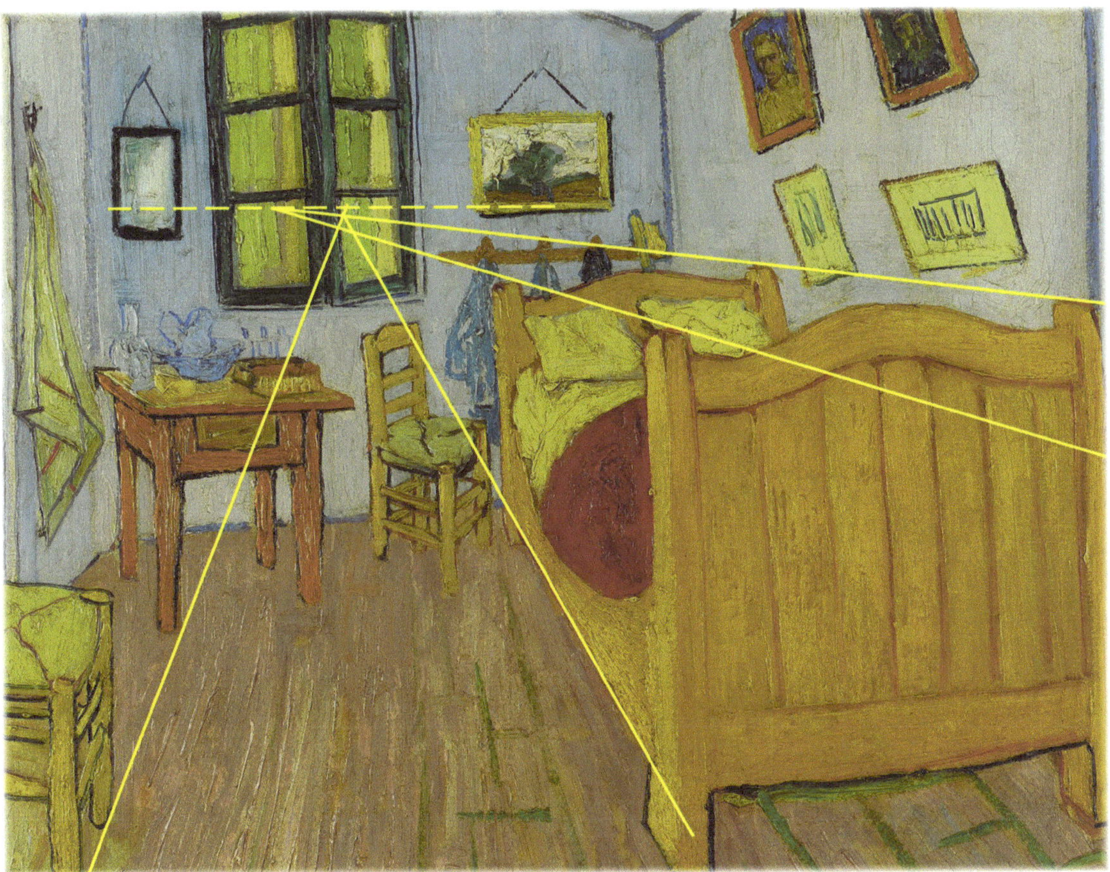

Fig. 75: *Bedroom in Arles,* with perspective lines and horizon

In fact, van Gogh was well-versed in the techniques of perspective, as can be particularly seen in some of his earlier works. He studied modeling and perspective while attending the Royal Academy of Fine Arts in Brussels in 1880 and earlier attended the Willem II College in Tilburg, where students were taught by the Dutch artist and teacher Constant Cornelius Huijsmans.

Now, as described earlier, a camera automatically captures depth and realism almost perfectly on a flat surface. During the latter half of the nineteenth century, photography became widespread and fashionable. Did this influence artists to move away from realistic representation?

By the early twentieth century one move away from the single viewpoint of a camera resulted in Cubism, which sought to show multiple viewpoints of a person or an object simultaneously.

Pioneered by Pablo Picasso and Georges Braque, Cubism was heavily influenced by the representation of three-dimensional form in the late works of Paul Cézanne.

Here is a quote from Jean Metzinger (a notable 20th-century French painter) from his *Note sur la peinture*, Pan (Paris), October–November 1910:

> *"In Cubist artwork, objects are analyzed, broken up and reassembled in an abstracted form. Instead of depicting objects from a single viewpoint, the artist depicts the subject from a multitude of viewpoints to represent the subject in a greater context."*

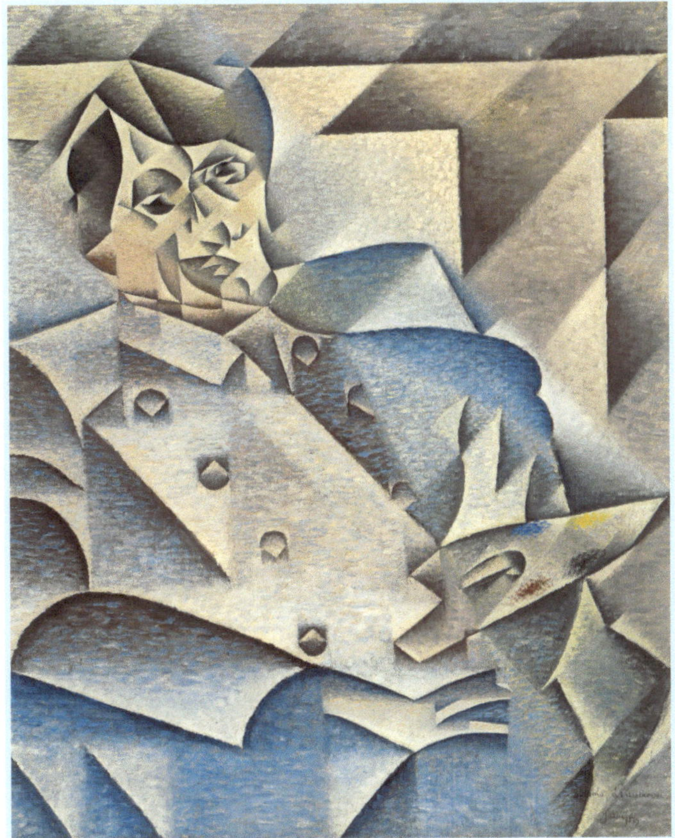

Fig. 76: Example of cubist art: *Portrait of Picasso,* Juan Gris, 1912
(oil on canvas, Art Institute of Chicago)

Abstract art, influenced by Cubism, went even further, completely removing any notion of realistic representation.

Interestingly, however, by the late twentieth century, we see a reversion to realistic representation, with movements such as photo-realism and hyper-realism, where the goal is to produce a work that is nearly indistinguishable from a photograph.

Below is a good example of photo-realism: *La hora del té*, an oil on canvas painting by Magda Torres Gurza. Admire the reflections in the pot surfaces!

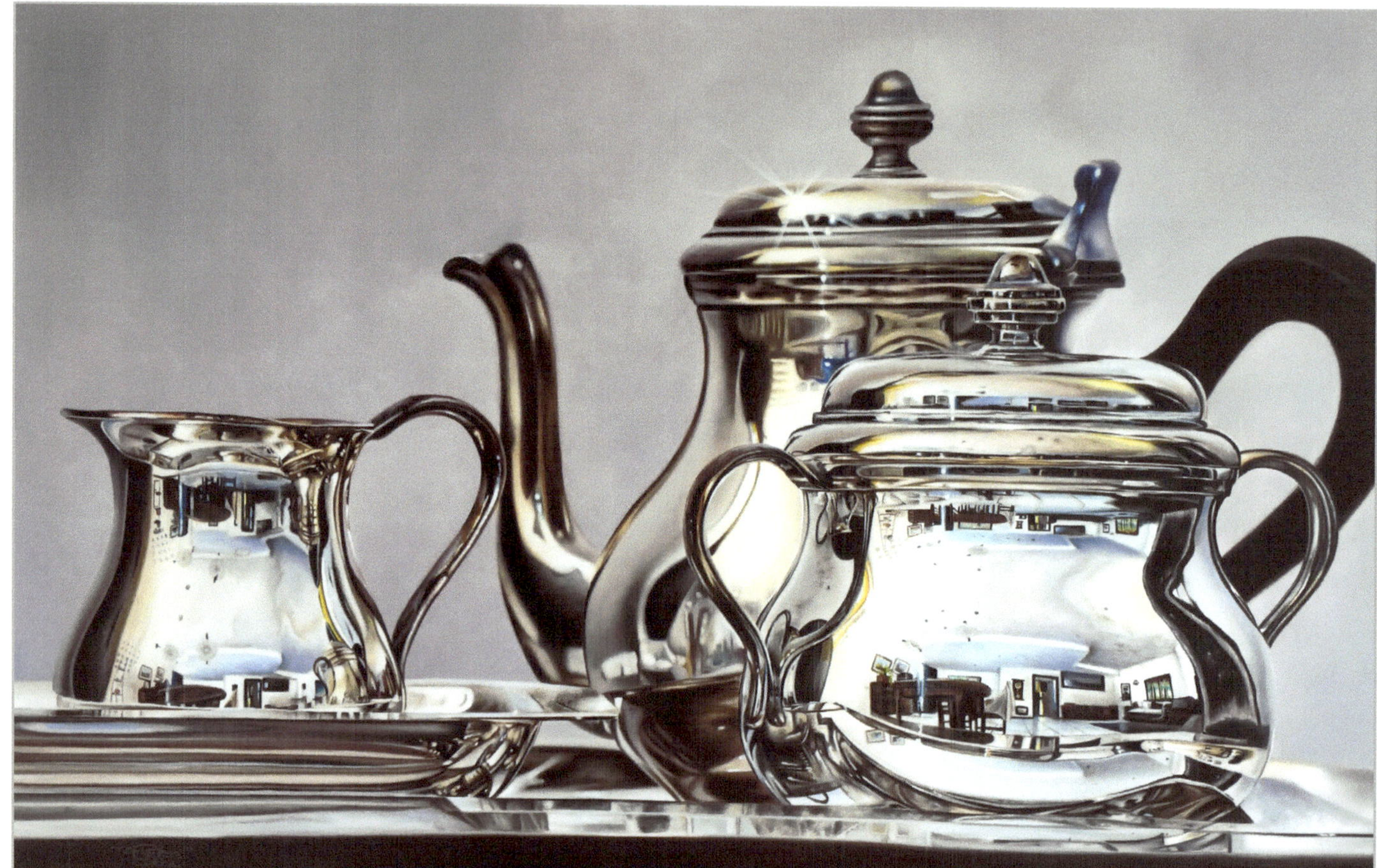

Fig. 77: *La hora del té,* Magda Torres Gurza, 2015

Some contemporary artists even go so far as to start from a large-scale photographic enlargement and then literally create a work of art by painting over the surface of the enlargement.

Multi-Point Perspective

You may have noticed that almost all of the paintings illustrated so far have only used single point perspective. That is, they have been created with only one vanishing point.

Single point perspective is by far the most common artistic approach because it is sufficient for the vast majority of subjects.

In the following sections we will look at some more examples of single point perspective, to illustrate the breadth of artists' works using this technique, then go on to illustrate two and three-point perspective.

As an aside, this book is not intended as a tutorial on the construction of linear perspective – there are plenty of texts [7,8] available to the artist seeking this information. However, for those readers interested, I have included an appendix that explains the basic concepts of one, two and three-point perspective, using simple wire cubes. Note that there is no upper limit to the number of vanishing points in a drawing but the complexity increases considerably and does not necessarily imply a more accurate representation.

One-Point Perspective

Here are a few more examples of strong one-point perspective art. I leave it to the reader to identify how the artist has created an illusion of depth and reality in the scene, and where the artist wishes us to focus our attention. This Dutch work by Meindert Hobbema, painted in 1689, illustrates an avenue leading to the village of Middelharnis on the island of Goeree-Overflakkee.

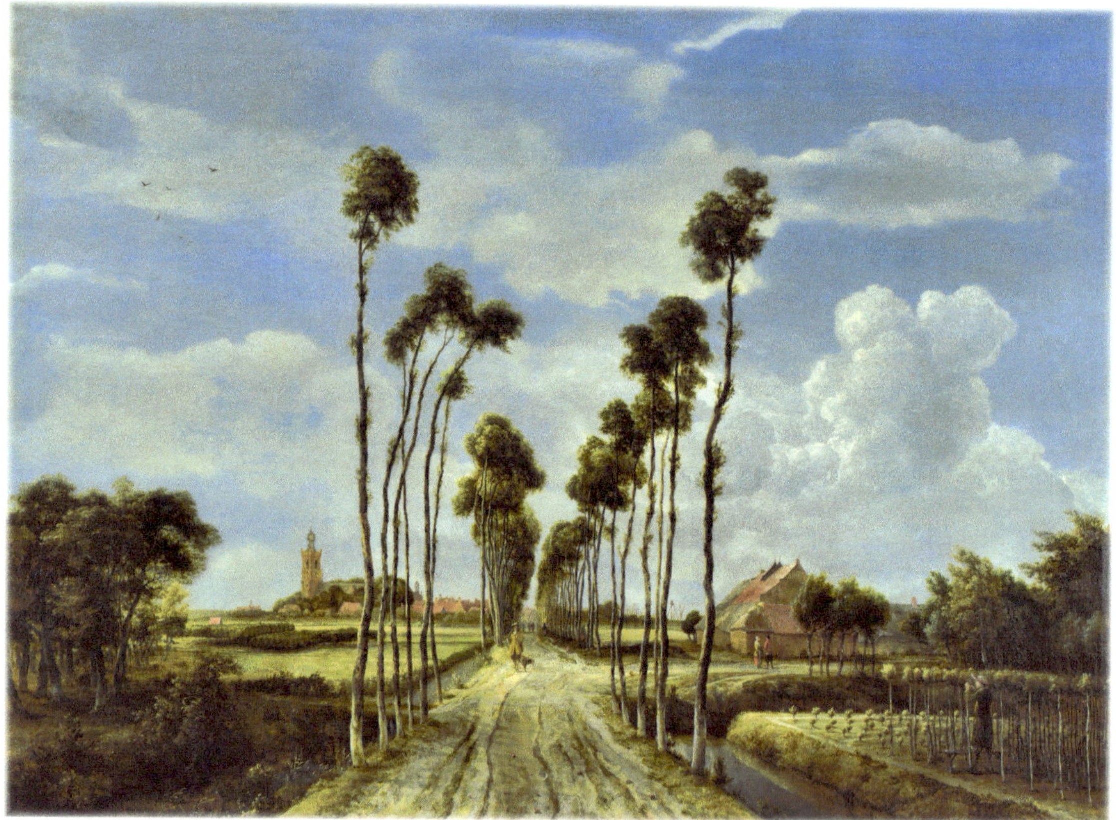

Fig. 78: *The Avenue at Middelharnis,* Meindert Hobbema, 1689, oil on canvas

Quoting from Rex Vicat Cole [9], this painting exhibits "*a strongly foreshortened road lined with trees in a wide flat landscape*". See the later chapter for a more detailed exploration of foreshortening.

The Danish-French impressionist Camille Pissarro painted many single-point perspective landscapes. It is interesting to compare his tree-lined avenue painting entitled *Entrée du village de Voisins* with Hobbema's *The Avenue at Middelharnis*, opposite, painted some 200 years earlier.

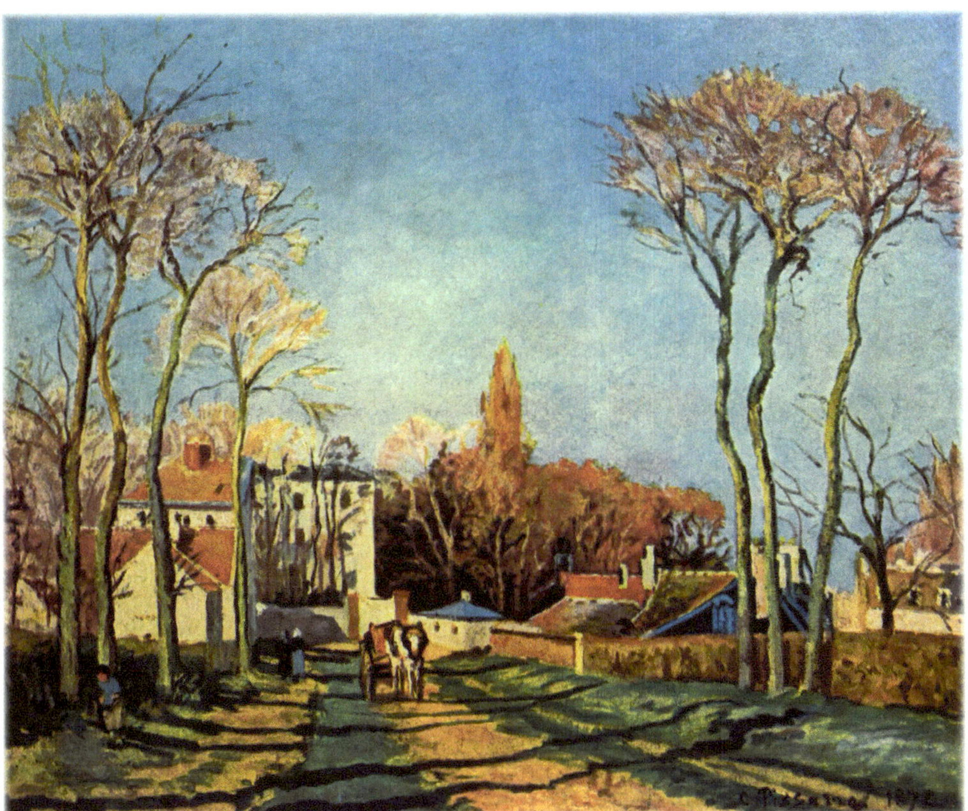

Fig. 79: *Entrée du village de Voisins,* 1872, Camille Pissarro, oil on canvas

Many impressionist works in fact use an underlying one-point perspective framework, capturing outdoor scenes of city and country life. The French-born British painter Alfred Sisley employed a clear sense of perspective in many of his paintings. *Langland Bay,* painted in 1872, is a good example.

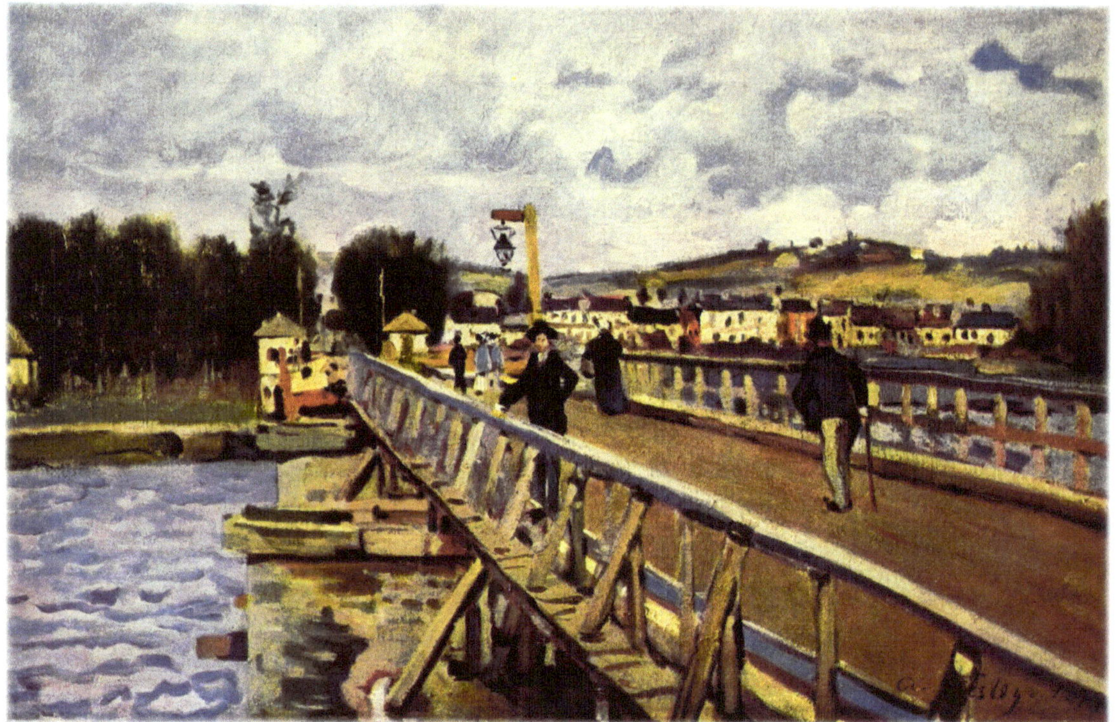

Fig. 80: *Langland Bay,* 1872, Alfred Sisley, oil on canvas

Despite the quick impressionist approach to the subject, we can still appreciate the sense of depth. We feel drawn into the scene. Camille Pissarro is also well-known for his many scenes of Paris streets, often painted from a high viewpoint. Compare his painting of the *Rue Saint-Honoré* in Paris, shown below, with Breughel's high viewpoint painting of *Children's Games*, shown earlier.

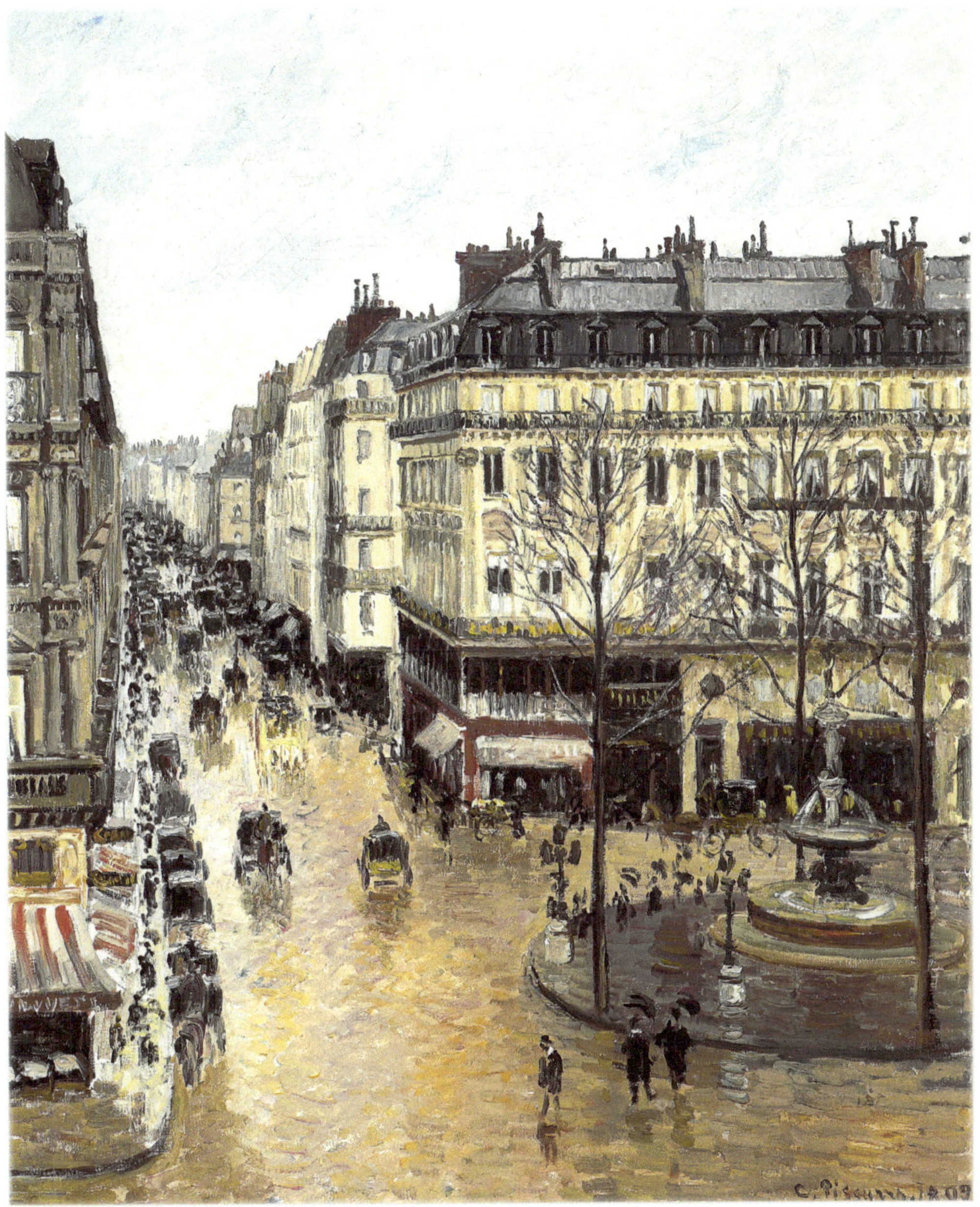

Fig. 81: *Rue Saint-Honoré, Après-midi, Effet de Pluie*, Camille Pissarro, 1897, oil on canvas

Two-Point Perspective

Two-point linear perspective is just an extension from single point linear perspective. Let me emphasize again that these are simply drawing techniques to approximate what we see in real life. *Ambulatory of the Nieuwe Kerk in Delft,* by Gerard Houckgeest is a good first example.

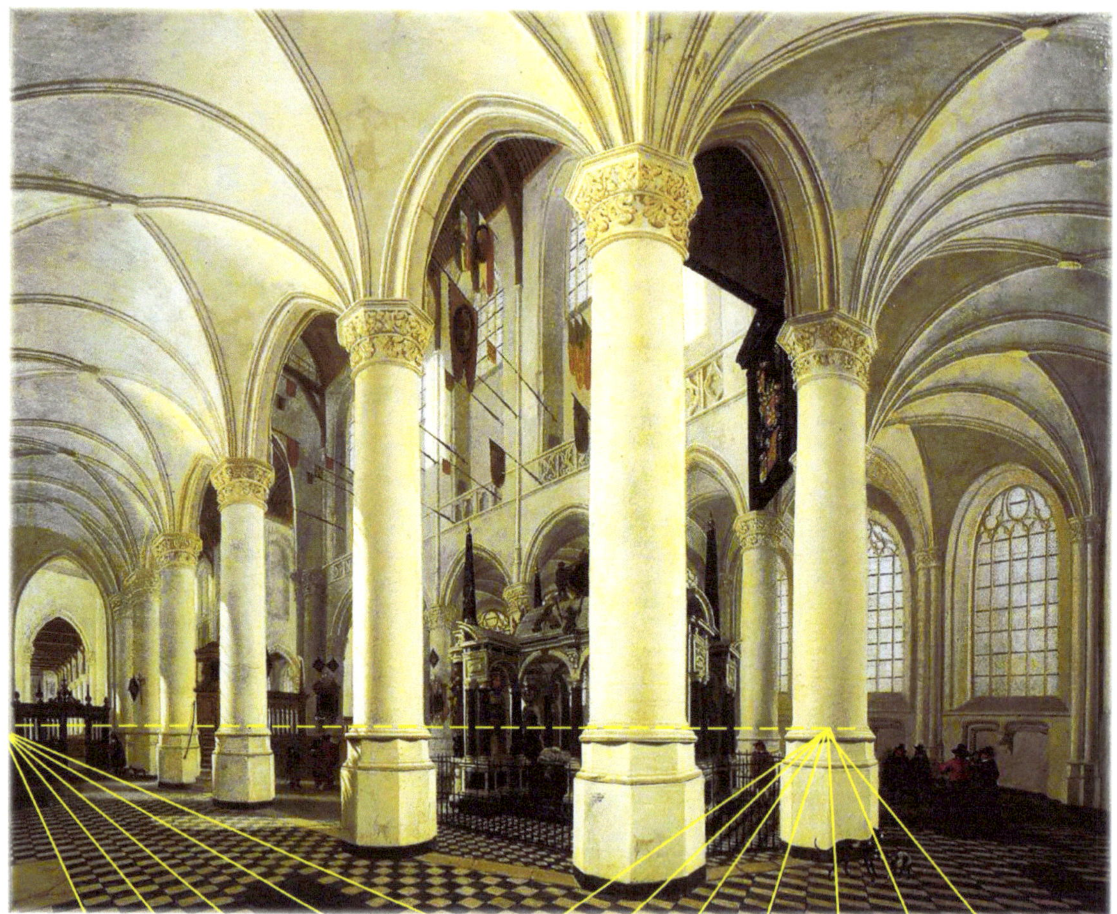

Fig. 82: *Ambulatory of the Nieuwe Kerk in Delft*, with perspective lines added

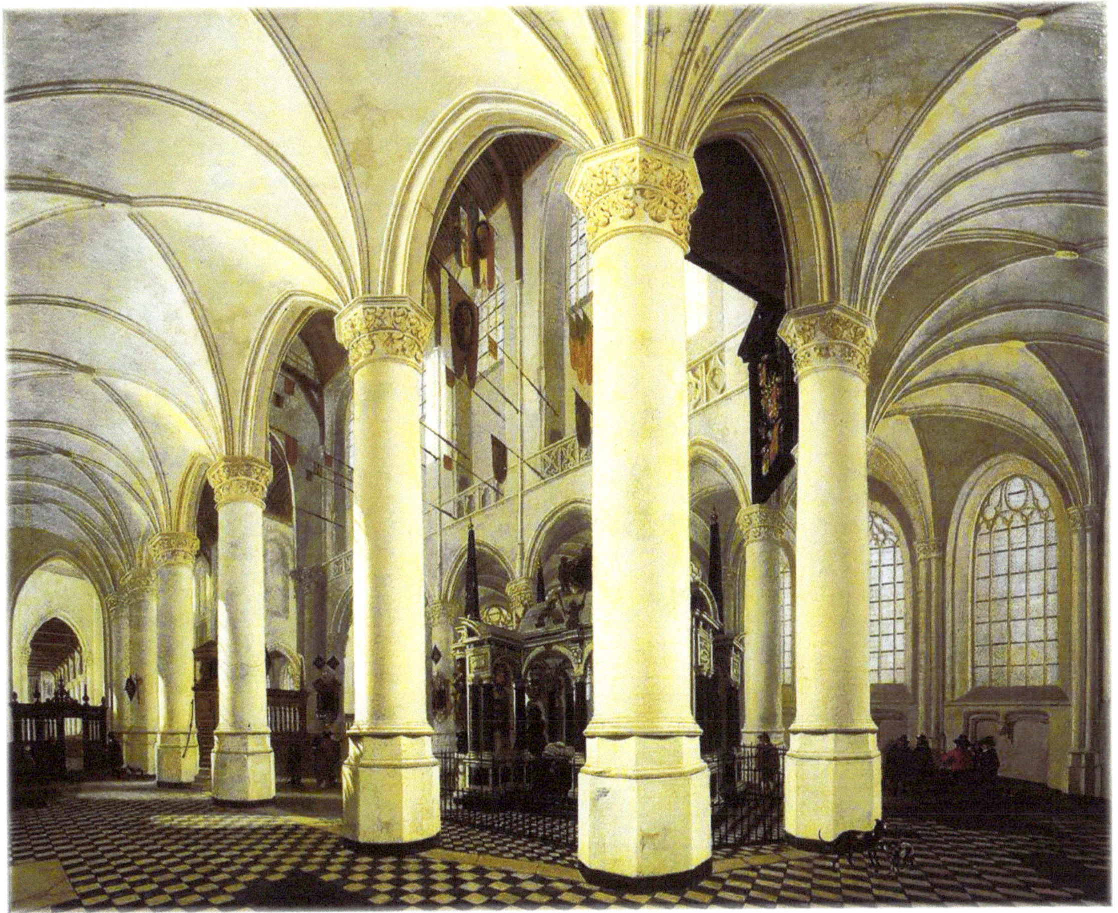

Fig. 83: *Ambulatory of the Nieuwe Kerk in Delft*, 1651, Gerard Houckgeest, oil on wood

You will notice that this church interior has a somewhat special appearance. In this example we are looking at a central pillar end-on and so have a good view down the aisles to the left and to the right of the adjacent pillars. Adding key perspective lines, we find two vanishing points on a single horizon line. We feel drawn into the church, and could choose to go down either aisle.

Next we have an image of the richly decorated bedroom of Louis XIV. Created around 1700, the various panels are embroidered with silk and wool in gros and petit point on a base of canvas. Stories from Ovid are depicted in the medallions, the secondary scenes represent fables from Ovid and La Fontaine.

In this instance, we are looking at the bed from a front corner. Adding perspective lines, we can find two vanishing points along the one horizon line. This is a classic example of a basic cube viewed close-up and end-on.

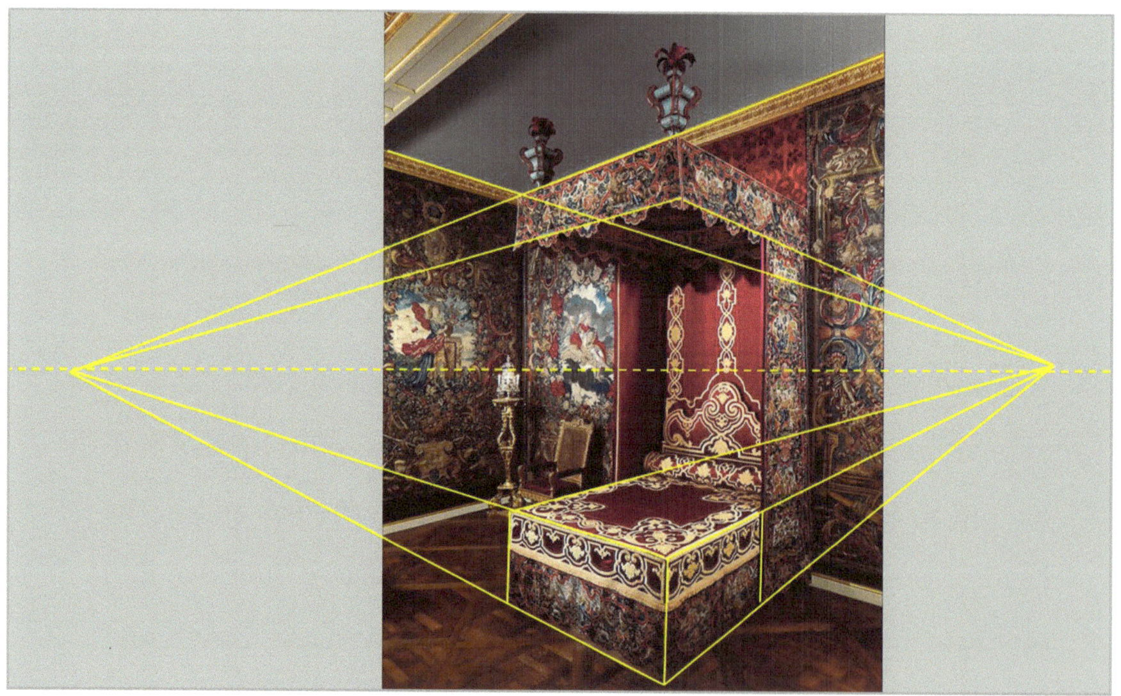

Fig. 84: *Bed valances and side curtains,* with perspective lines

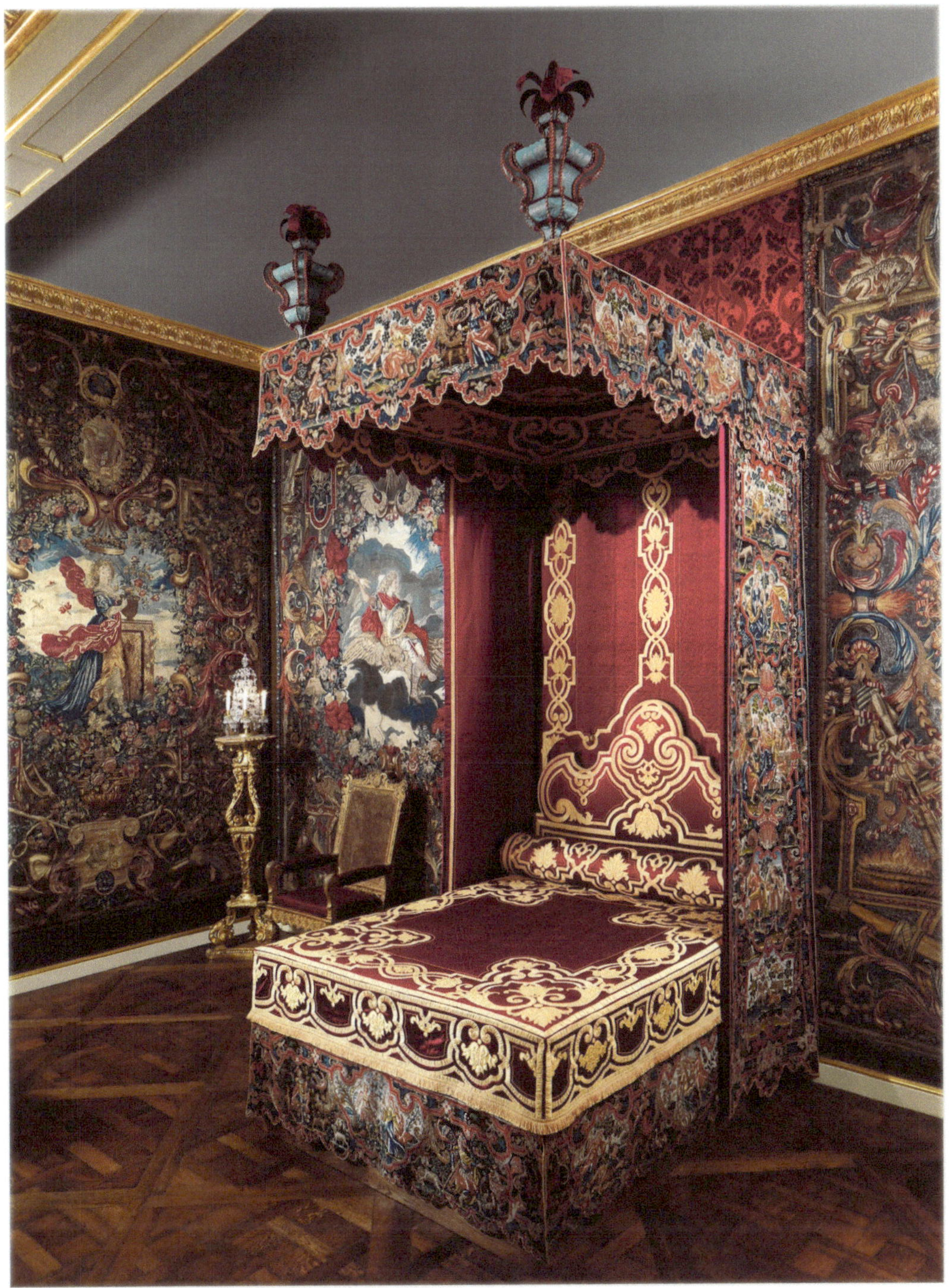

Fig. 85: *Bed valances and side curtains,* ca 1700, French, on canvas with silk and wool embroidery in gros and petit point

The next example of two-point perspective is Gustave Caillebotte's famous work, *Rue de Paris, temps de pluie*.

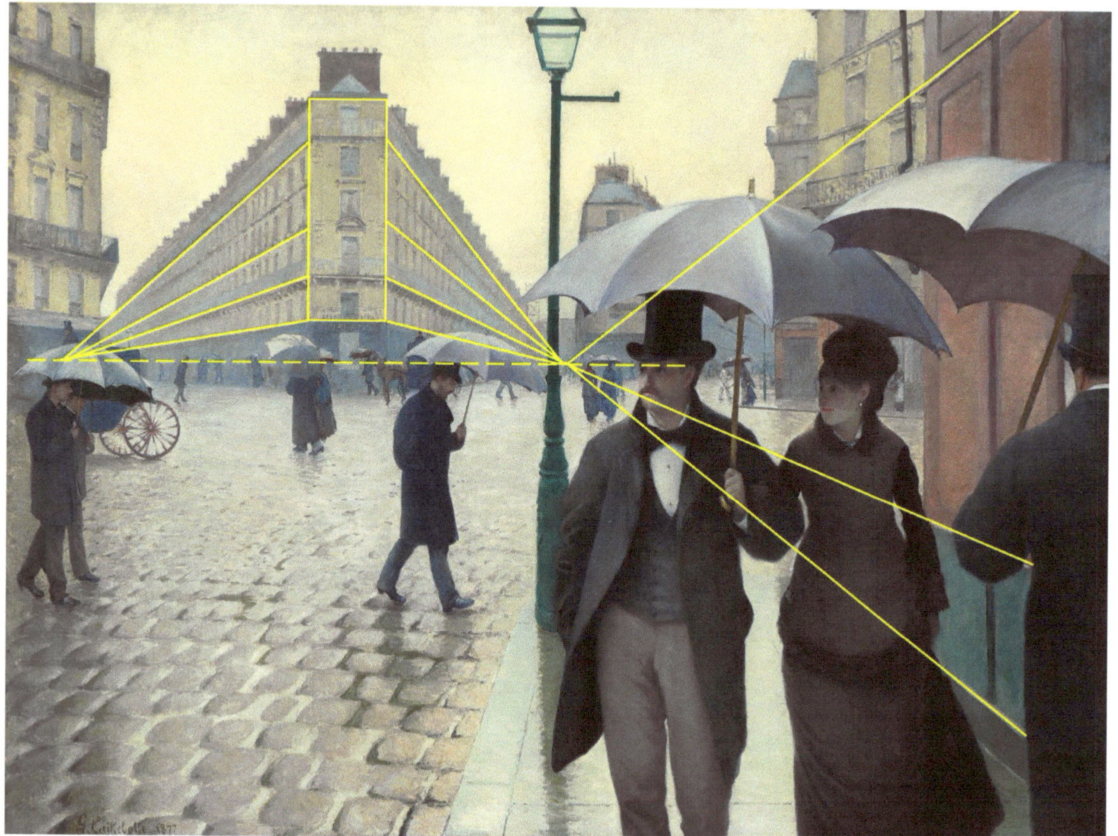

Fig. 86: *Rue de Paris, temps de pluie* with perspective lines

Adding key perspective lines, we can see that Caillebotte has cleverly positioned the horizon at the level of the foreground figures' eyes. So we are drawn to these main figures, particularly the gentleman holding the umbrella.

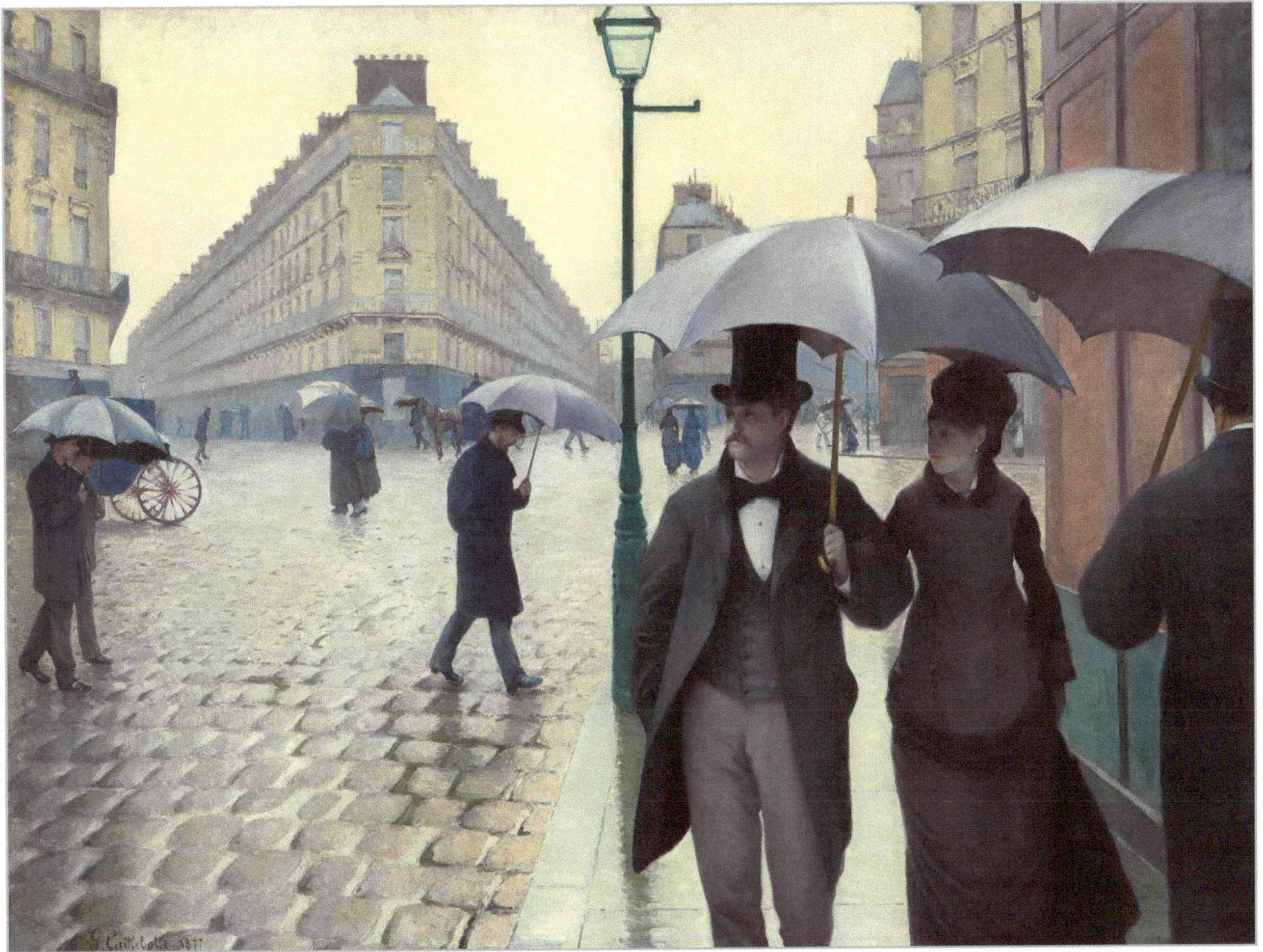

Fig. 87: *Rue de Paris, temps de pluie*, 1877, Gustave Caillebotte, oil on canvas

At the same time the second vanishing point invites our eyes to scan from these foreground figures towards the *place*, and the imposing, “flat-iron”, triangular-shaped building that is presented end-on, with its avenues disappearing into the top corners of the painting.

Here's a final, contemporary example of two-point perspective.

Briefly described earlier, see Figure 16, this particularly realistic oil-on-canvas painting, entitled *Lunch Specials,* was created in 2001 by Richard Estes, one of the foremost painters of art that is categorized under the heading of photorealism or sometimes hyperrealism, because of its near-photographic qualities.

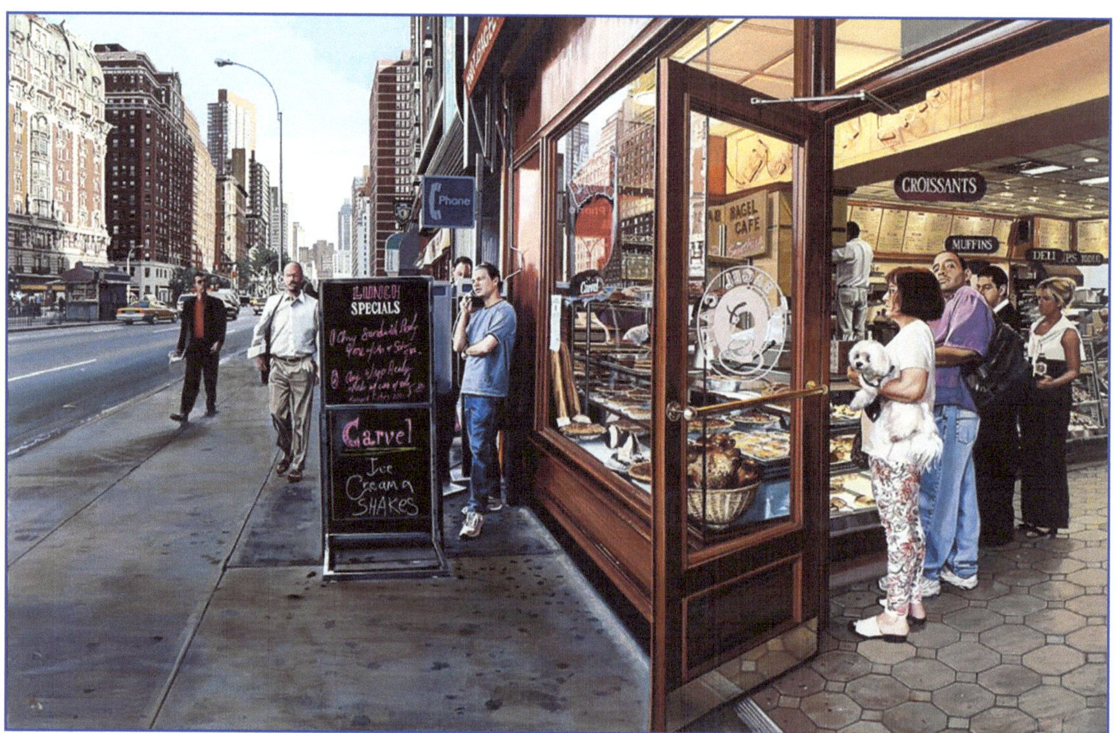

Fig. 88: *Lunch Specials*, © 2001 Richard Estes, oil on canvas

Adding perspective lines and finding the horizon line, we can

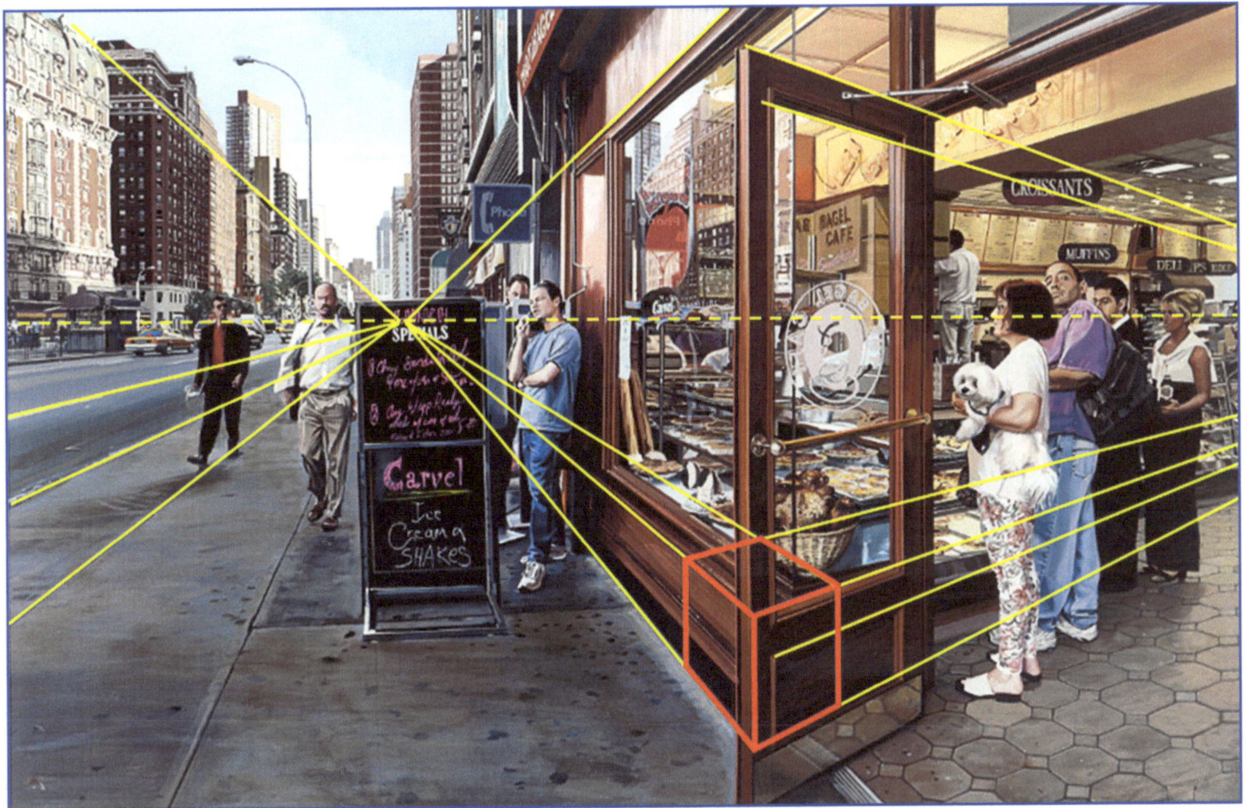

Fig. 89: *Lunch Specials*, © 2001 Richard Estes, with perspective lines added

see that the artist has placed the observer at the same height as customers inside the bakery. The overlaid red cube and perspective lines show one vanishing point inside the frame and one extending beyond the frame, both on approximately the same horizon line.

Again, our gaze moves from joining the customers inside the bakery to the street and the buildings as they disappear into the background.

Three-Point Perspective

Three Point Perspective is rare in art but applicable when viewing or drawing buildings from close-up, with a very low or very high viewpoint.

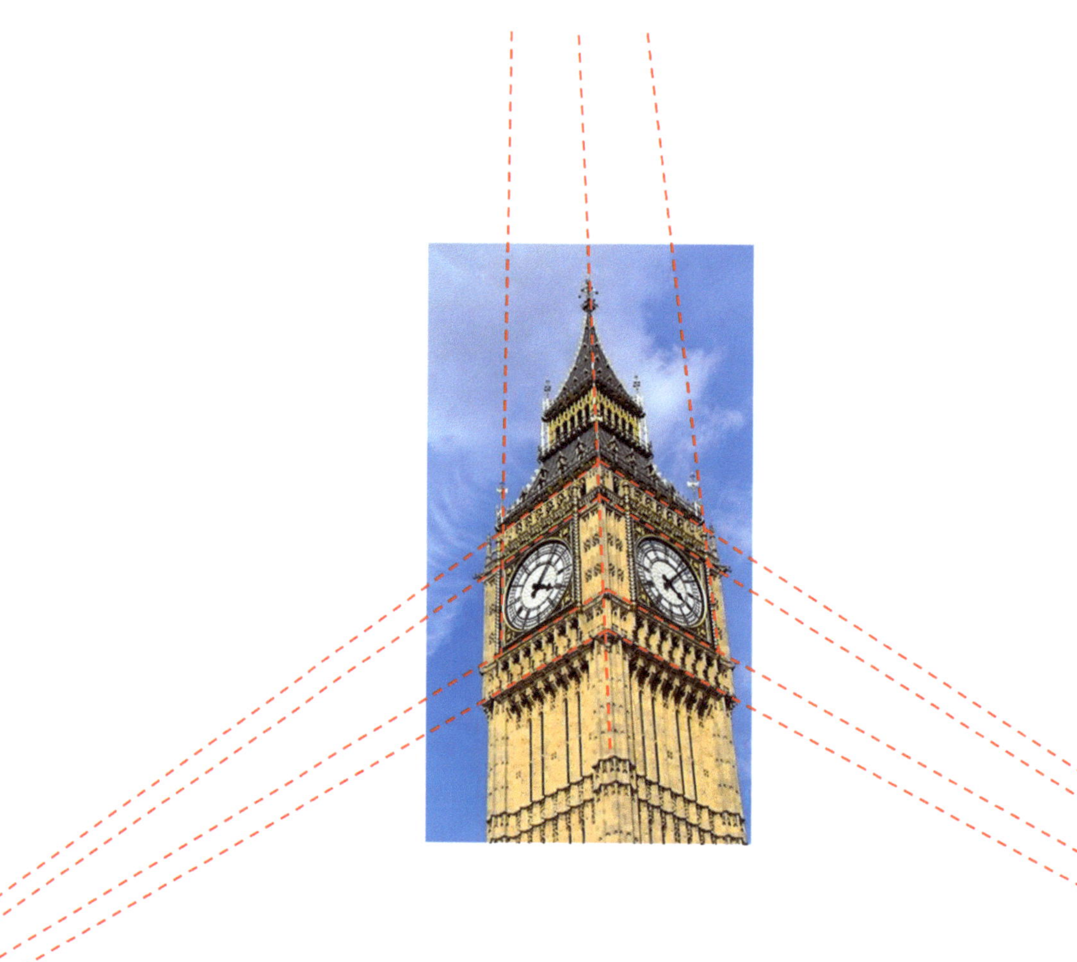

Fig. 90: London's Big Ben clock face with three-point perspective lines added

By way of example, here is an image of London's Big Ben, taken near to the base and looking up at the clock face.

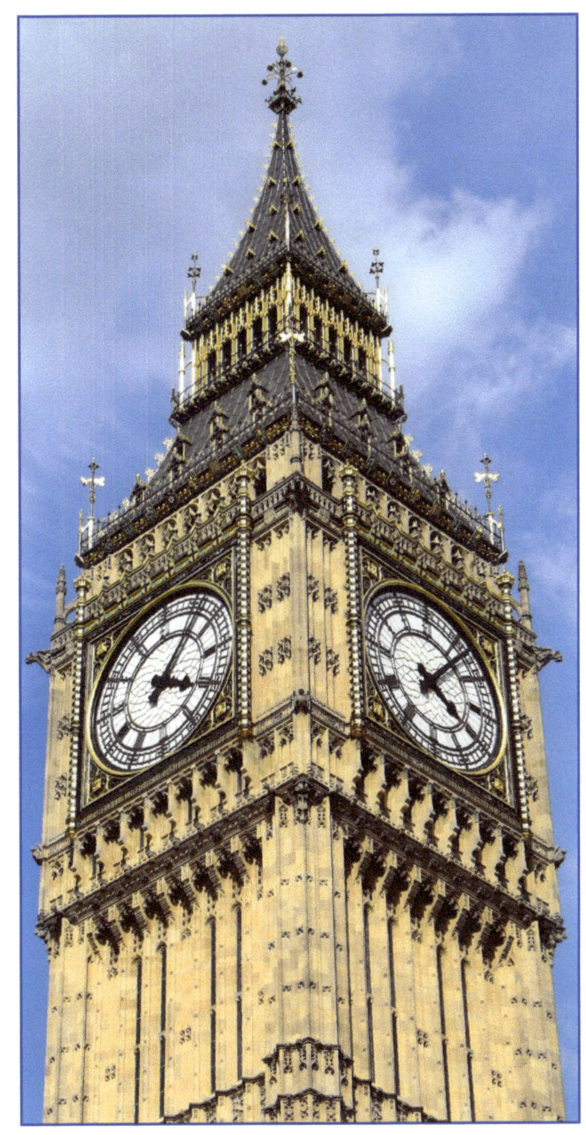
Fig. 91: London's Big Ben clock-face viewed from near the base

We can overlay three sets of perspective lines that eventually converge to their respective vanishing points.

We can envision that the lower two vanishing points create a horizon line that places us, as observer, close to the base of the tower.

So far, this is equivalent to two-point perspective.

The vertical uprights of the building will create an additional vanishing point that forms well above the building when it is viewed from below, and would form below the building, in the ground, if it were viewed from above.

Foreshortening

As we now know, objects in a real scene appear smaller with distance and closer together when projected onto a flat surface such as a canvas.

Let's focus for a moment on the *depth* of objects with distance, and the separation *between* objects with distance.

We assume the floor in this artwork is constructed of equal size tiles. If we draw our horizontal lines (transversals) at the juncture between each row of tiles, along with our perspective lines (orthogonals), we can clearly see how each tile's width becomes smaller with distance. More noticeably, we can see that each tile's *depth* (or the separation between rows of tiles) becomes much smaller with distance than its *width*.

This can be considered as a demonstration of foreshortening, although the term is usually applied to specific objects in a scene, and typically ones that are elongated with one end close to the observer.

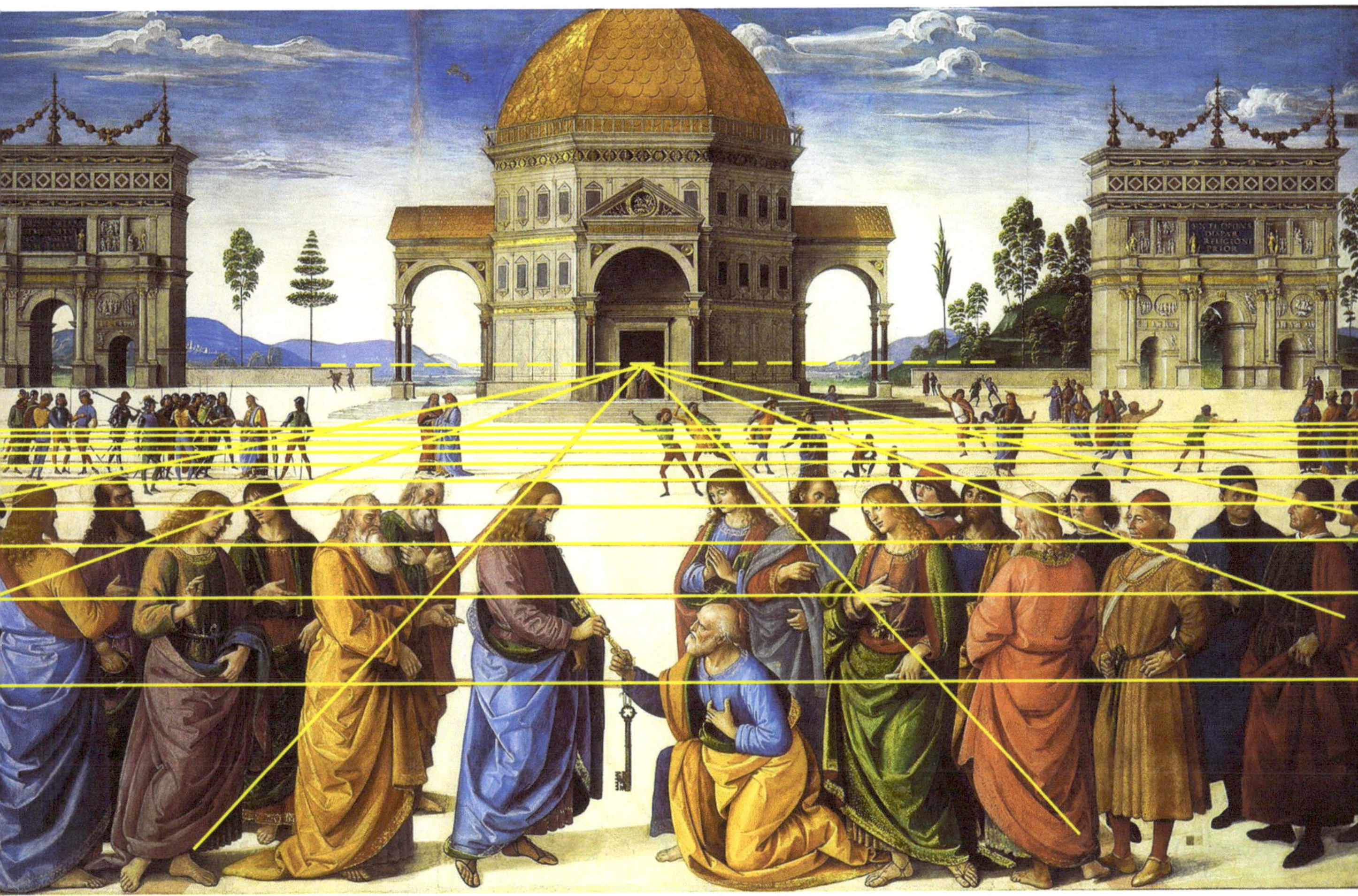

Fig. 92: *The Delivery of the Keys* from Fig. 10, with perspective and transversal lines added

Foreshortening is often treated separately in drawing and painting because it is quite difficult to correctly draw or paint a closely viewed object due to the extreme perspective view and the perspective correction the brain makes because it "knows" what the object should really look like in normal circumstances.

Consider this painting by Caravaggio, entitled *Supper at Emmaus*. At first sight, all looks well-proportioned. But observe the hands of the figure on the right, of Cleopas, a pilgrim.

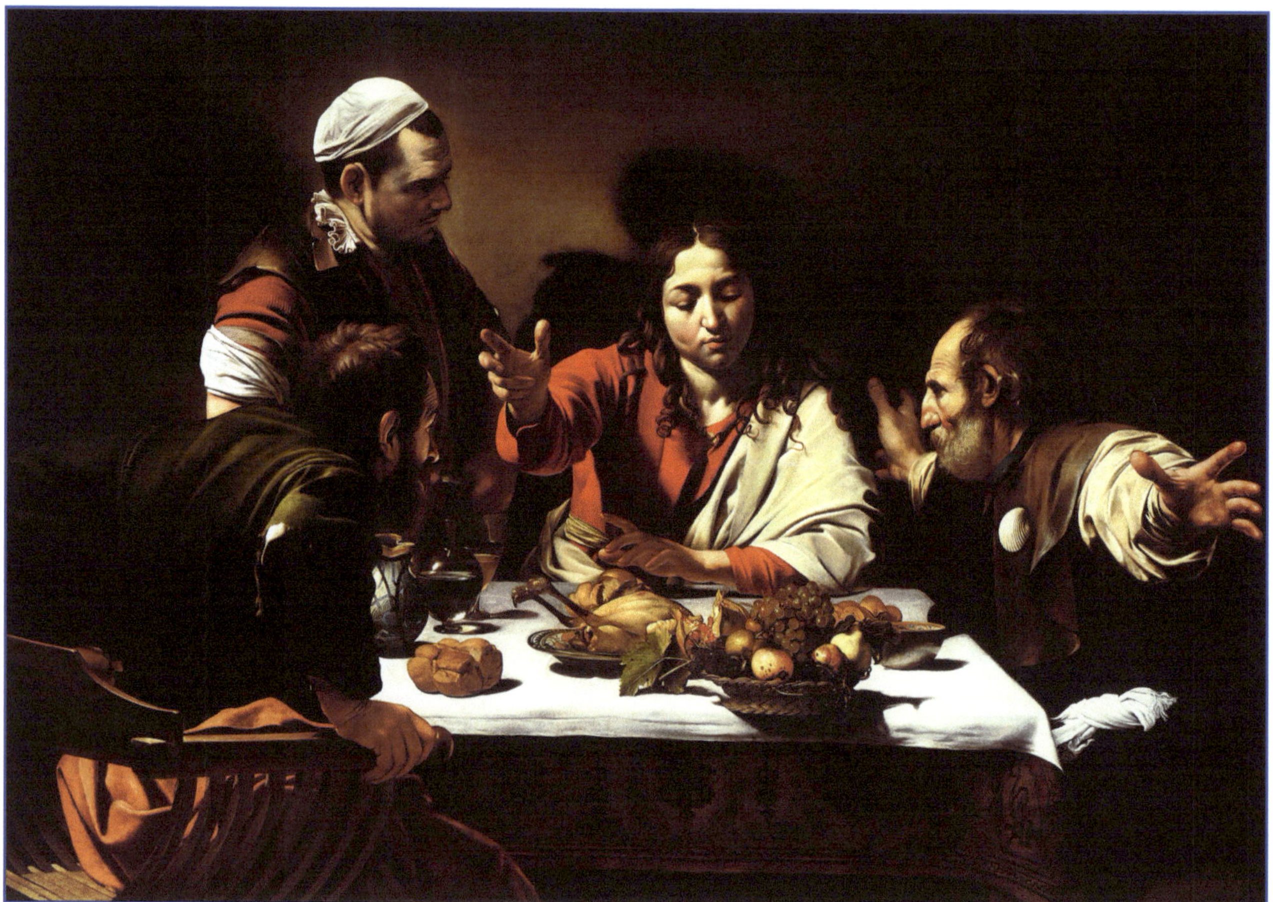

Fig. 93: *Supper at Emmaus,* 1601, Caravaggio, oil on canvas

His right hand, far back in the scene, appears unnaturally oversized, and in fact is painted larger than Christ's right hand which is much nearer to the observer.

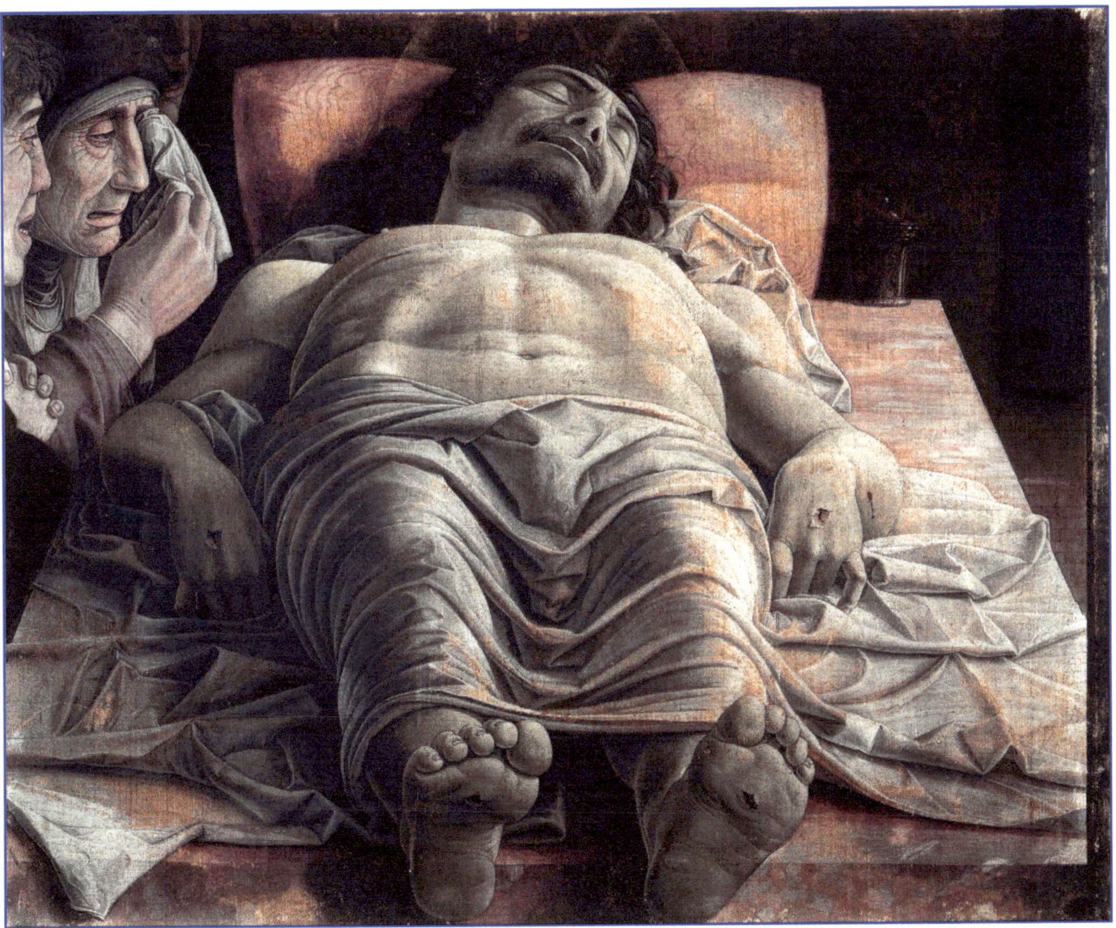

Fig. 94: *Lamentation of Christ,* c.1480, Andrea Mantegna, tempera on canvas

The above is an early example of an artist employing foreshortening to great effect: Mantegna's poignant *Lamentation of Christ*. Our eyes are drawn ineluctably upwards from the feet to Christ's head. But after a few moments of study we realize that the proportions seem a little odd. For example, from such a viewpoint, in reality the feet would appear much larger and the head smaller.

Salvador Dalí's *Christ of Saint John of the Cross*, opposite, is an excellent example of foreshortening. Look at the minimal distance between the head and feet of Christ.

Since it is extremely difficult to paint a suspended body in correct perspective without some form of aid, Dalí actually resorted to having a real person – a Hollywood stuntman – physically suspended from an overhead gantry. Dalí could then sketch the body from the desired angle, including the effect on gravity.

From a perspective viewpoint, we seem to be looking down from on high, onto the cross and the body of Christ. At the same time, we might seem to be looking at the cross from below, which appears sharply inclined away into the distance, while floating above us.

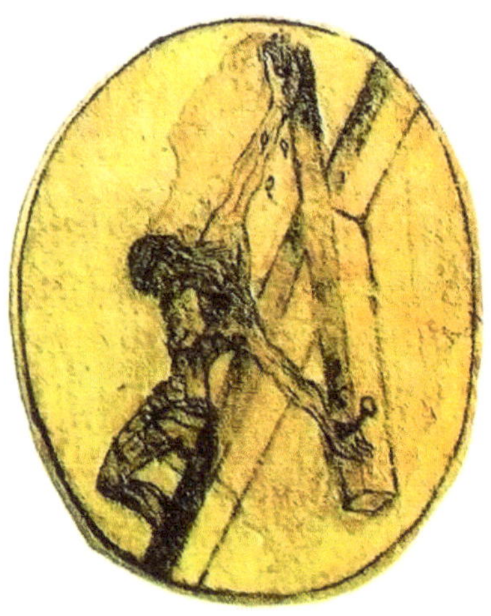

Fig. 95: *Drawing of the crucifixion,* John of the Cross, c.1550

Dalí was inspired by this drawing of the crucifixion. Created around 1550 by the 16th-century Spanish friar, John of the Cross, it shows Christ on the Cross, viewed from on high. The friar's name then served as the title for Dalí's inspired painting.

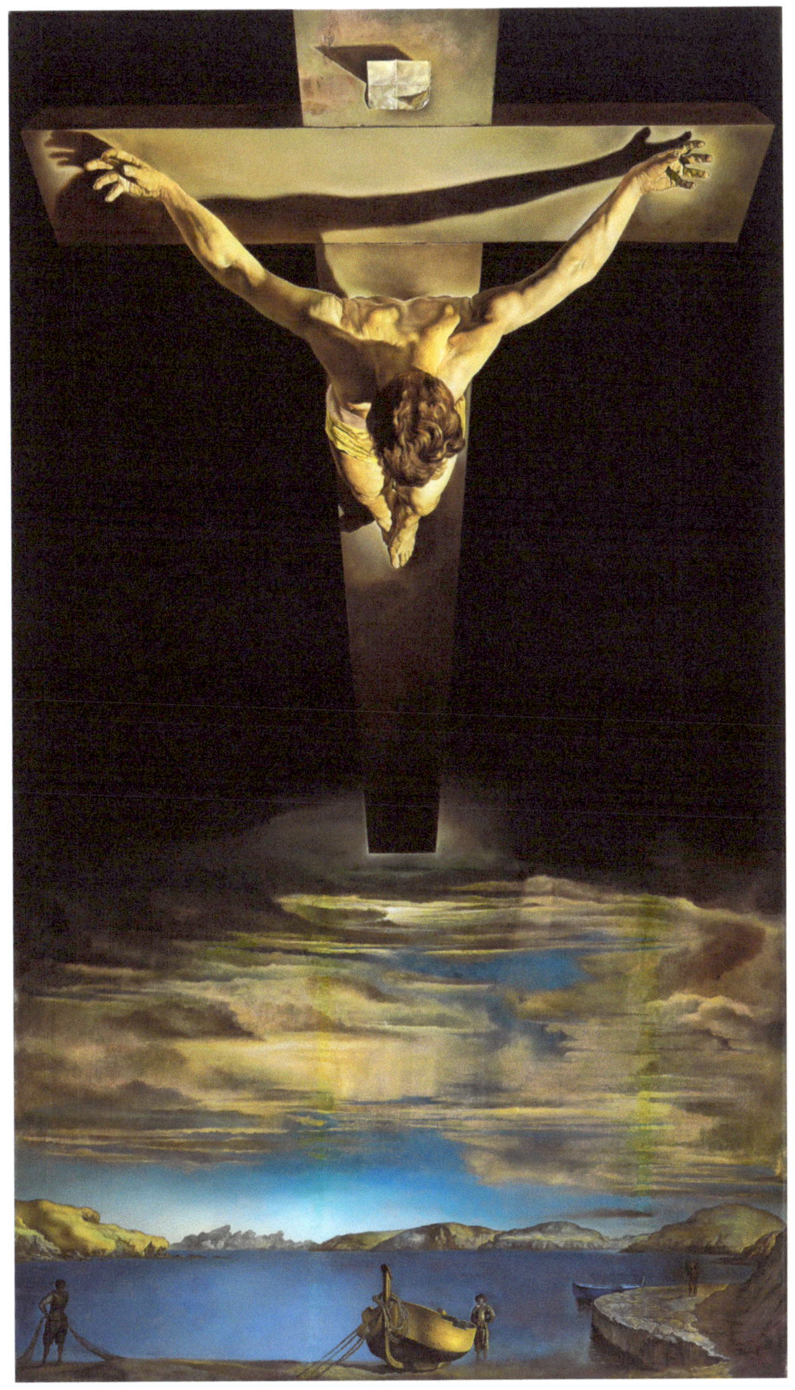

Fig. 96: *Christ of Saint John of the Cross,* Salvador Dalí, 1951

An interesting example of local foreshortening is presented in this painting by Paolo Uccello, entitled *Niccolò Mauruzi da Tolentino,* part of a series describing the *Battle of San Romano* (probably c. 1438–1440).

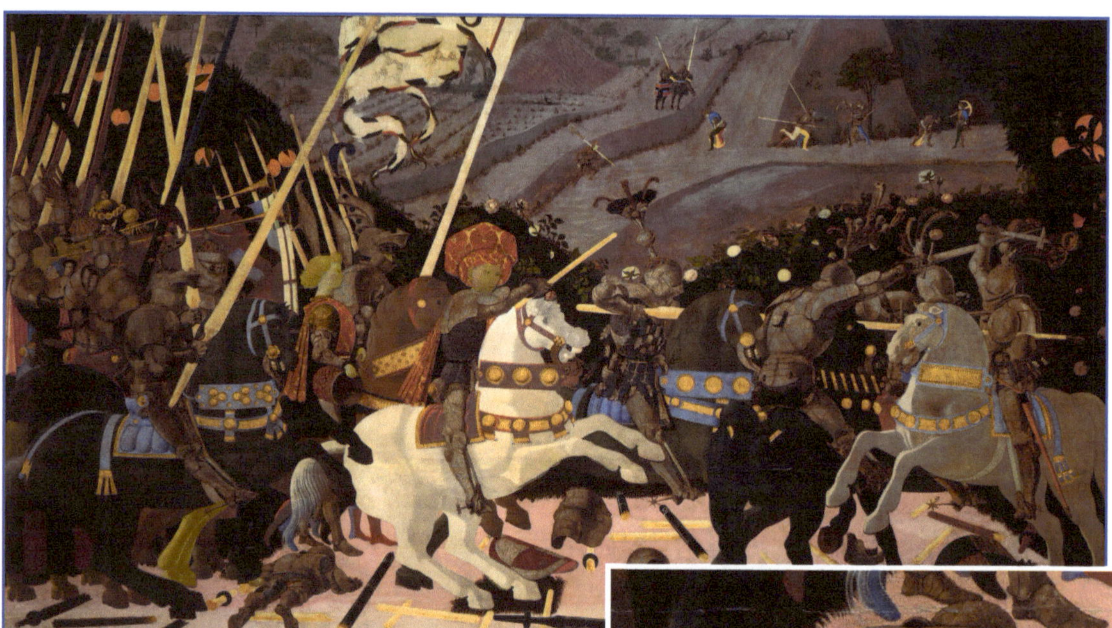

Fig. 97: *Niccolò Mauruzi da Tolentino,* c. 1438–1440, Paolo Uccello (part of the series entitled *Battle of San Romano)*

There is a fallen soldier in the lower left foreground whose form is heavily foreshortened, as can be seen in the enlarged view. However, his size and shape seem at odds with the overall scene.

To finish the topic of foreshortening, here is a good example of a close-up view of the human form in repose. The proportions seem exquisitely judged.

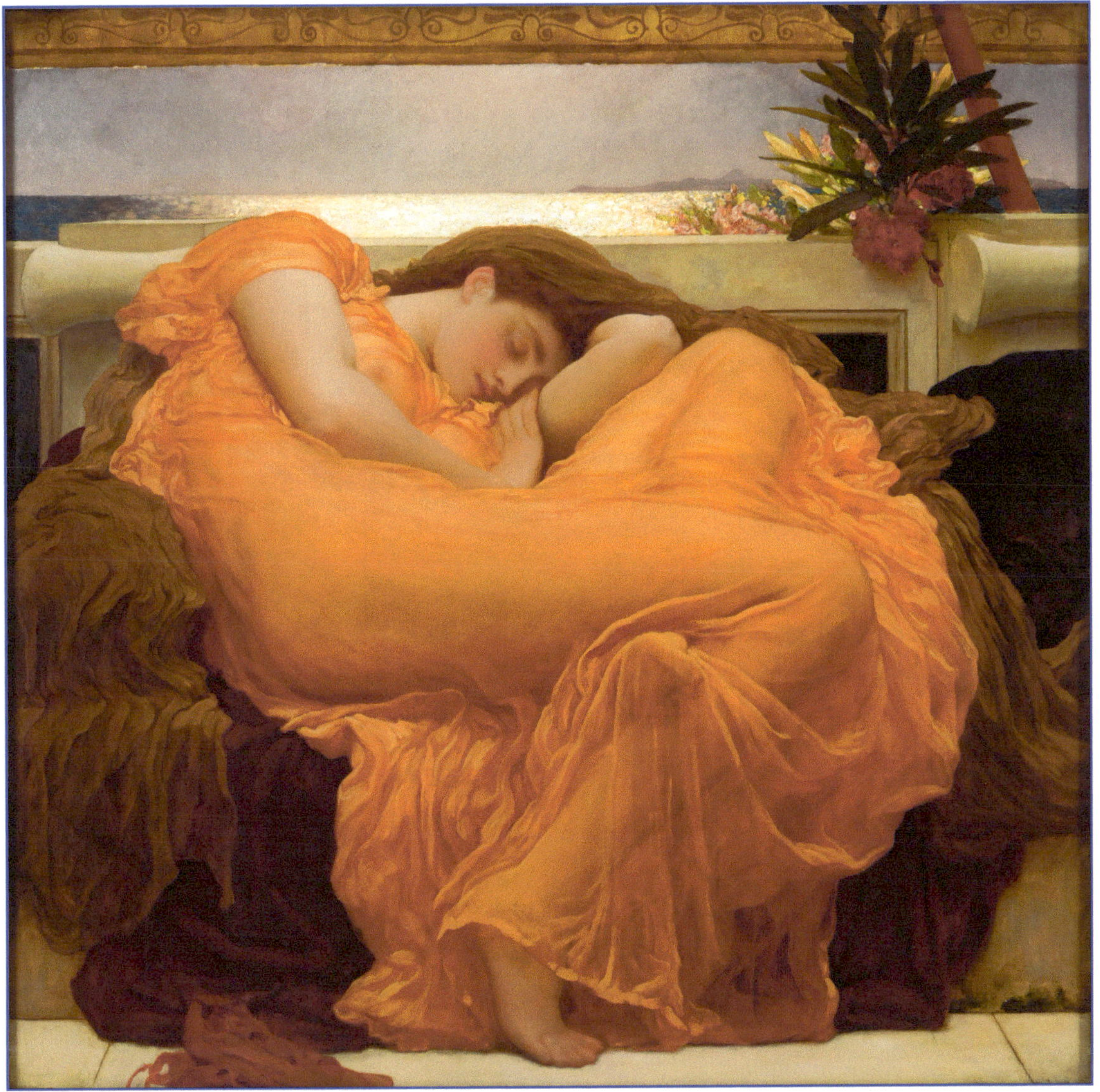

Fig. 98: *Flaming June,* 1895, Sir Frederic Leighton, oil on canvas

Trompe l'Oeil

Typically a *trompe l'oeil* painting will use a combination of the six monocular depth techniques described earlier, along with perspective, to provide an enhanced illusion of depth and reality. Below we have an end view of a real apartment block blending the real with the flat, painted imaginary. Can you tell the difference?

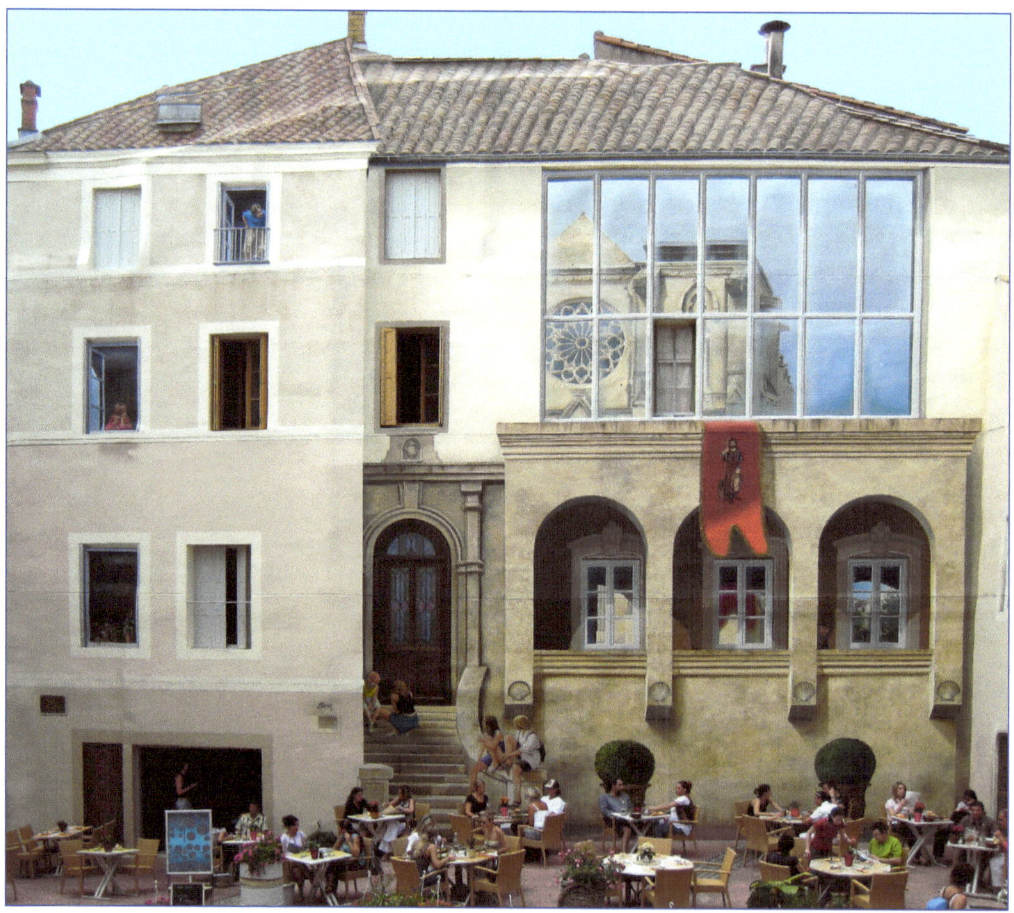

Fig. 99: *Trompe l'oeil mural*, 2007, madart.fr, Montpellier

Forced perspective is similar to *trompe l'oeil* and is a technique often used in stage, cinema and television. A famous early example exists in the Teatro Olimpico in Vicenza, with Vincenzo Scamozzi's seven forced-perspective "streets" (1585), which appear to recede into the distance.

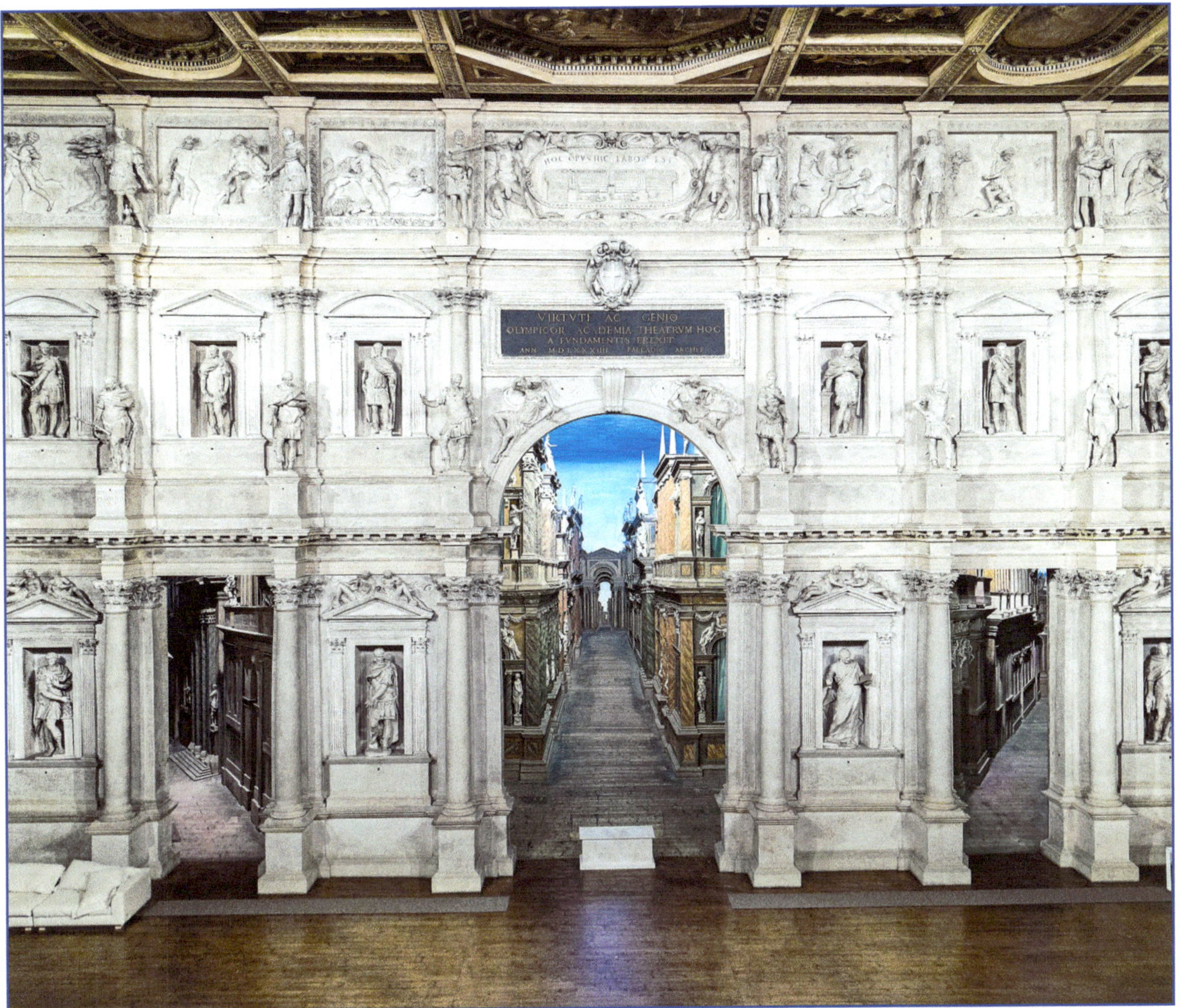

Fig. 100: *Street scene*, 1585, Vincenzo Scamozzi, view of the stage in the Teatro Olimpico, Vicenza

Perspective Tricks

Modern artists such as M C Escher, Viktor Vasarely and Jos De Mey often created art with contradictory clues to depth that lead us to puzzle over what we are really seeing. Such art often works by modifying perspective to create an ambiguous scene. Let's return to the ambiguous picture of the three cars parked along the curb as previously shown in Figure 24.

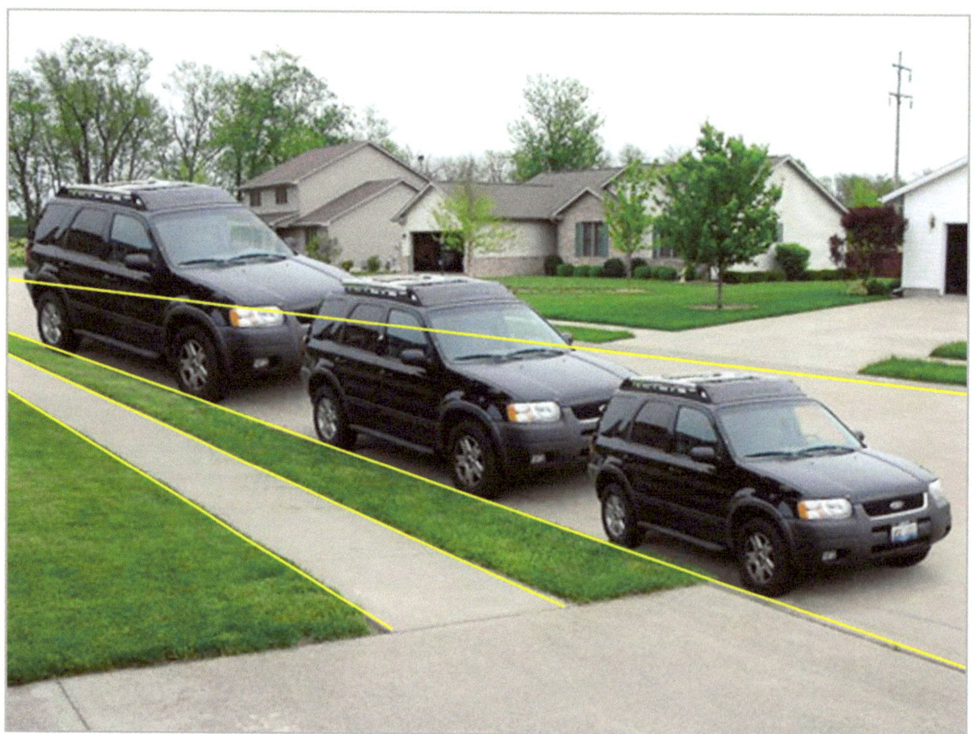

Fig. 101: *Three Car Size Illusion* - with background perspective lines

With our knowledge of linear perspective, we can explain why the cars appear to be getting larger with distance. In the opposite figure we show the perspective lines just from the path and the road. It's clear we have a vanishing point towards the upper left, suggesting we are looking up the road.

Now let's overlay perspective lines for the three cars. The lines are parallel, so no vanishing point! We have a depth clue contradiction. The brain prefers to believe in the perspective clues from the

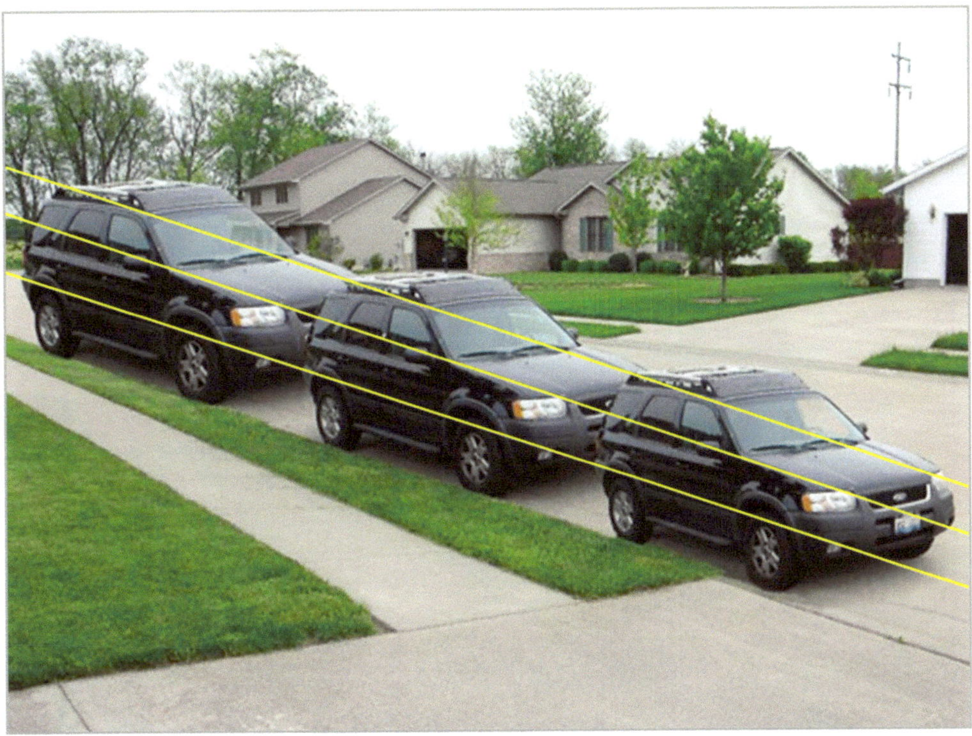

Fig. 102: *Three Car Size Illusion* - with vehicle perspective lines

surroundings, and knows that the three cars should thus become smaller with distance. The only way the brain can resolve the illusion is by forcing the cars to appear larger with distance.

Here's another example of illusory art. Entitled *Two Cubes*, it is a deceptively simple piece created by the author, and inspired by Viktor Vasarely. Do you see a large, solid cube with its front corner hollowed out by a smaller cube? Or a smaller, solid cube sitting inside an open room comprising two walls and a floor? Both versions are valid interpretations. There is a third possible

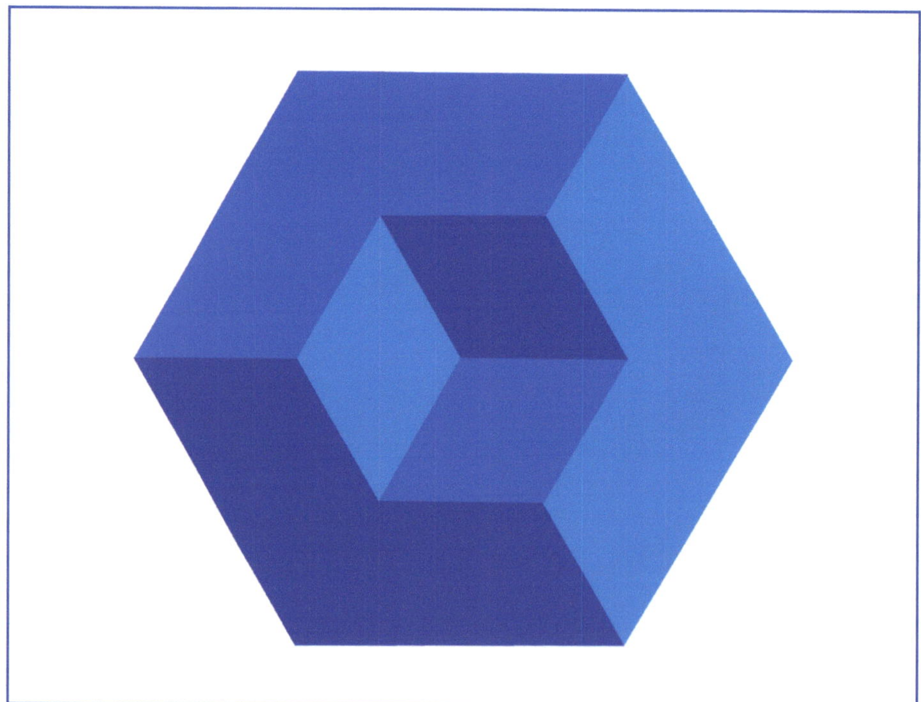

Fig. 103: *Two Cubes*, a deceptively simple piece inspired by Viktor Vasarely

interpretation of the smaller, solid cube situated in front of the large, solid cube but this can be more difficult to visualize.If you can only see one version or the other, simply continue looking at the image and after 15 seconds or so, the brain will automatically switch to the alternative version.

The illusion or ambiguity arises because Vasarely created cubes with no linear perspective. Let's draw some lines in as usual. Just like the three car illusion, we have no vanishing points, only parallel lines, and so the brain cannot decide which face

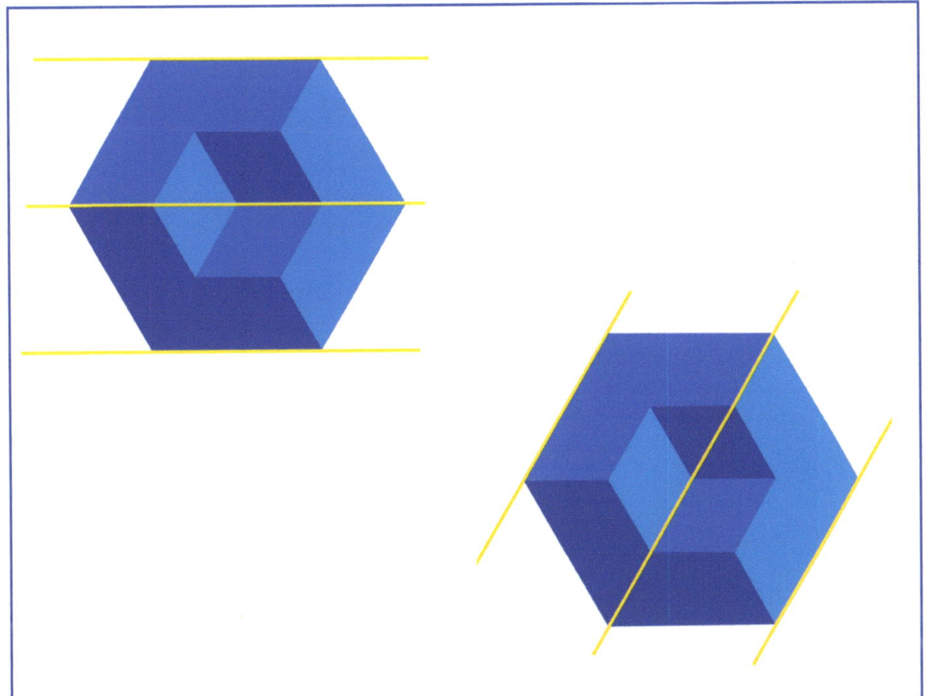

Fig. 104: *Two Cubes,* with perspective lines added

of each cube is to the front, and which face is to the back. The solution for the brain, therefore, is to decide on one interpretation then offer up an alternative. Of course, the various shades of blue on the cube's faces have been carefully chosen to enhance the contrast between the faces of the large and small cubes. The cubes are in fact classic isometric drawings, with all sides the same length, forming a perfect hexagon outline. See the appendix on isometric drawing for a more detailed explanation of this drawing technique.

Let's finish this section with an engraving by William Hogarth, produced in 1754, and entitled *Satire on False Perspective.* He created it on request from his good friend Joshua Kirby, who was producing a pamphlet on linear perspective. The engraving forms the frontispiece to this work. The scene contains multiple examples of depth clues that are ambiguous or contradictory. How many can you identify? [See the appendix for a list of the top ten!]

As an amusing aside, the intent of the work is evident from the subtitle at the base of the engraving:

Whoever makes a DESIGN, *without the Knowledge of* PERSPECTIVE, *will be liable to such Absurdities as are shewn in this* Frontispiece.

Since this may be difficult to read, the text is reproduced below:

Whoever makes a **DESIGN** *without the Knowledge of* **PERSPECTIVE** *will be liable to such Absurdities as are shewn in this Frontispiece*

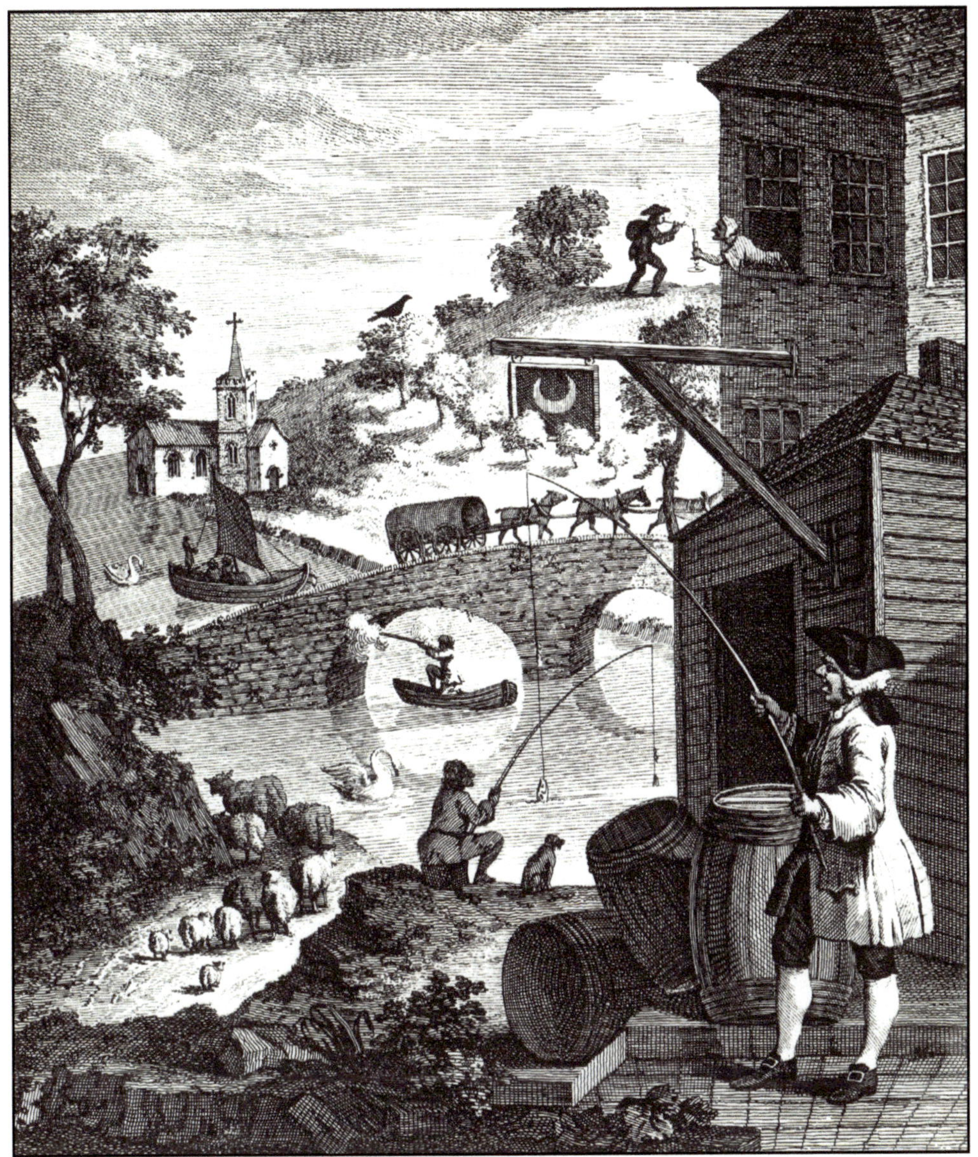

Fig. 105: *Satire on False Perspective*, William Hogarth 1754

Reverse Perspective

Reverse perspective, also known as inverse or inverted perspective, is a type of perspective drawing where the lines of perspective of a scene appear to point outwards rather than inwards, as in regular, linear perspective.

In other words, in inverse perspective, parallel lines that recede into the distance appear to diverge away from the viewer, rather than converge towards a vanishing point. This creates a distorted effect where objects at the center of the image appear to be farther away than those at the edges. The vanishing point or points appear to be in front of the painting, towards the observer.

Early, especially Russian, icons seem to exhibit some aspects of reverse perspective. An example of an icon often considered to be in reverse perspective is this 13th century painting of the *Madonna and Child Enthroned*.

Clearly the chair and stool seem distorted to our modern eye since they are not a faithful reproduction of what we would see in reality.

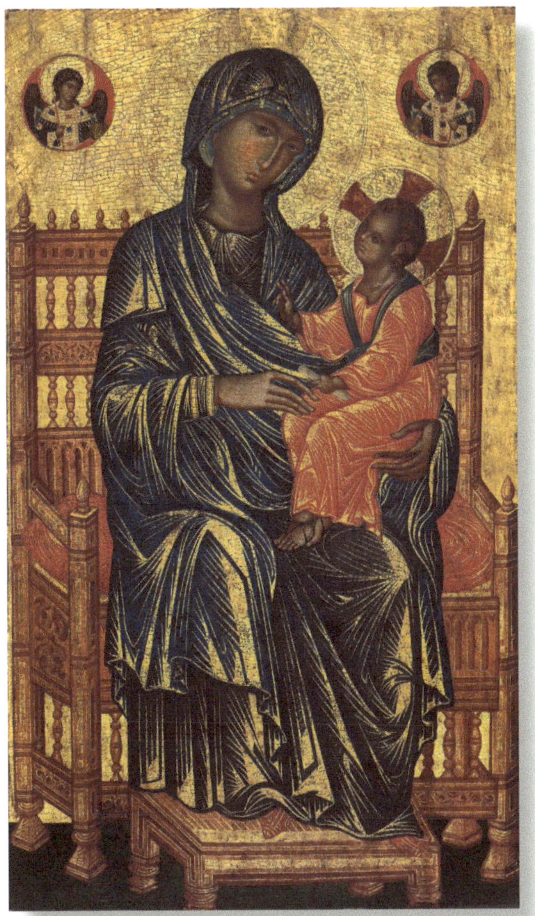

Fig. 106: *Madonna and Child Enthroned,* Byzantine 13th Century, tempera on poplar wood

The chair does appear wider at the back than the front, as does the stool, so implying reverse perspective. The story becomes a little more nuanced when we attempt to draw in lines of perspective.

We can see in Figure 107 (a), over, that lower elements of the left side of the chair (as viewed) show no perspective. In fact, the chair's left side seems to become distorted as we look from bottom to top. Similarly, taken on its own, the right side of the chair seems to offer no perspective either, as in (b).

However, overlaying lines from both sides of the chair, includng the feet, as in (c), reveals quite a strong reverse perspective, even if there is not one clear single vanishing point.

The stool (d) also shows a clear reverse perspective, but with a vanishing point a little closer in and to the left, compared with the chair vanishing points. As an aside, the back right foot of the stool seems completely misplaced!

Overall there appears to be a strong, overall sense of reverse perspective for the chair and stool while the Madonna and child seem to be painted in more conventional style of the period. It is not known of course whether the artist knowingly painted the throne and footstool in this mixed manner. Since the concepts of linear perspective had not been codified at this time, it would seem more likely that this was an attempt at a particular style.

See the appendix on this topic for a more detailed explanation and sketches illustrating a chair in linear and then reverse perspective that can be compared with the chair in this icon.

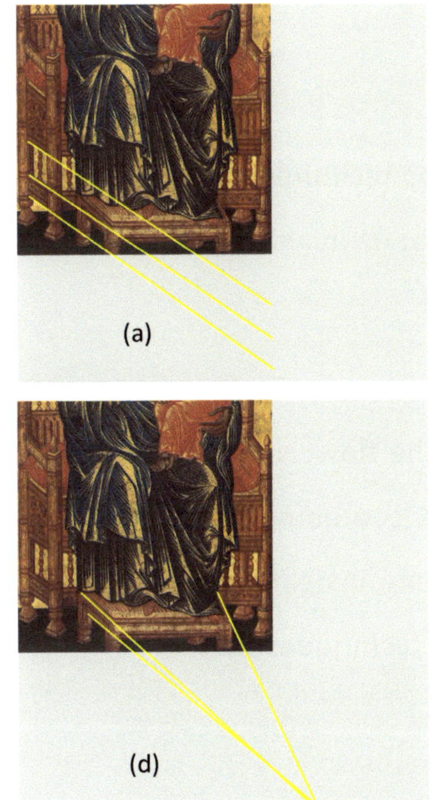
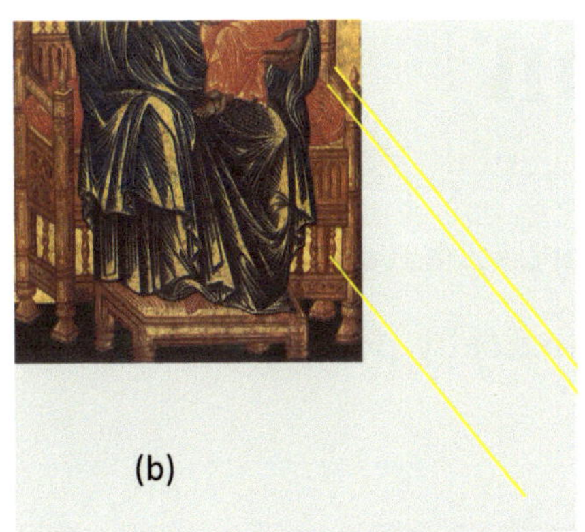
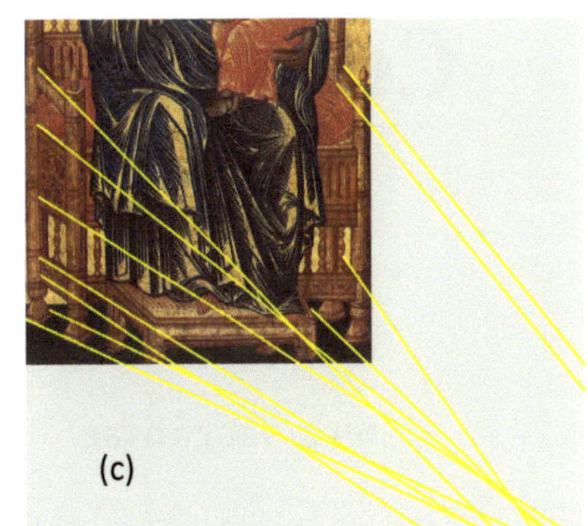

Fig. 107: *Madonna and Child Enthroned* with key perspective lines added

Reverse perspective may be deliberately used in art to create a sense of depth and space that is different from what we see in the real world, to create a disorienting or surreal effect.

Some modern artists such as David Hockney have experimented with reverse perspective, sometimes combining linear and reverse perspective in the same scene.

Note that recently the term reverse perspective has also been applied to a form of illusory *solid* art. Since this technique is not created on a flat, two-dimensional surface it falls outside the scope of this book.

Conclusion

Over the centuries, artists have struggled to develop techniques to ensure a way to realistically portray our world, real or imaginary, on a flat canvas.

As we progressed from prehistoric art, through the flowering in representational art during the Renaissance, to contemporary hyper-realism, I hope this book has given you some insight into the historical developments that occurred, and the techniques that eventually aided artists in their quest.

In summary, next time you're standing in front of a painting, ask yourself these questions:

Do I feel drawn into the scene?

Where are my eyes being directed?

Where is the horizon line?

What depth clues and techniques did the artist use?

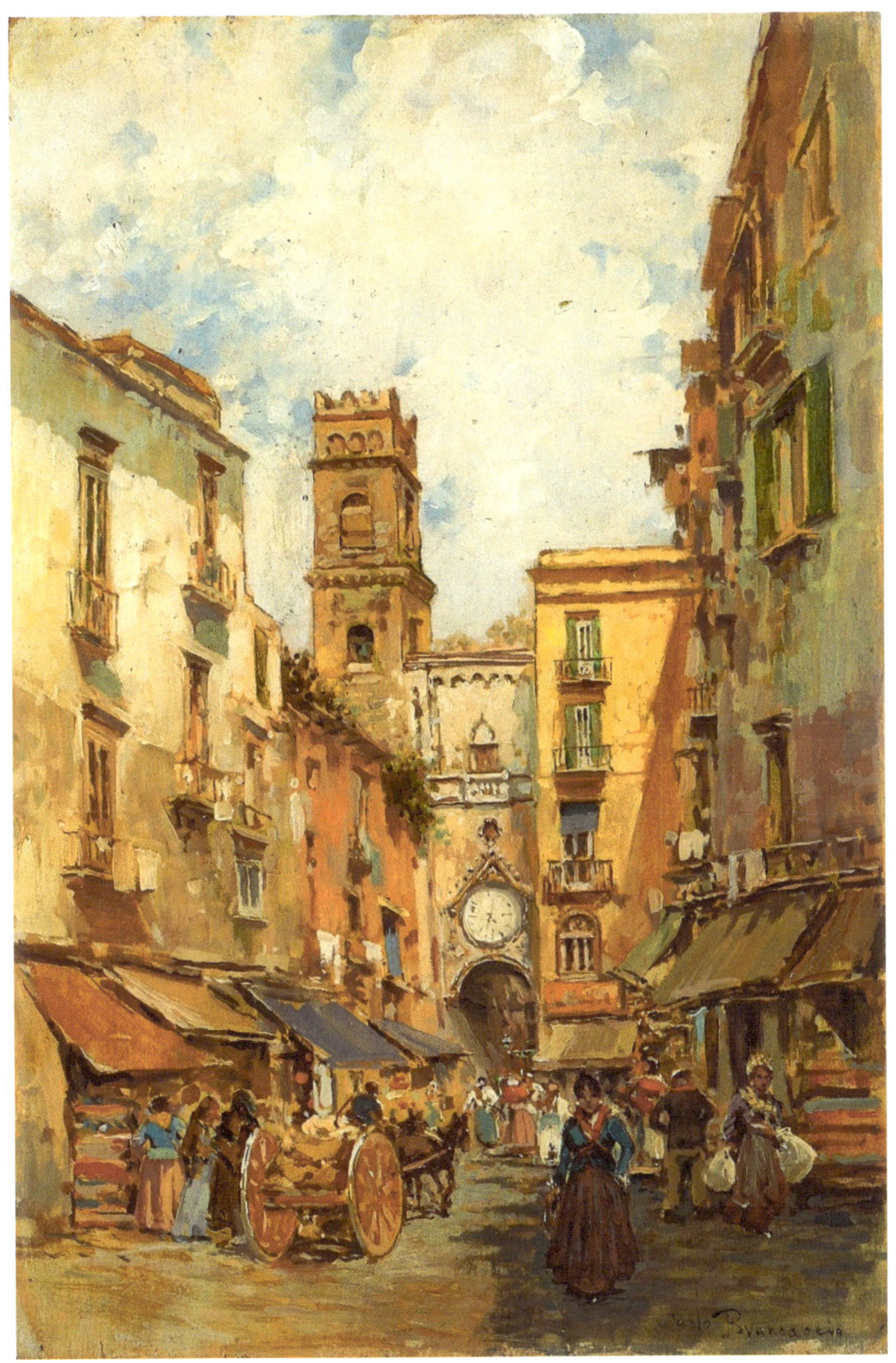

Fig. 108: *Street view in Naples*, Carlo Brancaccio

Appendices

Hogarth's Satire on Perspective

The following abbreviated list of deliberate depth errors in Hogarth's *Satire on False Perspective* is extracted from an article in Wikipedia:

1. The line of the fishing rod belonging to the man in the foreground passes behind that of the man behind him.
2. The sign is moored to two buildings, one in front of the other, with beams that show no difference in depth
3. The sign is overlapped by two distant trees.
4. The man climbing the hill is lighting his pipe with the candle of the woman leaning out of the upper story window.
5. The crow is massive in comparison to the tree on which it is perched.
6. The church appears to front onto the river. Both ends of the church are viewable at the same time.
7. The left horizon on the water declines precipitously.

8. The man in the boat under the bridge fires at the swan on the other side, which is impossible as he's aiming straight at the bridge abutments.

9. The right-hand end of the arch above the boat meets the water further from the viewer than does the left-hand end.

10. The two-story building, though viewed from below, shows the top of the roof. As does the church tower in the distance.

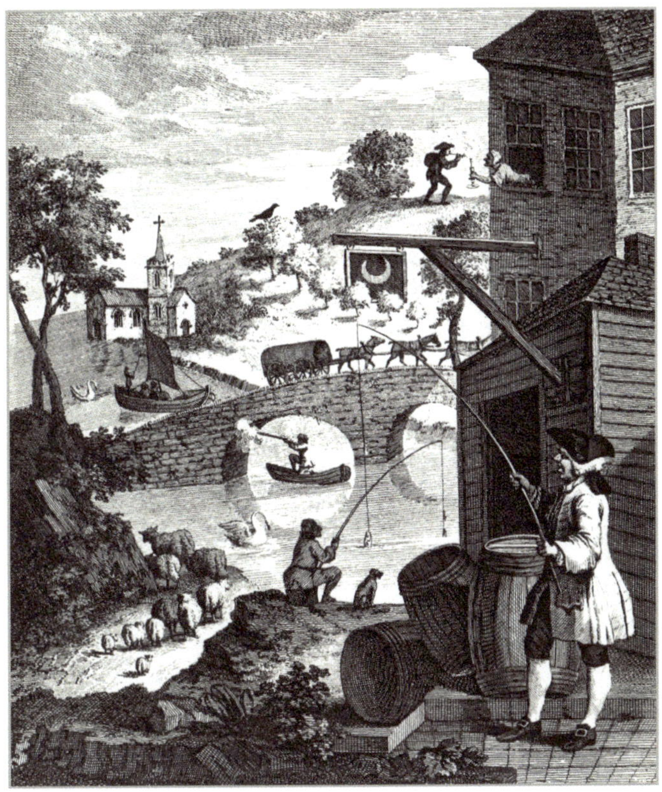

https://en.wikipedia.org/wiki/Satire_on_False_Perspective

Basics of Linear Perspective

Linear perspective uses a geometric system comprising a horizontal line (the horizon or eye level view), one or more vanishing points, and lines that converge toward those vanishing points. The artist places elements on the canvas, appropriately scaled by these so-called orthogonal lines.

In one-point perspective, elements recede into the distance in one direction, to one spot, one single point. The railroad track shown earlier narrows and then disappears to a single point at eye level in the distance. The viewer is essentially regarding the scene face-on.

If we were viewing a simple cube face-on, our eye level centered on that face, we would see only that face and nothing else. We would not, in fact, know it was a cube, it could simply be a flat panel.

Now imagine we view a cube face-on, but from slightly above.

Here is a simplified description of how an artist might construct such a view in one-point perspective:

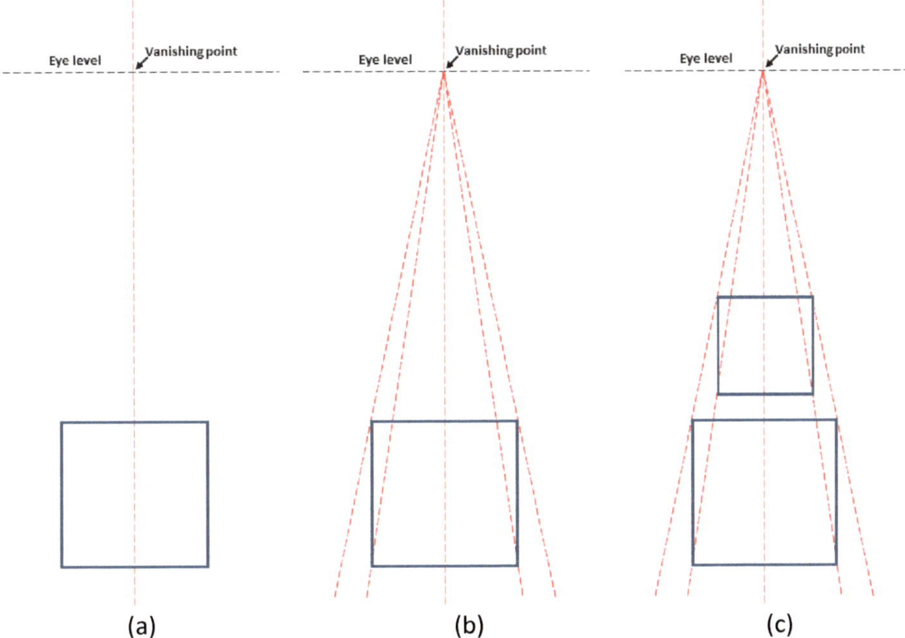

Fig. 109: One point perspective creation of a simple cube viewed from slightly above

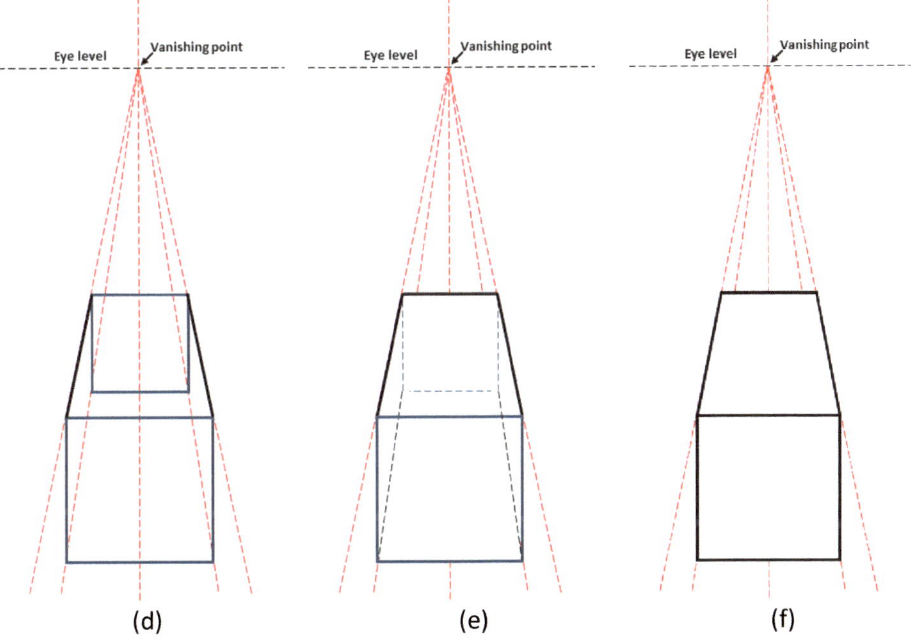

a. Create a one-point perspective framework of horizon line and vanishing point, then place a simple rectangle in the desired location

b. Draw an orthogonal line from each corner of the rectangle to the vanishing point

c. Add a second, smaller rectangle further up to represent the desired cube depth, its corners touching the four orthogonal, dashed lines

d. Join the top corners of each rectangle to create the top surface of the cube

e. Convert interior lines of the cube to dashed lines to create a transparent cube

alternatively

f. Fill the front and top faces to create a solid cube.

The intent of the above explanation is to help the reader generally appreciate the steps involved. In reality, we may wish to draw many different shapes in the scene, shapes that may not be well-structured, and continuous forms such as the human body. The interested reader is referred to selected texts [7,8].

Below is a practical example of a one-point perspective, geometric framework and the construction of key elements in the scene. This is typical of a how a computer game might rapidly generate a scene for a Formula 1 race circuit.

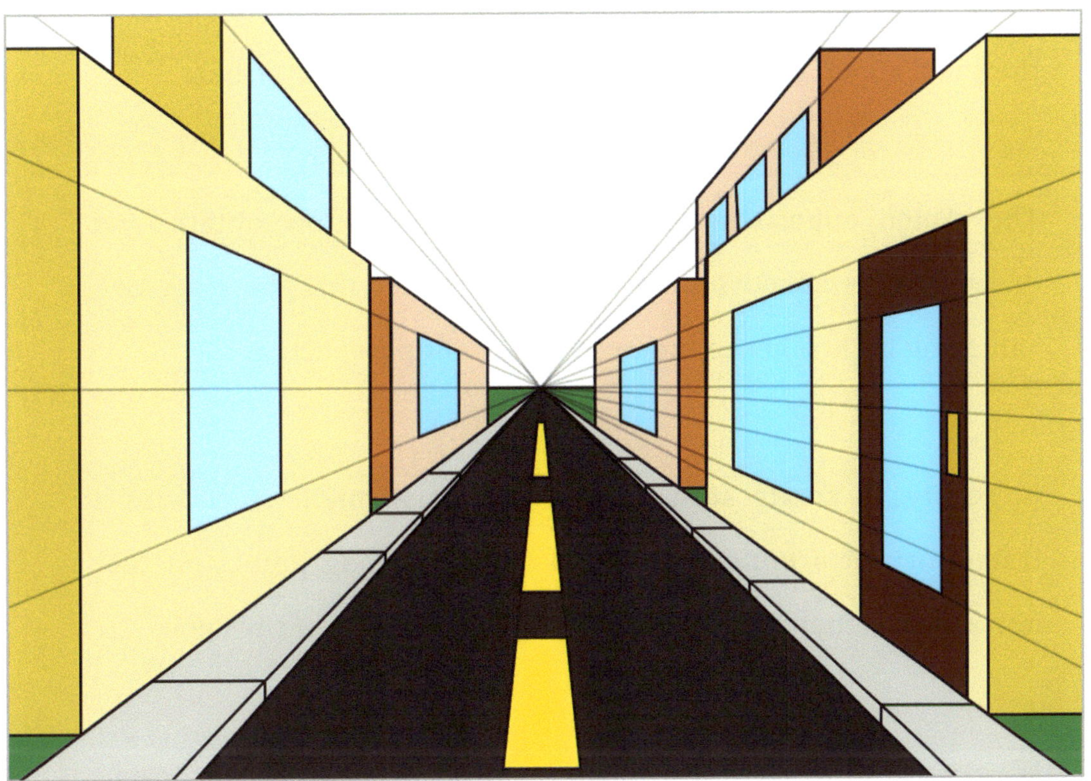

Fig. 110: *Demonstration of 1-point perspective drawing,* © 2008 Braindrain0000

One, Two and Three-point Perspective

One, two and three-point perspectives are mathematically identical. The difference is simply in the orientation of the scene relative to the "window" through which the viewer observes the scene.

Consider, for example, our basic cube viewed from slightly above in one-point perspective, as before, but now viewed from one vertical edge, rather than directly viewing one face. We have simply rotated the cube so that one vertical edge is visible in the forefront.

The sketch opposite illustrates the view we now obtain, and drawing in perspective lines enables us to see that there are two vanishing points, hence the term two-point perspective.

In reality, to create such a view, the artist might start with a framework of a horizon line and two vanishing points on that horizon line, then place just the front vertical line of the cube.

We can draw lines from the top and bottom of this front vertical to each vanishing point in turn.

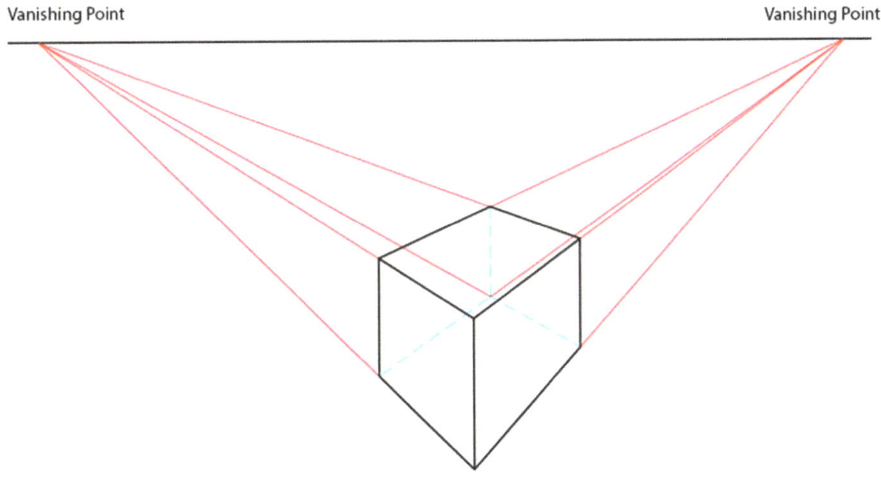

Fig. 111: Wire frame cube showing two-point perspective

Next we can create a vertical on one side of the front vertical, whose top and bottom touch the perspective lines on that side. This represents the back vertical of one visible side, and we can now draw in the top and bottom lines of that side. Finally, we draw perspective lines from this side upright to the opposite vanishing point, then repeat for the opposite side.

To better illustrate the approach, we have rotated the cube a little more than 45 degrees so that the back upright is slightly offset from the front upright being viewed, so one can see the set of perspective lines and how they touch the various corners of the cube.

And finally an illustration of three-point perspective. We now view our two-point perspective cube tilted from one corner, so that some uprights of the cube are no longer vertical.

The cube exhibits three vanishing points, two of which typically appear on the same horizon line. In three-point perspective, we are often looking from an odd angle or rather extreme viewpoint.

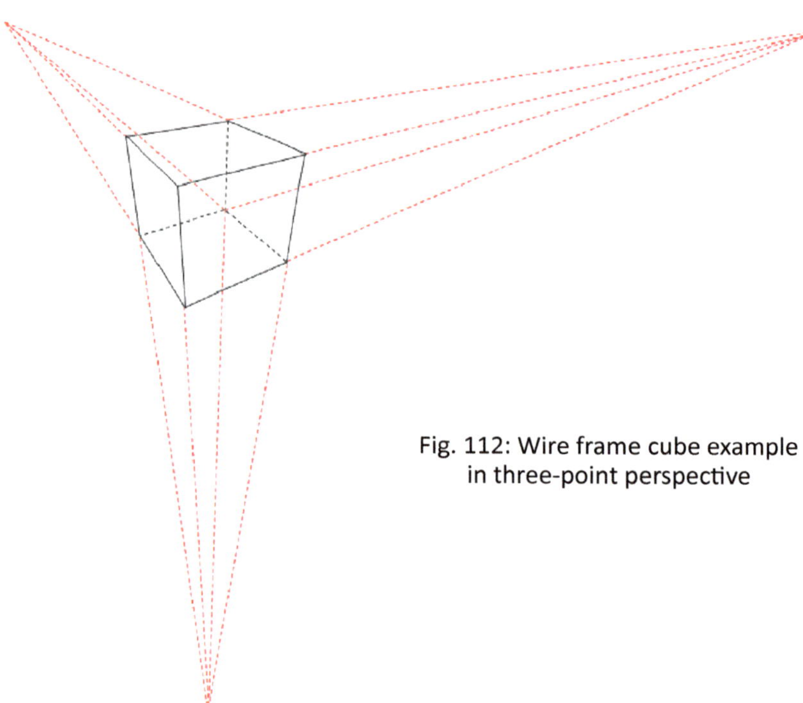

Fig. 112: Wire frame cube example in three-point perspective

In summary, we can compare the view and consequent shape of our basic cube in one, two and three-point perspective as illustrated opposite.

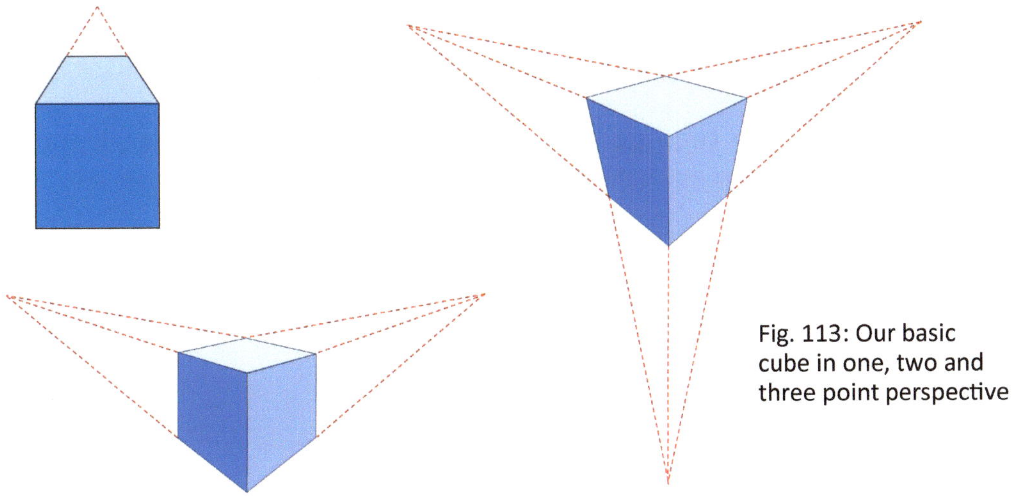

Fig. 113: Our basic cube in one, two and three point perspective

Parallel and Isometric Projections

Parallel projection (axonometric) is a graphical projection from our three dimensionsal world to a flat, two dimensional canvas, where opposing sides of an object remain parallel. No change in size occurs with distance, and therefore no vanishing point exists.

Let's take as an example the Necker cube. It is a basic wire-frame, two-dimensional drawing of a cube with no depth perspective, first described as a rhomboid in 1832 by Swiss crystallographer Louis Albert Necker. The back face is drawn the same size as the front face so the cube becomes an optical illusion where it is not clear which face is the front and which the back. See Figure 114, next. If you don't experience the illusion immediately, look at the two versions with a shaded face which illustrate which can be seen as the front face, then go back and observe the basic wire-frame version.

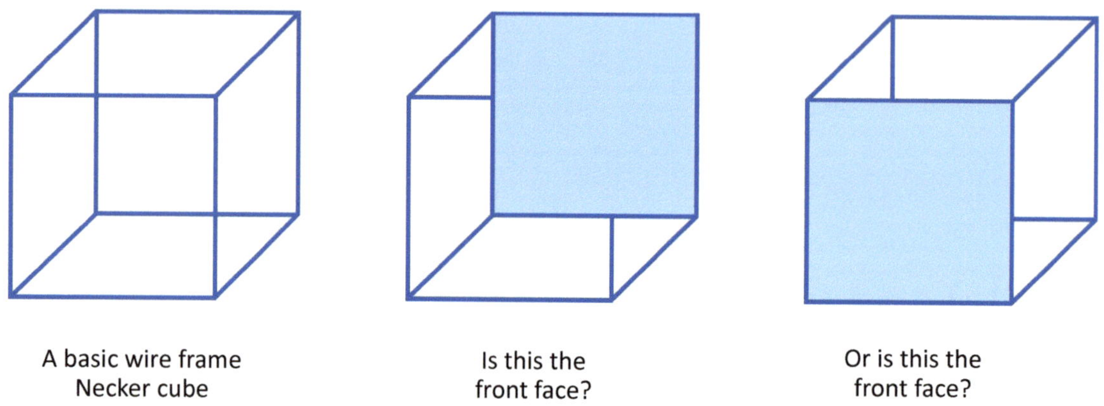

Fig. 114: A basic wire frame Necker cube showing ambiguous perspective

Isometric drawing is a specific type of axonometric projection where the direction of viewing is such that all three axes of space appear equally foreshortened, with a common angle of 120° between them.

In Figure 115 opposite, I have created a basic isometric cube using readily available isometric grid paper.

Since there is no perspective cue, the cube can be seen as a solid block with corner A coming towards you, or as an open room with three sides, with corner A farthest away.

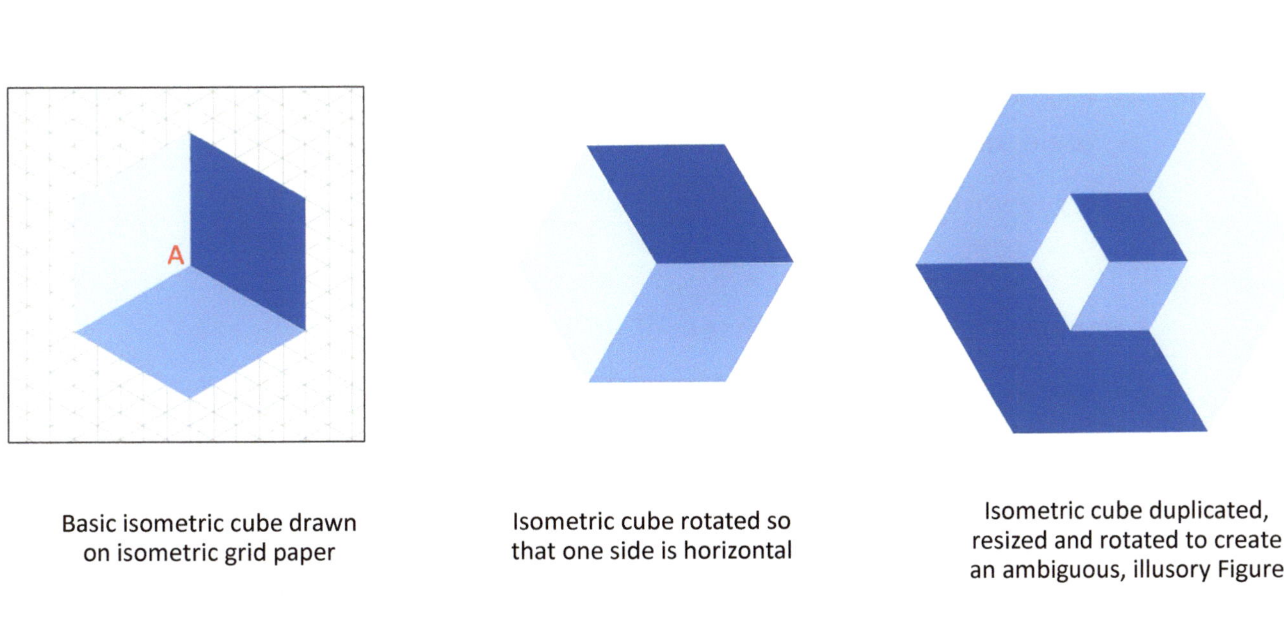

Basic isometric cube drawn on isometric grid paper

Isometric cube rotated so that one side is horizontal

Isometric cube duplicated, resized and rotated to create an ambiguous, illusory Figure

Fig. 115: A basic isometric cube and creation of an illusory figure

I have then simply rotated the cube so that one side is horizontal. Next, I have duplicated this cube, resized, rotated and overlaid the pair to create another optical illusion, inspired by the work of Vasarely. There are at least two interpretations of this combined drawing: a large cube with the near corner eaten away by the small cube, or a solid small cube inside three sides of a room.

Reverse Perspective

Essentially, in reverse perspective, elements farther away are drawn larger while elements nearby are drawn smaller, resulting in a vanishing point towards the observer and not more distant as would appear in a linear perspective construct, or in reality as observed with a camera or the eye.

Compare the change in shape of this simple chair in linear perspective, with that drawn in reverse perspective opposite.

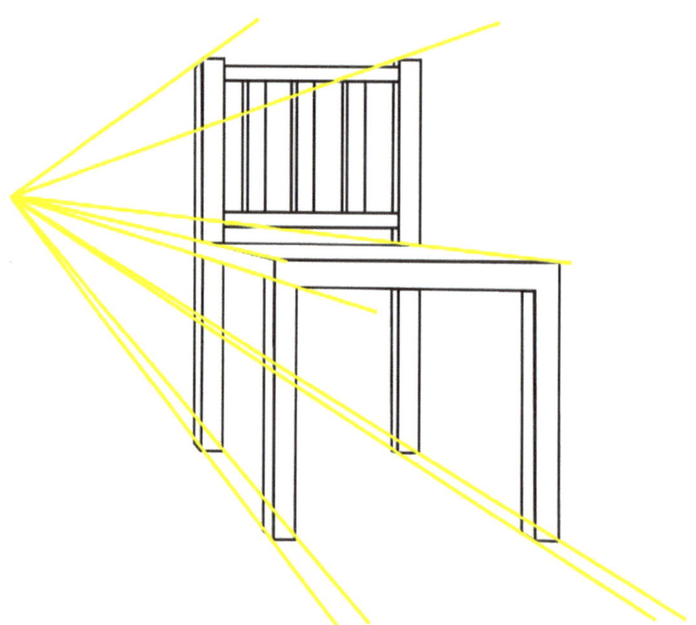

Fig. 116: Close-up view of a chair drawn in single-point linear perspective

Clearly, the chair in reverse perspective looks odd to our eyes, but as we said earlier, reverse perspective may be deliberately used to create a disorienting sense of space.

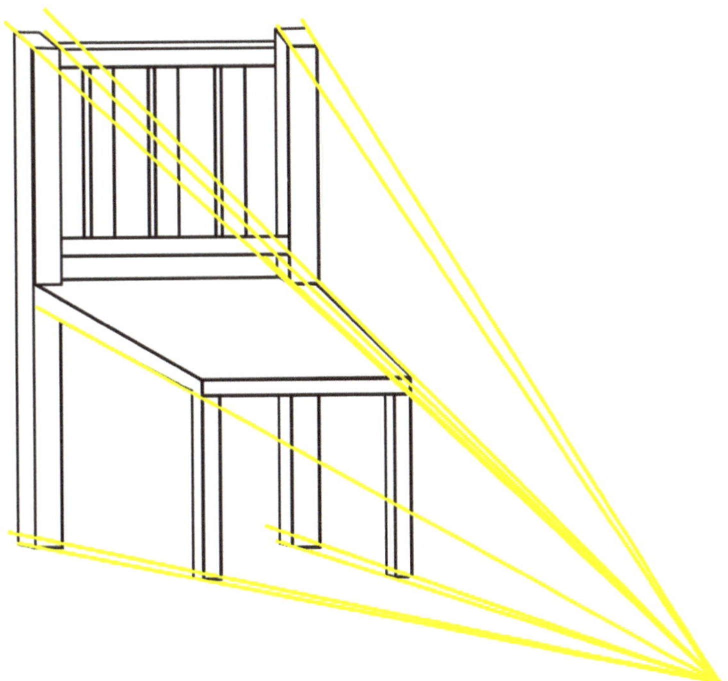

Fig. 117: Close-up view of a chair drawn in reverse perspective

Now compare and contrast the above sketch of a basic chair in reverse perspective with the 13th century icon of the *Madonna and Child Enthroned* (see Figure 106), often cited as an example of reverse perspective.

VISAGE PUBLICATIONS

Figures and Credits

Figures and credits are listed below, and are all copyright the author, unless otherwise indicated. Where required, every effort has been made to obtain copyright release but if any inaccuracy or omission is found, please contact the publisher for correction.

Cover art: The Arnolfini Portrait, Jan van Eyck, 1434 ⊜ ; Inset page 4: Holy Trinity, scheme of linear perspective, Masaccio c.1426-1428 ⊜ ; Fig. 1: Lions painted in the Chauvet Cave: a replica of the painting from the Brno museum Anthropos ⊜ ; Fig. 2: Fresco on the Villa of P. Fannius Synistor in Boscoreale 43-30 BCE showing primitive use of vanishing points ⊜ ; Fig. 3: Detail from another fresco on the Villa of P. Fannius Synistor in Boscoreale, 43-30 BCE ⊜ ; Fig. 4: Christ and Abbot Mena, 6-7-8th century, Fig tree wood panel ⊜ ; Fig. 5: Mary Magdalen announcing the resurrection to the apostles, 1120, St. Albans Psalter, St Godehard's Church, Hildesheim ⊜ ; Fig. 6: Meister des Codex Manesse, Manessische Liederhandschrift c.1305–1340 (water colors, parchment, Heidelberg Universitätsbibliothek) ⊜ ; Fig. 7: Paradiesgärtlein, Upper Rhenish Master c.1410-1420 (Egg tempera, oak, oil paint, Städel Museum, Frankfurt) ⊜ ; Fig. 8: Detail from Meister des Codex Manesse and Paradiesgärtlein, showing a view from on high ⊜ ; Fig.9: The Round Table © 1929 Georges Braque (oil, canvas, Philips Collection, Washington, DC, US, fair use) ; Fig. 10: The Delivery of the Keys, c. 1481–1482, Fresco, Perugino, Sistine Chapel, Vatican City ⊜ ; Fig. 11: The Marriage of Virgin Mary, Raphael, 1504, oil on roundheaded panel ⊜ ; Fig. 12: Children's Games, Pieter Bruegel the Elder, 1560, oil on panel ⊜ ; Fig. 13: The Piazzetta, Canaletto c.1734 (oil on canvas, Galleria Nazionale d'Arte Antica) ⊜ ; Fig. 14: Interior of Saint Peter's Rome, Giovanni Paolo Panini after 1754, oil on canvas (CC0) ; Fig. 15: Lavaburst, © 2008 Edgar Mueller, chalk on pavement ; Fig. 16: Lunch Specials, © 2001 Richard Estes (oil on canvas) ; Fig. 17: Just a drawn picture or a real scene? © Funatico.com, 2008 ; Fig. 18: Artist at work on Lavaburst, © 2008 Edgar Mueller ; Fig. 19: Example of partial overlap ; Fig. 20: Detail from the Chauvet cave art replica Brno museum Anthropos ⊜ ; Fig. 21: A Mediterranean scene ; Fig. 22: Brown birds flying in the sky, Pikrepo ; Fig. 23: Easter Island, © 2004 Phil Whitehouse ; Fig. 24: Three Cars Size Illusion - all the vehicles are the same size, © 2009, earthguide.blogspot.com ; Fig. 25: Modified Rano Raraku hillside, © 2002 Robert Nyman ; Fig. 26: Rano Raraku hillside (original, with man added), © 2002 Robert Nyman ; Fig. 27: Detail from a Mediterranean scene ; Fig. 28: Aerial perspective example, Provence, France ; Fig. 29: Depth from light and shadow on a ball ; Fig. 30: Field of cereal crop showing the reduction in texture with distance ; Fig. 31: Detail from Vase in perspective, Paolo Uccello, Pen on paper, 15th century ⊜ ; Fig. 32: Cover from Secret Knowledge, © 2001 David Hockney ; Fig. 33: Underweysung der Messung, Albrecht Dürer, 1525 ⊜ ; Fig. 34: The Ambassadors, 1533, Hans Holbein the Younger, oil on oak ⊜ ; Fig. 35: Der Zeichner des liegenden Weibes, Albrecht Dürer 1510-1525 ⊜ ; Fig. 36: An Artist Drawing a Seated Man, Albrecht Dürer, 1510-1525 ⊜ ; Fig. 37: First published picture of camera obscura in Gemma Frisius' 1545 book De Radio Astronomica et Geometrica ⊜ ; Fig. 38: Camera Obscura box, c.1850, 19th Century Dictionary Illustration ⊜ ; Fig. 39: Camera Obscura Tent, Edmund Atkinson, 1875 ⊜ ; Fig. 40: Camera Obscura, Edinburgh, Scotland, © Camera Obscura & World of Illusions, Edinburgh ; Fig. 41: Illustration of a full-size camera obscura with a panoramic rotating mirror, adapted from A. Rees, Cyclopoedia Universal Dictionary of Arts and Sciences 1778, © National Maritime Museum, Greenwich ; Fig. 42: A splendid view from inside, © Camera Obscura & World of Illusions, Edinburgh ; Fig. 43: Image capture in a camera ; Fig. 44: Image capture in the eye ; Fig. 45: A camera lucida in use ⊜ ; Fig. 46 The superbly painted convex mirror from Jan van Eyck's 1434 Arnolfini Portrait ⊜ ; Fig. 47: Filippo Brunelleschi, Sailko, CC BY-SA 3.0 ; Fig. 48: Brunelleschi's demonstration of painting a real scene in perspective, then comparing with the real building, (unknown artist) ; Fig. 49: Della Pittura , Leon Alberti (later version) ⊜ ; Fig. 50: Leon Battista Alberti ⊜ ; Fig. 51-52: Sample perspective pages from Della Pittura ⊜ ; Fig. 53: Della Pittura, da Vinci, Rhododendrites, CC BY-SA 4.0 ; Fig. 54: Railroad Track Perspective ⊜ ; Fig. 55: Extract from 1804 edition of Della Pittura, Alberti, 1435-6 ⊜ ; Fig. 56: Holy Trinity, scheme of linear perspective, Masaccio c.1426-1428 ⊜ ; Fig. 57: Holy Trinity, fresco, Masaccio c.1426-1428 ⊜ ; Fig. 58: Healing of the Cripple and Raising of Tabitha, fresco, c. 1424, Masolino & Masaccio ⊜ ; Fig. 59: Healing of the Cripple and Raising of Tabitha showing perspective lines ; Fig. 60: A Woman Drinking with Two Men, Pieter de Hooch, c.1658, oil on canvas ⊜ ; Fig. 61: A Woman Drinking with Two Men, showing perspective lines from ceiling, window and floor, together with horizon line ⊜ ; Fig. 62: Het melkmeisje (The Milkmaid), Johannes Vermeer, c.1660 (oil on canvas, Rijksmuseum) ⊜ ; Fig. 63: Het melkmeisje (The Milkmaid), Johannes Vermeer, c.1660 showing perspective lines and horizon line ⊜ ; Fig. 64: Children's Games, Pieter Bruegel the Elder, 1560 (oil on wood, Kunsthistorisches Museum) ⊜ ; Fig. 65: Children's Games, Pieter Bruegel the Elder, 1560 with perspective lines added, together with the horizon line ⊜ ; Fig. 66: The Arnolfini Portrait, Jan van Eyck, 1434 (oil on oak panel, National Gallery, London) ⊜ ; Fig. 67: The Arnolfini Portrait, Jan van Eyck, 1434 with ceiling and floor perspective lines added ⊜ ; Fig. 68: The Last Supper Restored, Leonardo Da Vinci, 1495 – 1498 (painted on the refectory wall of Santa Maria delle Grazie, Milan) ⊜ ; Fig. 69: Refectory view from the outside, Marcin Białek, CC BY-SA 3.0 ; Fig. 70: Refectory view from the inside showing the illusion of perspective, AI coolTIM CC BY-SA 4.0 ; Fig. 71: The Last Supper Restored with perspective lines and horizon line ; Fig. 72: Interior of Saint Peter's Basilica, Rome, Giovanni Paolo Panini, after 1754, oil on canvas ⊜ ; Fig. 73: Interior of Saint Peter's Basilica, Rome with perspective lines and horizon ; Fig. 74: Bedroom in Arles, 1888, Vincent van Gogh, oil on canvas (first version) ⊜ ; Fig. 75:Bedroom in Arles, with perspective lines and horizon ; Fig. 76: Example of cubist art: Portrait of Picasso, Juan Gris, 1912 (oil on canvas, Art Institute of Chicago) ⊜ ; Fig. 77: La hora del té, Magda Torres Gurza, 2015 CC-BY-SA 4.0 ; Fig. 78: The Avenue at Middelharnis, Meindert Hobbema, 1689, oil on canvas ⊜ ; Fig. 79: Entrée du village de Voisins, 1872, Camille Pissarro, oil on canvas ⊜ ; Fig. 80: Langland Bay, 1872, Alfred Sisley, oil on canvas ⊜ ; Fig. 81: Rue Saint-Honoré, Après-midi, Effet de Pluie, Camille Pissarro, 1897, oil on canvas ⊜ ; Fig. 82: Ambulatory of the Nieuwe Kerk in Delft, with perspective lines added ; Fig. 83: Ambulatory of the Nieuwe Kerk in Delft, 1651, Gerard Houckgeest, oil on wood ⊜ ; Fig. 84: Bed valances and side curtains, with perspective lines (The Metropolitan Museum of Art) ; Fig. 85: Bed valances and side curtains, ca 1700, French, on canvas with silk and wool embroidery in gros and petit point (The Metropolitan Museum of Art) ⊜ ; Fig. 86: Rue de Paris, temps de pluie with perspective lines ; Fig. 87: Rue de Paris, temps de pluie, 1877, Gustave Caillebotte, oil on canvas ⊜ ; Fig. 88: Lunch Specials, with perspective lines added, © 2001 Richard Estes, oil on canvas ; Fig. 89: Lunch Specials, © 2001 Richard Estes, oil on canvas ; Fig. 90: London's Big Ben clock face with three-point perspective lines added ⊜ ; Fig. 91: London's Big Ben clock-face viewed from near the base ⊜ ; Fig. 92: The Delivery of the Keys from Fig. 10, with perspective and transversal lines added ; Fig. 93: Supper at Emmaus, 1601, Caravaggio, oil on canvas ⊜ ; Fig. 94: Lamentation of Christ, c.1480, Andrea Mantegna, tempera on canvas ⊜ ; Fig. 95: Drawing of the crucifixion, John of the Cross, c.1550 ⊜ ; Fig. 96: Christ of Saint John of the Cross, Salvador Dalí, 1951 © CSG CIC Glasgow Museums and Libraries Collections ; Fig. 97: Niccolò Mauruzi da Tolentino, c. 1438–1440, Paolo Uccello (part of the series entitled Battle of San Romano) ⊜ ; Fig. 98: Flaming June, 1895, Sir Frederic Leighton, oil on canvas ⊜ ; Fig. 99: Trompe l'oeil mural, 2007, madart.fr, Montpellier ; Fig. 100: Street scene, 1585, Vincenzo Scamozzi, view of the stage in the Teatro Olimpico, Vicenza, Didier Descouens CC-BY-SA 4.0 ; Fig. 101: Three Car Size Illusion - with background perspective lines ; Fig. 102: Three Car Size Illusion - with vehicle perspective lines ; Fig. 103: Two Cubes, a deceptively simple piece inspired by Viktor Vasarely ; Fig. 104: Two Cubes, with perspective lines added ; Fig. 105: Satire on False Perspective, William Hogarth 1754 ⊜ ; Fig. 106: Madonna and Child Enthroned, Byzantine 13th Century, tempera on poplar wood ⊜ ; Fig. 107: Madonna and Child, with perspective lines added ; Fig.108: Street view in Naples, Carlo Brancaccio ⊜ ; Fig. 109: One point perspective creation of a simple cube viewed from slightly above ; Fig. 110: Demonstration of 1-point perspective drawing, © 2008 Braindrain0000 ; Fig. 111: Wire frame cube showing two-point perspective, Ejahng CC BY-SA 3.0 ; Fig. 112: Wire frame cube example in three-point perspective ; Fig. 113: Our basic cube in one, two and three-point perspective ; Fig. 114: A basic wire frame Necker cube showing ambiguous perspective ; Fig. 115: A basic isometric cube and creation of an illusory figure ; Fig. 116: Close-up view of a chair drawn in linear perspective ; Fig. 117: Close-up view of a chair drawn in reverse perspective.

References

1. *Secret Knowledge: Rediscovering the Lost Techniques of the Old Masters,* 2001, David Hockney, 978-0670030262

2. *Vermeer's Camera,* 2001 Philip Steadman, Oxford University Press, ISBN 0-19-280302-6

3. *The Notebooks of Leonardo da Vinci*, Jean Paul Richter , editor 1880, Dover, 1970, ISBN 0486225720

4. *X-rays and Vermeer's painting technique,* Petria Noble and Ige Verslype, section 2.5 of RKD Studies, Netherlands Institute for Art History, https://rkdstudies.nl/

5. *Renaissance Perspectives,* James Elkins, University of Pennsylvania Press, Journal of the History of Ideas, Vol. 53, No. 2 (Apr. - Jun., 1992), pp. 209-230

6. *On the Arnolfini portrait and the Luca Madonna: Did Jan van Eyck have a Perspectival System?,* James Elkins, The Art Bulletin, Vol. 73, No. 1 (March 1991), pp 53-62

7. *Perspective Made Easy,* 1939 & 1967, Ernest R. Norling, ISBN 9563100166

8. *The Art of Perspective: The Ultimate Guide for Artists in Every Medium,* 2007, Phil Metzger, ISBN 1581808550

9. *Perspective*, Rex Vicat Cole, 1921, Seeley Service & Co., Ltd., London

Further Reading

1. *Never Trust Your Eyes,* 2017, Trevor A White, Visage Publications, ISBN 0999093304

2. *The Geometry of an Art: The History of the Mathematical Theory of Perspective from Alberti to Monge (Sources and Studies in the History of Mathematics and Physical Sciences),* 2007 Kirsti Andersen, ISBN 0387259619

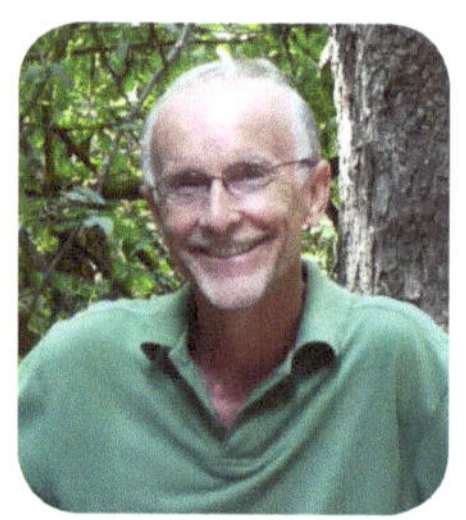

This book on ***Art and Perspective*** grew out of an understanding of how a camera captures our real three-dimensional world and displays it on a flat two-dimensional screen, and then how the eye can still perceive depth and reality when looking at that flat surface - whether a TV screen, a photograph, or a painting.

Trevor White has an academic background in visual science and electronics. During his years of research into Visual Telecommunications at British Telecom Research Labs, he compared and contrasted our human sense of vision with the functioning of modern-day cameras and video systems. He holds a Master's degree in Visual Science and Ophthalmic Optics, an Executive Master's degree in Business Administration and a Bachelor's degree in Electronics.

Previous publications include ***Never Trust Your Eyes*** (ISBN 0999093304), and articles in professional journals such as ***Nature*** and ***Proceedings of the IEE***.

www.ingramcontent.com/pod-product-compliance
Ingram Content Group UK Ltd.
Pitfield, Milton Keynes, MK11 3LW, UK
UKHW060117300726
14090UKWH00002B/247

* 9 7 8 0 9 9 9 0 9 3 3 6 8 *